The Agricultural
Development
of Mexico

This volume is No. 2 in the series entitled *Bench Mark Studies on Agricultural Development in Latin America*. For publication dates of the other books in the series, listed below, contact the publisher.

THE AGRICULTURAL DEVELOPMENT OF ARGENTINA
A Policy and Development Perspective
by Darrell F. Fienup
Russell H. Brannon
Frank A. Fender

THE AGRICULTURAL DEVELOPMENT OF BRAZIL
by G. Edward Schuh, in collaboration
with Eliseu Roberto Alves

THE AGRICULTURAL DEVELOPMENT OF PERU
by Arthur J. Coutu
Richard A. King

THE AGRICULTURAL DEVELOPMENT OF URUGUAY
Problems of Government Policy
by Russell H. Brannon

THE AGRICULTURAL DEVELOPMENT OF VENEZUELA
by Louis E. Heaton

PRAEGER SPECIAL STUDIES IN
INTERNATIONAL ECONOMICS AND DEVELOPMENT

The Agricultural Development of Mexico

ITS STRUCTURE AND GROWTH
SINCE 1950

Eduardo L. Venezian
William K. Gamble

Foreword by Lowell S. Hardin,
The Ford Foundation

FREDERICK A. PRAEGER, Publishers
New York · Washington · London

The purpose of the Praeger Special Studies is to make specialized research monographs in U.S. and international economics and politics available to the academic, business, and government communities. For further information, write to the Special Projects Division, Frederick A. Praeger, Publishers, 111 Fourth Avenue, New York, N.Y. 10003.

FREDERICK A. PRAEGER, PUBLISHERS
111 Fourth Avenue, New York, N.Y. 10003, U.S.A.
5, Cromwell Place, London S.W.7, England

Published in the United States of America in 1969
by Frederick A. Praeger, Inc., Publishers

FOREWORD

This book is based on one of several agricultural "bench mark" studies undertaken under Ford
Foundation sponsorship in Latin American countries
during 1966 and 1967. The researchers addressed
themselves to questions such as: What changes are
taking place in each country's agricultural output
and productivity? Are levels of per capita food
production, human nutrition, and rural living
rising? What relationships exist between the performance of the agricultural sector and the nation's
total economic development? Can the strengths and
weaknesses of the agricultural sector be identified?
What are the major impediments to more rapid rates
of advance? Among the means of accelerating agricultural development, which should be given priority? Subjective judgments necessarily are involved
in the analysis of such questions. The potential
for improvement, however, is substantial and real.

If the potential is great, why has it not been
realized? A partial answer is that much of today's
advanced technology for food and fiber production
is developed to meet the needs of production within
a specific geographical area. Modern agricultural
production techniques developed in temperate zones
generally do not transfer directly to different
environments. Moreover, it is difficult to project
the rate at which new, well-adapted technology may
be developed in a particular country. This, in
turn, complicates attempts to estimate a nation's
future comparative advantage in the production of
a crop or an animal product. Historically, it was
presumed that developing nations had relative ad-
vantages in agriculture, compared with industry;

v

92537

these countries were important exporters of agricultural products, including the food grains. In recent years, however, the net flow of trade in basic food crops has been from the developed to the less-developed nations.

Public and private investments in production research, educational programs, provision of fertilizer and other inputs, and infrastructure development compete for scarce resources. In the absence of systematic evaluation and policy guidelines, therefore, policy decisions concerning resource development and use may be the product of short-run pressures, rather than contributions to a rational plan.

This study of Mexico (and related studies in the series) indicates that several nations that formerly gave top priority to industrialization now are re-examining the potential contribution of agriculture to balanced development. Research in agricultural production technology carried on in tropical and subtropical regions has been greatly stimulated by the performance of the new Mexican wheat and Philippine rice varieties. Multidisciplinary teams have shown that substantial yield increases can be profitably obtained.

Although capacity to advance production technology is necessary, this capability in itself constitutes only part of the total effort needed for rapid economic growth. Structural, institutional, policy, and organizational changes often are equally important. Work in the policy area, however, is often more controversial and harder to evaluate than is production research. As this study demonstrates, key questions in the policy-organization-planning area remain to be answered. It is at the interface where agriculture, industry, and public policy meet that the most significant questions are raised.

Lowell S. Hardin
The Ford Foundation
June, 1968

PREFACE

This analysis of the agricultural development
of Mexico was completed during 1966 and revised in
1968. It seeks to present a fairly complete description of the structure and performance of the
agricultural sector in recent years, especially
from 1950 to 1967, as a reference for institutions,
agencies, or individuals who are interested in the
agriculture of Mexico, as well as in general agricultural development problems.

Mexico is among the few countries in the world
that have managed to achieve rapid and sustained
agricultural development during the last quarter of
a century, increasing the availability of agricultural and livestock products per person, even in
the face of an explosive population growth. Furthermore, of all the Latin American countries, Mexico
has experienced the fastest uninterrupted development in agriculture during this period of time.
Because Mexico is still counted among the relatively underdeveloped countries, it is extremely interesting to analyze the factors relating to the evolution of its agriculture, with the aim not only
of understanding the elements which have made this
development possible, but also of understanding
the value that the Mexican experience may have for
other countries at similar development stages.

Although this book emphasizes the economic aspects of agricultural development, an effort has
been made to cover institutional, sociological,
educational, and other aspects which constitute
very important elements in the over-all study of

agricultural development in order to present a non-technical, panoramic view of the subject that will be of interest to a wide range of "agriculturists."

For the most part, the data used in this study are from readily available, published material supplemented at times by information contained in unpublished reports or obtained through personal interviews. It should be noted, however, that serious discrepancies are often found in the data published by different authors or agencies. Given the objectives of this study, an effort was made to use primarily official statistics in the analysis; no attempt was made to adjust the data when they were inconsistent with those reported from other sources. Nevertheless, where the figures showed major differences, attention has been brought to the problem so that the reader may exercise caution in their interpretation.

The presentation, analysis, and interpretation of the statistical data and the conclusions and recommendations put forward are naturally the sole responsibility of the authors. Credit must be given, however, to Lic. Miguel A. Alvarez for preparing a preliminary version of the second chapter. At all times an effort has been made to maintain an objective and unprejudiced view of the subject under review and to include divergent points of view regarding those aspects on which there has not been a consensus in Mexico.

Given the scope and complexity of the problem of agricultural development, it is recognized that this study on Mexican agriculture suffers many limitations, but no pretense has been made to cover the subject completely. Rather, it is hoped that this study will indicate the various areas where further research is most needed and will stimulate discussion and new studies on a topic of such importance in the world today.

CONTENTS

	Page
FOREWORD	v
PREFACE	vii
LIST OF TABLES	xiii
LIST OF MAPS AND FIGURES	xviii
LIST OF ABBREVIATIONS	xix
GLOSSARY	xxi

Chapter

1 GEOGRAPHY, RESOURCES, AND POPULATION — 1

    Background — 1
    Area, Topography, and Climate — 3
    Regions and Resources — 5
    Population — 9

2 DEVELOPMENT OF THE MEXICAN ECONOMY — 12

    The Porfirio Díaz Era — 12
    From 1910 to 1934 — 14
    From 1934 to 1950 — 16
    Economic Development Since 1950 — 20
        Consumption, Savings, Investments,
            Foreign Debt, and Financing — 21
        Gross Internal Product and
            Productivity — 25
        Industrial Activities — 27

Chapter   Page

      Transportation and Communications   31
      Agricultural Activities   32
      Prices and Living Standards   33
      Foreign Trade and Balance of
        Payments   35
      Development Programming   38

3   STRUCTURE AND CHARACTERISTICS OF
    AGRICULTURE   40

      Land Use   40
      Agricultural (Cropping) Regions   41
      Land Tenure   44

4   LONG-RUN EVOLUTION AND SPECIAL FEATURES
    OF MEXICAN AGRICULTURAL DEVELOPMENT   51

      From 1900 to 1930   51
      Land Reform in the 1930's   54
      From 1940 to 1950   58
      Development Since 1950   59

5   GROWTH OF AGRICULTURAL OUTPUT AND
    EXPORTS SINCE 1950   63

      Agricultural GNP and Population Growth   63
      Agricultural Production by Sectors
        and Regions   66
      Growth of Individual Crops   70
      Expansion of Cultivated Land Area   72
      Increases in Crop Yields   74
      Agricultural Production and Yields
        by Tenure Groups   77
      Evolution of Livestock Production   86
      Agricultural Exports and Imports   89

6   FACTORS INFLUENCING MEXICAN
    AGRICULTURAL DEVELOPMENT   92

      Expansion of the Area Under Cultivation   95
      Agricultural Labor Force   96
      Irrigation Water   98
      Fertilizer Use   102

x

Improved Seeds   105
Plant Protection   108
Agricultural Capital and Credit   108
Agricultural Education, Research,
  and Extension Services   115
Marketing and Prices   115
Land Redistribution   118

7   GOVERNMENT POLICIES AND PROGRAMS
    FOR AGRICULTURE   121

    Public Investment and Planning
      in Agriculture   121
    Land Distribution   128
    Land Reclamation and Improvement   130
    Market Regulations and Price Controls   132
    Foreign Trade Regulation   134
    Agricultural Credit   135
    Crop and Livestock Insurance   136
    Education, Research, and Extension
      Services   136
    Other   138

8   AGRICULTURAL EDUCATION, RESEARCH, AND
    EXTENSION SERVICES   139

    Agricultural Education   142
      Elementary Agricultural Education   143
      Practical Agricultural Education   143
      Advanced Agricultural Education   145
    Agricultural Research   152
    Agricultural Extension Services   164

9   PROJECTED NEEDS FOR AGRICULTURAL
    PRODUCTION IN MEXICO   171

    The Balance of Production and
      Demand in 1970 and 1975   173
    Limitations of the Projections Study   179
      The Data Problem   179
      The Assumptions   179
      The Methodology   180

Chapter   Page

10   LIMITING FACTORS AND ALTERNATIVE
     OPPORTUNITIES IN MEXICAN
     AGRICULTURAL DEVELOPMENT   181

     Agrarian Problems   183
     Capital Shortage   185
     Scarce Educational Facilities   185
     Technical Assistance to Farmers   187
     Gaps in Research   187
     Salaries of Technical Personnel   189
     Marketing Problems   190
     Agricultural Policy and Planning   191
     Possibilities for Growth   193
     Alternative Programs and Investments
        for Growth   197
        Irrigation   197
        Tropical Areas   198
        Technological Improvements   199
        Better Resource Allocation   200
        Improved Product Distribution   201

11   SUMMARY AND CONCLUSIONS   203

STATISTICAL APPENDIX   215

NOTES
     Chapter 1   245
     Chapter 2   245
     Chapter 3   249
     Chapter 4   249
     Chapter 5   250
     Chapter 6   251
     Chapter 7   254
     Chapter 8   256
     Chapter 9   256
     Chapter 10   257

SELECTED BIBLIOGRAPHY   261

ABOUT THE AUTHORS   283

LIST OF TABLES

Table		Page
1	Gross Internal Product and Productivity	26
2	Distribution of Monthly Income in Mexico in 1964	35
3	Land Distribution by Tenure Groups, 1960	49
4	Agricultural and Gross National Product	64
5	Change in Rural and Urban Population, 1950-65	67
6	Changes in Value of Agricultural Production, 1949-51 to 1960-62, by Regions	68
7	Increase in Production (Tonnage) of Important Crops	71
8	Increase in Area of Major Crops Harvested	73
9	Average Yields of Important Crops	75
10	Yield Increases of the Major Crops by Regions	76
11	Value of Agricultural Production by Tenure Groups, 1960	78
12	Productivity of Private Farms and Ejidos in El Bajio, 1954	81

Table   Page

13   Value of Sales by Tenure Groups, 1960   83

14   Farm Groups by Volume of Crop Sales,
         1960   84

15   Yields of Major Crops by Tenure Groups,
         1960   85

16   Mexico: Livestock Numbers, 1950-64   87

17   Regional Distribution of Livestock,
         1960   89

18   Mexico: Value of Exports   90

19   Contribution of Area and Yield
         Increments to Agricultural Output,
         1949-51 to 1964-66   94

20   Mexico: Expansion of Irrigation,
         1926-67   99

21   Expansion of Irrigation, by Regions   100

22   Main Crops Grown Under Irrigation,
         1960   101

23   Consumption of Fertilizers, 1948-66   103

24   Production of Improved Seeds for
         Selected Crops   106

25   Amount and Composition of Capital in
         Agriculture, 1950 and 1960   109

26   Agricultural and Livestock Loans
         Granted by Mexican Government Banks,
         1950 to 1963, at Current Prices   111

27   Volume of Agricultural Credit Out-
         standing at End of Year   112

28   Agricultural Credit Granted by
         Term and Purpose   114

Table   Page

29   Education Level: Active Population in
     Agriculture by Major Skills, 1950
     and 1960   116

30   Index of Wholesale Prices in Mexico
     City, 1951-66   118

31   Agrarian Reform: Land Redistribution,
     1916-67   119

32   Agriculture's Share in the Federal
     Budget   122

33   Distribution of the Federal Budget   124

34   Transfers of the Federal Government to
     Consumption and Social Aid by
     National Agricultural Agencies and
     Enterprises   125

35   Agricultural Education Institutions at
     the Elementary and Practical Levels   144

36   Schools of Agriculture and Animal
     Husbandry   146

37   Postgraduate Education   148

38   Higher Education: Enrollment in
     Agriculture and Other Careers   153

39   Agricultural Research: Institutions,
     Staff, and Fields, 1964-68   155

40   Agricultural Extension: Personnel   166

41   Projected Rates of Growth of Supply
     and Demand of Crop and Livestock
     Products   173

42   Balance of Supply and Demand of
     Agricultural Products in 1970
     and 1975   175

xv

Table   Page

43   Balance of Supply and Demand of Animal
     Products, 1970 and 1975   176

44   Average and Maximum Yields of Important
     Crops, by Regions, 1966   196

                    TABLES IN STATISTICAL APPENDIX

1   Gross National Product   214

2   Gross National Product by Principal
     Sectors   218

3   Exports by Groups and Most Important
     Products   219

4   Imports by Groups and Most Important
     Products   220

5   Geographical Distribution of Commerce   221

6   Balance of Payments   222

7   Total Financing Provided by Banking
     System   228

8   Supply of Money and Means of
     Circulation   229

9   Price Index of Wholesale Prices in
     Mexico City   230

10   Index of the Volume of Industrial
     Production   231

11   Total Production of Principal
     Manufacturing Industries   232

12   Production of Principal Minerals   233

13   Land Use   234

Table   Page

14   Land Tenure and Value of Agricultural
         Production, 1950   235

15   Land Tenure and Value of Agricultural
         Production, 1960   236

16   Area, Production, and Yield of
         Principal Crops   237

17   Livestock Slaughtered, 1956-65   239

18   Volume and Value of Important
         Agricultural Exports   240

19   Mexico: Schools of Veterinary
         Medicine and Animal Husbandry   241

LIST OF MAPS AND FIGURES

Map   Page

1   Political Subdivisions of Mexico   2

2   Major Climatic Regions of Mexico   4

3   Natural Regions of Mexico   6

4   Mexican States and Boundaries of
       Census Regions   10

5   Agricultural Regions of Mexico   42

6   Agricultural Experiment Stations of
       INIA, State Governments, and
       Agricultural Schools   158

7   Regions of Supervision of Agricultural
       Extension Service   169

Figure

1   Growth of Agricultural Production,
       Land, and Labor   53

2   Mexico: Growth of Total GNP,
       Agricultural GNP, and Population   65

3   Organization of the Secretariat of
       Agriculture and Livestock of Mexico   140

4   Organization of the Federal
       Agricultural Extension Service   168

LIST OF ABBREVIATIONS

AID — Agency for International Development

BNCA — Banco Nacional de Crédito Agrícola--
National Agriculture Credit Bank

BNCE — Banco Nacional de Crédito Ejidal--
National Bank of Ejidal Credit

CEA — Centro de Estudios Agrarios--Center for
Agrarian Research

CIANE — Agricultural Research Center for the
Northeast

CIANO — Agricultural Research Center for the
Northwest

CIAS — Agricultural Research Center for Sinaloa

CIASE — Agricultural and Livestock Center for
the Southeast

CIAPY — Agricultural Research Center for the
Yucatán Peninsula

CIB — Basic Research Center

CIMMYT — Centro Internacional de Mejoramiento de
Maiz y Trigo--International Maize and
Wheat Improvement Center

CNIP — Centro Nacional de Investigaciones
Pecurias--National Center for Livestock
Research

CONASUPO	Compañía Nacional de Subsistencias Populares
FAO	Food and Agriculture Organization (United Nations)
GATT	General Agreement on Tariffs and Trade
GNP	gross national product
IBRD	International Board for Reconstruction and Development
IMF	International Monetary Fund
INIA	Instituto Nacional de Investigaciones Agrícolas--National Agricultural Research Institute
INIF	Instituto Nacional de Investigaciones Forestales--National Forestry Research Institute
INIP	Instituto Nacional de Investigaciones Pecurias--National Livestock Research Institute
IMIT	Instituto Mexicano de Investigaciones Tecnológicas--Mexican Institute of Technological Research
ITESM	Monterrey Institute of Technology and Advanced Study
LAFTA	Latin Free Trade Association
PEMEX	Petroleas Mexicanos
PNS	Productora Nacional de Semillas
SAG	Secretaría de Agricultura y Ganadería--Secretariat of Agriculture and Livestock
SHR	Secretaría de Recursos Hídraulicos--Secretariat of Hydraulic Resources
UNAM	Universidad Nacional Aútonoma de México

GLOSSARY

aftosa	hoof and mouth disease
agrónomo	degree in agriculture obtained after four years of college or university study
avio	production
bracero	migrant agricultural worker
ejido	communally owned village and surrounding lands
ejidatario	worker on an ejido
en descanso	(lands) untilled or infrequently tilled
ingeniero agrónomo	degree in agriculture obtained after five years of college or university study and presentation of thesis
minifundia	farms of less than five hectares
parcelamientos legales	legalization of land rights of present holders of land
poblaciones	production in urban areas
refaccionario	equipment, livestock, etc.

<u>tierras de labor</u>	tillable land
<u>zootecnista</u>	degree in animal husbandry obtained after three years of college or university study

The Agricultural
Development
of Mexico

CHAPTER **1** GEOGRAPHY, RESOURCES,

AND POPULATION

BACKGROUND

The United Mexican States, usually known as
Mexico, constitute a single nation, located in the
North American continent, between the United States
on the north and Guatemala and Belice (British Honduras) on the south, and bordered on the east and
west by the Atlantic and Pacific Oceans, respectively. This geographic position is economically favorable and strategically valuable in the physical and
cultural integration of the American continent.

The country is politically organized as a republic and is divided into twenty-nine states, two
federal territories, and the Federal District,
which contains Mexico City, the nation's capital
(see Map 1).

Much of what is now Mexico was originally in-
habited by numerous indigenous peoples that had
developed high cultures, such as the Mayas, Toltecs,
Tarascans, Aztecs, and others. These peoples are
estimated to have numbered over 7 million at the
time the land was conquered by Spain, early in the
sixteenth century. Spanish rule extended until
1821 when Mexico achieved independence. The Indian
people and much of their culture survived this
period and came to constitute a basic element of
Mexican civilization. The superimposition of Spanish culture--language, religion, and institutions--
upon the existing Indian civilizations is of great
importance in understanding many of the characteristics of present-day Mexico (especially in the rural

1

MAP 1

Political Subdivisions of Mexico

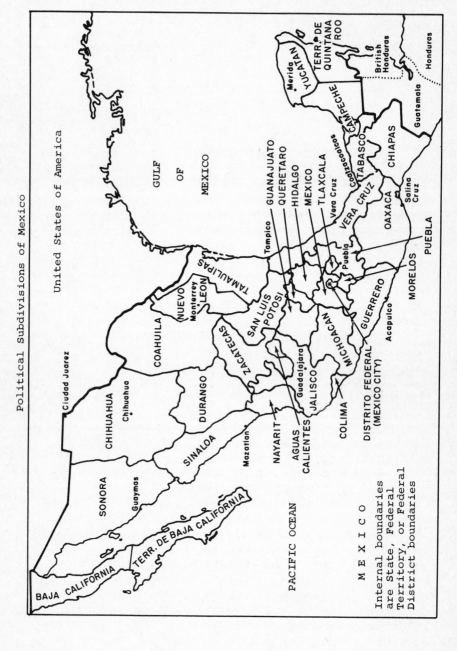

Internal boundaries
are State, Federal
Territory, or Federal
District boundaries

sector) and the problems the nation has had to face
throughout its history. This situation, paralleled
only in a few other Latin American countries, such
as Guatemala and Peru, is the cause of basic differences, all too often overlooked, in the cultural and
institutional evolution of the various countries of
the Western Hemisphere.

AREA, TOPOGRAPHY, AND CLIMATE

Mexico has a total area of 1,967,183 square
kilometers (approximately 762,000 square miles),
which is about one fifth the size of the United
States. It is the third largest country in Latin
America. Most of the country is mountainous and of
high altitude. Two mountain ranges, containing
numerous peaks and volcanoes of over 10,000 feet,
extend along the two maritime sides, enclosing an
elevated plateau, open in the direction of the
north, and converge southeast of Mexico City. The
plateau (or mesa) is also cut by smaller mountain
ranges, thus forming many separate basins and valleys. Aside from this plateau, level lands are
found mostly in the Yucatán Peninsula, which, however, has limited agricultural value because of its
poor soil.

Because of the country's topography, the rivers
are short and torrential. They are important as
sources of hydroelectric power and irrigation but
insignificant as means of transportation. The most
important watershed systems are the Lerma-Chapala-
Santiago and the Balsas on the Pacific side, and
the Pánuco and Papaloapan on the Gulf Coast.

Characteristic of Mexico is its great diversity
of climates, ranging from arid to tropical. This
diversity is due partly to the geographical location
of the country, which extends from approximately 15°
to 32° north latitude, and partly to the variations
in altitude. Roughly three major climatic zones
can be distinguished (see Map 2): a dry zone
(steppes and deserts) covering most of the northern

MAP 2

Major Climatic Regions of Mexico

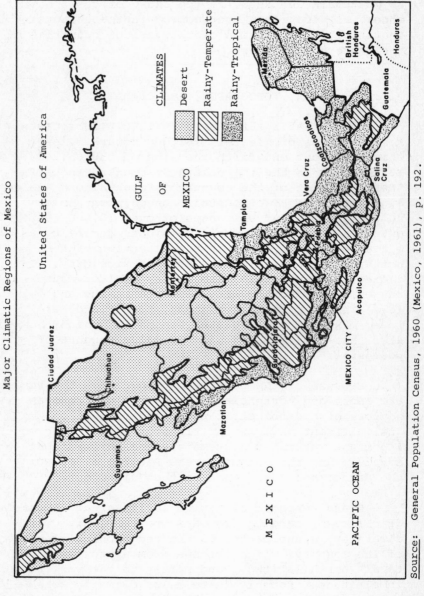

CLIMATES

Desert

Rainy-Temperate

Rainy-Tropical

United States of America

GULF
OF
MEXICO

MEXICO

PACIFIC OCEAN

Ciudad Juarez

Chihuahua

Guaymas

Mazatlan

Guadalajara

MEXICO CITY

Acapulco

Monterrey

Tampico

Puebla

Vera Cruz

Coatzacoalcos

Salina
Cruz

Merida

Guatemala

British
Honduras

Honduras

Source: General Population Census, 1960 (Mexico, 1961), p. 192.

4

half of the country; a rainy-temperate zone, corresponding mainly to the southern portion of the central plateau and the mountain ranges; and a rainy-
tropical zone, corresponding to the southern half
of the two coastal areas and the Yucatán Peninsula.
Rainfall is greatest in southeast Mexico, averaging
from 40 inches to over 120 inches per year; it
diminishes gradually toward the north, where rainfall averages 16 inches or less per year. There
are also marked differences between the mountains,
which receive frequent and intense rainfall, and
the plains, with scattered rains. In general, the
main rainfalls occur during the summer and early
fall throughout the country, thus dividing the year
into a rainy season and a dry season.

Temperatures are affected mainly by altitude;
thus along the coasts and in the Yucatán Peninsula,
the weather is hot, and temperatures drop as one
moves up to the plateau and the mountain ranges.
Variations in temperature, however, never represent
a limiting factor for Mexican agriculture; the
critical climatic element for agriculture is rainfall, which is insufficient in most of the country
and varies greatly from year to year.

REGIONS AND RESOURCES[1]

The combination of topography and climates
gives rise to several distinct natural regions in
Mexico (see Map 3).

The central plateau (or central mesa) occupies
the central part of the country from the northern
border to south of Mexico City. It rises gradually
from 3,600 feet in the north to about 8,000 feet
near Mexico City. The northern part of the plateau
is very dry; the vegetation consists of desert
plants and small trees. Since water is scarce,
agriculture is conducted on a limited scale under
irrigation. This region is used mostly for livestock grazing. There is also considerable exploitation of natural desert plants that produce wax

MAP 3

Natural Regions of Mexico

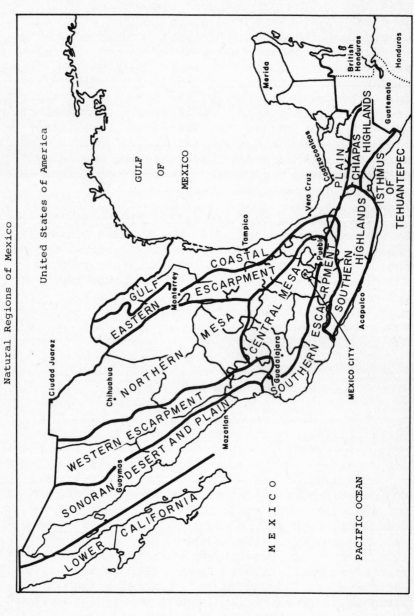

Source: Nathan Whetten, <u>Rural Mexico</u> (Chicago: The University of Chicago Press, 1948).

6

and fibers. Important mineral deposits are also found here.

The southern part of the plateau contains seven separate basins and valleys, all located at an elevation of more than 5,000 feet. This region receives more rainfall in the summer, but not always enough for good crops; thus, in some areas irrigation facilities have been developed. This region has been settled for the past ten centuries and subjected to intensive agricultural exploitation, which still continues. Corn is the most important crop, and there is a sizable livestock industry. Forest and mineral resources have been largely exhausted, and soil erosion is a serious problem. However, this region is still potentially rich, containing nearly one half the population and some of the most important industrial centers of Mexico.

The escarpments represent serious obstacles to communications, especially in an east-west direction, and for the most part are of no agricultural value. They do, however, contain good forestry resources and mineral deposits and are used for some grazing.

The southern highlands are a very mountainous region, containing narrow valleys and little level land. The climate varies from dry to rainy tropical, and the region is severely affected by erosion. Agriculture is limited; carried on in the valleys and hillsides along with some livestock-raising, it is generally subsistence agriculture. There is also some small-scale forestry and mineral exploitation. The population of this region is still mostly Indian racially and culturally; their standards of living are the lowest in the country.

The coastal lowlands extend in narrow strips of land along both coasts of Mexico and into the Yucatán Peninsula. The Pacific lowlands are arid in the north (including the Lower California peninsula), and agriculture is conducted only under

irrigation, which has been extensively developed in
this region.   Livestock production is important in
drylands that present favorable range conditions.
The region is rich in mineral deposits, especially
iron ore.   In the southern portion of the Pacific
lowlands, there is more rainfall, but there is
little flat land suited for agricultural use, except in the area of the Tehuantepec Isthmus.

The Gulf coastal plains are the most rainy
area of Mexico and generally have a hot climate,
although they enclose a mosaic of microclimates in
the valleys and hills that cut the plains along
their expanse.   The vegetation is exuberant and
varied.   This region is very important agricultural-
ly and still offers much potential for further development, especially for livestock-raising.   The
principal agricultural products are sugar cane and
coffee.   This region contains most of the oil deposits of Mexico.

The Gulf coastal plains flatten out at the
isthmus and extend into the Yucatán Peninsula,
which is practically all level ground.   Northern
Yucatán is dry, but the rest of the region has
abundant rainfall.   There are no surface streams
and soils are mostly of poor quality and present
drainage problems, thus limiting agricultural production.   Important crops are bananas in the
Tabasco area and henequen in northern Yucatán; corn
is cultivated in nomadic-type agriculture.   The region is rich in forest resources.   Many areas of
this tropical land may have good agricultural potential, but, at present, lack of communications
and small population make it a poor and isolated
region.

The foregoing description of natural regions
unfortunately has no counterpart in the form of
statistical regions in Mexico.   Agricultural statistics are compiled according to state boundaries and
grouped into five major census regions, namely,
North, Gulf, North Pacific, South Pacific, and Central, that correspond only roughly with the major

natural regions (see Map 4). The census regions
are used later in this book to analyze the regional
pattern of Mexican agricultural development.

POPULATION

The rugged nature of the Mexican territory historically has separated its population into isolated
communities and has thus influenced the character of
the people and the economic and political life of
the nation. Only in the last three decades has
greater integration been achieved through a marked
improvement in communications.[2]

The original population of what is today
Mexico is estimated to have numbered over 7 million
at the time of the Spanish Conquest; subsequently
the Indians appear to have diminished considerably
because of diseases introduced by the Spaniards and
the ill treatment of the conquerors. In the middle
1800's, the population was estimated at only 8 million. Since then, population has increased steadily,
except for the years around 1920, when the revolutionary wars produced an actual decrease in population, then estimated at about 14 million.

Total population, at present, is estimated at
45.7 million people, representing an increase of
approximately 19.3 million since 1950 and more than
a doubling since 1940. Because of the sustained
high birth rate and a substantial decline in mor-
tality rates, mainly among infants, the average
annual rate of population growth was 3.3 per cent
in 1950-67, compared with 2.8 per cent for 1940-50
and 1.7 per cent for 1930-40. Currently, this rate
is estimated at 3.4 per cent and is expected to
reach 3.6 per cent in the 1970's. This extremely
fast rate of population growth poses a serious problem for the improvement of average standards of living in Mexico and makes clear the crucial importance
of continued rapid development of agricultural production, if the nation is to be able to feed itself
at adequate nutritional levels.

MAP 4

Mexican States and Boundaries of Census Regions

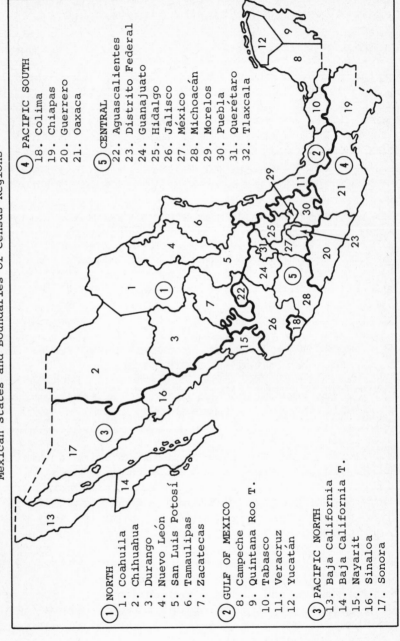

① NORTH
1. Coahuila
2. Chihuahua
3. Durango
4. Nuevo León
5. San Luis Potosí
6. Tamaulipas
7. Zacatecas

② GULF OF MEXICO
8. Campeche
9. Quintana Roo T.
10. Tabasco
11. Veracruz
12. Yucatán

③ PACIFIC NORTH
13. Baja California
14. Baja California T.
15. Nayarit
16. Sinaloa
17. Sonora

④ PACIFIC SOUTH
18. Colima
19. Chiapas
20. Guerrero
21. Oaxaca

⑤ CENTRAL
22. Aguascalientes
23. Distrito Federal
24. Guanajuato
25. Hidalgo
26. Jalisco
27. México
28. Michoacán
29. Morelos
30. Puebla
31. Querétaro
32. Tlaxcala

The average density of population in Mexico in
1967 was twenty-three persons per square kilometer
(60 per square mile), but density differs considerably between the heavily populated central states
and the sparsely settled northern and southeastern
states. More than one half of Mexico's population
is concentrated in the Federal District and the
eleven states surrounding it, which correspond
roughly to the central mesa described previously.

Rural population, defined as those living in
communities of less than 2,500 inhabitants, was
estimated to be about 43 per cent of the total population in 1967, whereas it was 57 per cent in 1950.
The annual rate of growth of rural population between these two years was 1.6 per cent, as compared
with 5 per cent for the urban population (see Table
5). The five largest urban centers of the country
are Mexico City, with over 6 million inhabitants,
Guadalajara and Monterrey, with approximately 1 million each, and Puebla and Ciudad Juárez, with approximately 400,000 each.

An important feature of the present Mexican
population is its age composition. About one half
of the population is under sixteen years of age,
and only 40 per cent is between the ages twenty to
sixty, the bulk of the labor force. This structure
imposes a heavy burden on the national economy to
support, educate, and create new job opportunities
for the throngs of youngsters who year after year
are being added to the population.

CHAPTER **2** DEVELOPMENT OF THE

MEXICAN ECONOMY

THE PORFIRIO DÍAZ ERA

From colonial times on through its first half
century of independent life, Mexico's economy was
essentially agricultural, with some important mineral exploitations oriented to foreign markets and
industrial activity limited to handicrafts. The
first significant efforts at developing an infrastructure and industrial base appeared during the
prolonged dictatorship of General Porfirio Díaz
from 1876 to 1910. During this period, the political instability that had colored Mexican life since
independence was repressed by force. The ensuing
peace did not result in improved living standards
for most Mexicans, but, at least, it allowed the
gross national product (GNP) to increase; this is
estimated to have grown at an annual rate of 2.9
per cent (1.6 per cent per inhabitant) between 1895
and 1910. The most important expanding activities
were mining, manufacture, and transportation.[1]

Several conditions made this economic growth
possible. Tariff protection to incipient industries
and franchises for certain imports helped the development of industries producing for the domestic
market. Small factories and workshops were established or enlarged to manufacture clothing, cotton
and wool fabrics, silver goods and ceramics, sugar,
cigarettes and cigars, some metal products, etc.
Although these products partially substituted for
imports, purchases of capital and consumer goods
from abroad continued to increase.

12

External demand for some Mexican commodities expanded, especially cattle and leather, cotton, sugar, henequen, chicle, and istle, as well as precious metals and other minerals. This external demand was stimulated by continued monetary devaluation up to the beginning of this century, thus allowing foreign income from exports to increase more or less steadily.

Direct foreign investment was especially attracted by the government, and its volume became quite important. This investment[2] was devoted to construction of railways, mine exploitation, and other export activities. About 20,000 kilometers of railway tracks were built, connecting the center of the country with the United States and the Gulf of Mexico, and the southeast with the Pacific Coast, thus facilitating transportation of raw materials and tropical products abroad.

Production of agricultural raw materials and export crops increased through the expansion of cultivated areas, but domestic food production continually decreased. The characteristics of latifundia agriculture, such as landlord absenteeism, their political power, and foreign interests in agriculture, as well as other factors are considered responsible for this situation. For instance, it is estimated that at the turn of the century only 3.1 per cent of the population owned any land; the remaining 96.9 per cent (over 14 million people) owned none. The State owned 19.4 per cent of the total land area of the country, 64.4 per cent was owned by Mexican citizens, and 22.2 per cent was owned by foreigners.[3]

During the Díaz era, the living conditions of the lower classes worsened in contrast with the general economic progress. As a result of population growth and diminishing domestic food production, per-capita consumption of corn, beans, sugar, brown sugar, tobacco, and cotton was reduced. From 1897 to 1910, salaries are considered to have fallen in real terms, from 0.92 to 0.36 pesos per day.[4]

Thus, in the last decade of the Díaz regime, a process of falling real income set in, shrinking internal demand and limiting the expansion of incipient industry. This was aggravated by monetary policies. The price of silver was stabilized in 1905,
and a monetary reform set the rate of exchange,
slightly revaluating the currency, eliminating previous protection and stimulus provided by the exchange market, and discouraging further export expansion. Instability in the international market
of minerals increased, and the prices of henequen
collapsed in 1907. In addition, the terms of trade
began to deteriorate, again reducing the capacity
to import.

The indifference of the governing oligarchy
represented by the dictator, the army, intellec-
tuals, foreigners, and landowners, their negligence
toward the needs of the great masses of rural population, was made more acute by the continued debt
of the laborers and the mistreatment and injustices
perpetrated by the landowners. This, combined with
population growth and lack of employment, caused
strikes that were violently repressed, which fos-
tered the Revolution of 1910.

FROM 1910 TO 1934

Revolutionary fighting lasted until 1921,
bringing with it destruction that interrupted the
country's growth. The 1910 population of 15.2
million inhabitants had decreased by 1 million by
1921 (including those who had migrated). During
the next eight years, very little was done to re-
pair the damage. However, there were significant
increases in the production of export items such
as minerals and petroleum. (In 1921, 30.7 million
cubic meters were extracted, as compared with 0.5
million in 1910.) Crop production decreased, except for henequen, which was also an export crop;
railroads were reconstructed. When Mexico was in
the middle of a slow recovery, the world crisis of
1929 had a strong impact on its economy, because

of its dependence on foreign trade. In 1933, another monetary devaluation was effected. The GNP
in 1932 was lower than in 1910, but by 1934 it had
reached again the 1929 level.

Although the Revolution caused a temporary
setback in development, it established the bases
for a new social order and conditions for progress
that may have been impossible otherwise. The 1917
Constitution, still in effect, contains some very
advanced provisions on social rights, aimed at pro-
tecting and improving the living standards of the
majority of the people. Article 27 of the Constitution, which modified the property system (see Chapter 3), became the basis of the agrarian-reform
program, the most far-reaching structural transformation accomplished by the Revolution. The agrarian
reform was put into effect slowly and hesitantly between 1916 and 1934, creating much uncertainty in
property rights and consequently hampering agricultural production. During this period, about 10 per
cent of the total land available for cultivation
was distributed among individual ejidatarios and to
collective ejidos.*

Because of the military campaigns throughout
the revolutionary years, inflation had taken place.
Gold and silver were taken out of circulation.
Article 27 of the Constitution conferred control of
monetary and fiscal policy exclusively on the Federal Government, which then created official credit
institutions to reorganize the country's finances,
controlled the printing of money, and moved to curb
the increase in the public debt. The Bank of Mexico,
created in 1925, later became the central bank and
the only one allowed to issue money. The National
Banking Commission was created in 1924 to supervise
banking institutions; between 1924 and 1934 the
National Agriculture Credit Bank (Banco Nacional
de Crédito Agrícola, BNCA), the National Mortgage,

---

*For an explanation of these concepts, see
Chapter 3, "Land Tenure."

Urban, and Public Works Bank, and the National
Financing Company were founded. The last institution was to become of central importance for the
future industrialization program; it, as well as
the banks, was used extensively to promote economic
development in the country.[5]

Because of expropriation of land owned by
foreigners and suspension of the public debt service by the government in 1926, direct foreign investments began to leave the country; the great
crash of 1929 furthered this trend. As a result,
foreign investment has never again acquired the importance it had before the Revolution.

FROM 1934 TO 1950

Once the world-wide depression was over in
1934, Mexico's economic development speeded up.
GNP increased by approximately 160 per cent between
1934 and 1950. The agricultural (crop), construction, and transportation sectors increased at about
the same rate. During these sixteen years, the manufacturing industry expanded almost 2-1/2 times.
Petroleum, mining products, and livestock-raising
had a lower rate of growth.[6] Population increased
only 45 per cent during the same period.

Among the most important factors deemed responsible for this progress are the policy of land
redistribution and the construction of public works.
With the distribution of feudal property, income
was also redistributed, and the political power of
large landowners was eliminated. The army was reorganized and after 1934 ceased to referee political and social conflicts. The problem of government-
church relations (the Catholic Church had been against
agrarian reform, progressive labor legislation, and
popular education) also was successfully resolved.
As the country developed, foreign investment and
hence influence became weaker, while domestic investment grew stronger. World demand for Mexican
products increased steadily after the depression

and received special stimulus during World War II
and the Korean conflict. Domestic manufacturers
benefited particularly by these events; they were
able to maximize the utilization of industrial
capacity, because the war eliminated competition
in the international market. This permitted a
faster substitution of imported goods by locally
manufactured ones and allowed larger exports as
well. Domestic production of iron, steel, cement,
paper, sugar, chemicals, and textiles expanded considerably.

In the years prior to 1934, financial policy
had been principally concerned with limiting monetary circulation and obtaining a balanced budget.
When confidence was restored and the banking system
acquired more liquidity, a new financial policy began to evolve. Large amounts were spent by the government on communications and transportation, irrigation, and promotion of agriculture and industry,
which helped raise the productive capacity of the
economy. This public investment (from 1926 to 1947)
was almost totally financed through internal resources, and budgetary deficits were covered by
overdrawing at the central bank and by emission of
government bonds. By 1939, foreign resources
financed only 15 per cent of the total national
investment, whereas internal savings financed 85
per cent; domestic savings were 39 per cent public
and 46 per cent private.[7]

During the first three years of deficit financing, increases in production and employment were obtained, but with an upward movement in the price
level. Inflationary pressures became stronger, so
that by 1950 the general price level had tripled
with respect to 1940. Lagging salaries vis-à-vis
prices led to wider profit margins without much
pressure from unions, thus allowing for greater
savings and investments, which raised the capitalization rate of the country.

Between 1939 and 1944, scarcity of capital
goods caused by World War II limited the rate of

investment, which remained at approximately 10 per
cent of the GNP. However, after the war, investment
increased much faster than GNP; in 1947 it represented 14 per cent of the GNP and remained at this
level up to 1950.[8] Thus, with relatively small investments up to 1945, a considerable expansion in
industrial production was achieved; at the same
time, services expanded at the expense of railways,
plants, and communications equipment. Investment
in the petroleum and electric-energy industries, on
the other hand, was virtually suspended, limiting
production in these fields. The large investments
for irrigation works during the war did not yield
important results until much later.

Expropriation of the oil fields in 1938 is another institutional change considered important in
fostering Mexican economic development, because the
petroleum industry then was linked to the domestic
market and directed in accordance with the long-
term interests of the nation.

Government policy for agriculture between 1935
and 1940 concentrated on land redistribution. In
this period, millions of hectares of land were
given to landless peasants. At the same time the
National Bank of Ejidal Credit (Banco Nacional de
Crédito Ejidal, BNCE) and the National Bank of
Foreign Trade, both concerned with agricultural
promotion, began operations. From 1939 to 1950,
on the other hand, most government investments in
agriculture were devoted to large irrigation projects, such as the Papaloapan and the Tecaltepec
works. The area benefiting from the irrigation
facilities exceeded 1 million hectares. The increase in production since 1939 was due primarily
to greater use of available tillable land. During
this period, traditional crops in certain regions
were substituted by other, high-value crops. However, it was not until the second half of the
1940's that agricultural yields increased modestly.

In 1938, the fixed exchange rate was abandoned
and re-established in 1940 at 4.85 pesos to the

dollar. Exchange rate difficulties were due to the
expropriation of oil fields and railways, and the
1937 U.S. economic recession. Devaluation was re-
sorted to again in 1948 and 1949, when the exchange
rate was set at 8.65 pesos to the dollar. Large
deficits in the balance of trade, arising from the
backlog of imports after the war, forced this action, despite the increase in exports, the establishment of quantitative controls on imports, and
the rise in customs tariffs.

Mexico's foreign trade increased considerably
from 1934 to 1950, as a combined result of World
War II, the stimulus of higher prices, elasticity
of national production, and devaluation. Between
1939 and 1950, the value of exports expanded from
$156 to $534 million. The composition of exports
also changed, with the traditional mineral products
(including silver, lead, copper, and zinc) decreasing relatively from two thirds of the total value
of exports in 1939 to only one third in 1950. On
the other hand, agricultural exports (such as cotton, coffee, tomatoes, fish, seafood, and henequen
fiber) increased during the same period from a
mere 28 per cent to 55 per cent of the total exports.

Imports increased parallel to exports up to
1945; after the war, however, they were generally
higher than exports. The value of imports expanded
from $121 million in 1939 to $509 million in 1950.
The composition of imports changed, with capital
assets becoming more important at the expense of
consumer goods and semiprocessed raw materials.
Capital goods increased from 24 to 38 per cent of
total imports in these eleven years, whereas consumer goods decreased their share from 24 to 18 per
cent, and semiprocessed raw materials from 39 to
30 per cent.

Throughout this period, Mexico's foreign trade
became increasingly concentrated toward the United
States. The U.S. share in the value of Mexican
foreign trade grew from about 60 per cent before
the war to about 85 per cent in 1950.[9]

ECONOMIC DEVELOPMENT SINCE 1950

By the end of the 1940's, Mexico had developed its characteristic institutions, had achieved substantial political stability, and had found its path to growth. Between 1950 and 1967, the gross national product, expressed in 1950 prices, increased at an annual average rate of 6.2 per cent whereas population expanded at 3.3 per cent per year, resulting in a 2.9 per cent average rate of growth in per-capita income. Real per-capita income increased approximately 60 per cent; in dollar terms, it rose from $259 to $450 per year. This growth was accompanied by important changes in the structure of the economy, which moved toward more capitalized forms of production and toward greater concentration of the labor force in industry. In spite of this, half of Mexico's economically active population still depends on primary activities (mainly agriculture) and the distribution of income still is heavily skewed in favor of a small minority of the population.

The Mexican economy is considered to be a "mixed economy," that is, a market economy with private enterprise and strong state intervention. Government participation has been outstanding in the development of the infrastructure (communications, transportation, irrigation, public education), in industrial promotion, and in its sensible financial policy. This, coupled with the elastic supply of the private sector, has allowed the country to grow steadily and achieve price stability after 1956.

Private enterprise has been able to take advantage of external economies and of opportunities offered by the expanding market, thus increasing employment and use of productive resources. At the same time, more savings have been generated and channeled largely toward productive activities. Also, foreign demand for Mexican goods and services has tended to increase (though with strong variations), with tourism becoming increasingly important.

However, the terms of trade during most of this period have been unfavorable. The sustained growth of the economy has permitted greater foreign indebtedness, which has increased both the country's capacity to import and the level of investment. Although importation of goods and services has increased substantially, their share in the total supply of goods and services of the country diminished from around 17 per cent in 1950-55 to 12.5 per cent in recent years, indicating a greater contribution of domestic production.

Consumption, Savings, Investments, Foreign Debt, and Financing

Internal consumption has been growing at a rate higher than population and equal to GNP (see Appendix Table 1). Private consumption represents four fifths of the total product, whereas consumption by the public sector is less than 6 per cent of GNP. Internal savings amount to 13 per cent of GNP,[10] a proportion that has remained stable for the past fifteen years. On the other hand, although there are some statistical discrepancies on this, gross fixed investment may have increased from 14 per cent to about 16 per cent of GNP in the last few years* because of the contribution of foreign savings; the portion financed with domestic savings has diminished from 94.3 per cent in early 1950 to 91 per cent in 1960-65.

Although government participation in consumption is fairly unimportant, its role in investment activities has been significant for it has been involved in strategic lines of production. Savings of the Federal Government and public enterprises have represented less than a fifth of total domestic savings in the past fifteen years; but their participation in total gross fixed investment has fluctuated between one third and one half. This has

---

*Excluding the inventory addition estimated at 3 per cent of GNP.

been possible because the public sector has tapped
savings from the private sector and obtained loans
from international organizations and foreign governments. Fluctuations in public investment are influenced mainly by the course of private investment
and government policy; for instance, when private
investment was reduced because of the Caribbean
crisis (early 1960's) the government stepped up its
own investment.

The Mexican fiscal system is weak compared to
that of other countries in the same developmental
stage. The Federal Government's income represents
only between 8 to 12 per cent of GNP; the equivalent figure, in 1964, for Argentina was 18.1,
Brazil, 16.8, and Chile, 21.3.[11] Only about 40 per
cent of the Mexican government revenue comes from
progressive income taxes. Apparently, the government has not wished to impose taxes on accumulated
capital of private enterprise and individuals in
order to avoid discouraging productive investing.

The government has tapped private savings
through various means, but primarily through monetary policy. Before 1950 and during 1952-54, the
Bank of Mexico financed the public-sector deficit
mainly by creating money (forced savings). In subsequent years, the central bank substantially reduced its government credits by compelling private
banking institutions to increase their holdings of
government titles, at low returns.

Mexico has made extensive use of foreign resources to complement domestic savings. The foreign debt (especially that of public enterprises)
has increased in recent years from $1,130.8 million
at the end of 1962 to $1,777 million at the end of
1965.[12] The strict fulfillment of current financial obligations, the payment of old debts, the
sustained growth of the economy, and the country's
capacity to accept the requirements imposed by
foreign grants have given Mexico access (after
fifty years) to international financial centers.
Moreover, since July, 1963, Mexico has sold $127.5
million worth of government bonds abroad.

This rapid growth of foreign indebtedness
could have been excessive in terms of repayment
capacity, but the sources of credit have been diversified and lower interest rates and longer terms
have been obtained, which has helped to refinance
part of the debt. Debt service for 1966 (as of
May 31, 1965) was estimated to amount to $403.2
million; this represents about one fourth of the
value of Mexican exports.

Public-sector investment in Mexico is carried
out principally by the Federal Government; less
than 5 per cent of total public investment is effected by the states and municipalities.[13] This
control of public expenditures by the central authorities indicates the tremendous economic and political power held by the State.

The manner in which federal public investment
has been channeled has varied through time. In the
early 1950's, 40 per cent of this investment was
channeled through the Secretariat of the Treasury's
budget;* at present, slightly over one quarter of
the investment goes through this Secretariat. The
largest part (almost 60 per cent) is invested by
semi-autonomous official enterprises. These have
continually increased in importance and numbers,
amounting to 471 enterprises[14] in 1964, engaged in
the most diverse activities. The most important
are the official banks, Petroleos Mexicanos (PEMEX),
Federal Electricity Commission, railways, and the
Mexican Institute of Social Security.

Federal spending fundamentally affects the
productive activities of the country; hence it is
interesting to know its distribution. Almost 40
per cent of the total federal investment has been
devoted to industrial promotion in the past few
years. The principal industries benefited have

---

*Up to 1965, the Federal Government's budget,
controlled by the Treasury and Public Credit Ministry, included the budget of several official agencies.

been electrical energy, petroleum and natural gas,
and steel. About 20 per cent of investment has
been used for communications and transportation
facilities (highways and railways) and a similar
proportion for social benefit works (hospitals,
social aid centers, education, and housing projects).
Agriculture received a small proportion of federal
investments, mainly for irrigation, in contrast
with 1950, when the allocation for agriculture was
almost 20 per cent of the total.

Another general way of determining the relative support that the various sectors of the economy receive is through the financing granted by
the banking system (see Appendix Table 7). Great
importance is given to the financing of production,
especially industry; large sums are also used by
the Federal Government, whereas agriculture and
livestock receive only about 12 per cent of the
total bank credits.

Money supply has maintained a more or less
constant relation to GNP. Its volume has been determined by the requirements of expanding production and trade, in addition to the state of
Mexico's foreign economic relations and the financing of federal budget deficits. Abundant monetary
circulation contributed to inflationary pressures
up to 1955, but money supply expansion later diminished and price inflation was practically checked.
This coincided with vigorous application of selective controls on credits granted by the private
banking systems (directed by a few huge financial
groups) and greater control of the capital and
money markets, which resulted in a rise of real interest rates. These increased from an annual average of 10.7 per cent in 1950 to 14 per cent in
1960, and recently dropped to 12 per cent. The
Mexican economy is becoming increasingly more
monetized, with more savings channeled to the financial system and with demand deposits increasing
relative to the total money supply.

In the financial sphere of Mexican economic
development, given the present heavy dependence on

foreign credit and the difficulty of enlarging foreign indebtedness, further capital formation will
have to be mainly internally generated. The rate
of savings will have to be increased and investment
funds allocated more rationally. The State should
contribute to this effort by raising the savings
rate of its enterprises, whether by adjusting prices
to their true cost, lowering costs, or instituting
a progressive taxation system.

Gross Internal Product
and Productivity

All the activities which contribute to GNP
showed significant increases in the period 1960-67,
except for mining and forestry (see Appendix Table
2 and Table 1). Sectors outstanding because of annual average increments of over 7 per cent were
electric power, manufacturing industries, petroleum
and by-products, services, and construction. Smaller increases were obtained by commerce, transportation, and agricultural and livestock activities,
although these were larger than population growth.

As a result of sustained efforts directed at
stimulating industrial activities, the industrial
sector (manufacturing, electricity, oil, mining,
and construction) has increased its share of GNP
from 30 to 35 per cent in the past seventeen years.
Only mining has continued to decrease in importance.
On the other hand, despite the expansion of primary
activities (agriculture, livestock, forestry, and
fishing), their contribution to GNP dropped from
22.5 per cent in 1950 to 16.1 per cent in 1967.
Commerce, services, and transportation have maintained their relative shares of GNP throughout the
period.

The product per worker, in 1950 pesos, increased from 4,969 in 1950 to 7,283 in 1965, indicating a substantial improvement in average productivity. This has been more marked in the service
and industrial sectors, because of greater availability of capital, use of modern techniques, and
good management.

TABLE 1

Gross Internal Product and Productivity
(values at 1950 prices)

Item	Total	Primary Activities	Industrial Sector	Services and Others
1950				
Internal gross product (billions of 1950 pesos)	41.1	9.2	12.5	19.4
Labor force (thousands)	8,272	4,824	1,319	2,129
Productivity (1950 pesos)	4,969	1,907	9,477	9,112
1965				
Internal gross product (billions of 1950 pesos)	99.6	17.3	35.0	47.3
Labor force (thousands)	13,676	7,092	2,779	3,805
Productivity (1950 pesos)	7,283	2,439	12,594	12,431

Source: Nacional Financiera, S.A.

In the early 1940's, additions to capital resulted in large increments of output, reflecting the
intensive utilization of industrial capacity and de-
ferral of plant maintenance and replacement. The
capital-output ratio is estimated to have been 1.5
at that time. In the early 1960's, the ratio had
increased to 2.5,[15] and at present it may well be
2.8. These increments can be explained by the fact
that at least one quarter of Mexico's gross fixed investments are long-term (i.e., slow-repayment) projects such as large-scale irrigation, communication,
and transportation facilities. This may be partly
due to the relative scarcity of short-term, high-
profit projects. Also, the establishment of modern
large-scale industries requires heavier capital investments, which have been undertaken in Mexico,
even if new capital intensive techniques may not be
the most adequate, given the country's abundant
labor supply. Investment allocation has resulted
in surplus productive capacity in some industries
(e.g., automobiles) and also has a bearing on the
magnitude of the capital-output ratio.

Industrial Activities

Mexico has plentiful reserves of natural resources for industry. It has sufficient mineral resources including petroleum, natural gas and their
by-products, forest products, hard fibers, agricultural raw materials, and the fish and sea products.
Only a few important resources are lacking, such as
bauxite, phosphorus, potassium, natural rubber, and
wool.

Growth of industrial activities in Mexico has
been largely based on import substitution and response to domestic demand, helped by protective
policies and support of the government, as well as
a progressive attitude on the part of entrepreneurs.
Addition of new industries has made possible a more
coordinated and sustained development and a better
occupational distribution, with enlargement of better paid and more stable sources of employment, as
is reflected in the increase in the number of industrial workers from 1.3 to 2.8 million between

1950 and 1965. Government intervention in this sector stimulated industry through federal and state subsidies and franchises;[16] a moderate tax structure; credit facilities for industrial development (mainly through Nacional Financiera); legal provisions to aid industries with excessive capacity; cheap energy (electrical and fuels); improvement and enlargement of transportation and communication facilities; and price and exchange-rate stability.

Mexican industry has been successful in supplying practically all the durable consumer goods needed by the domestic market and, in recent years, has moved to produce certain goods that unfavorably affected the balance of payments, such as petrochemical products and automobiles, which require much capital and complicated technologies.[17]

The volume of industrial production showed the fastest rates of growth of all activities in the Mexican economy in the period 1950-65. The General Index of Industrial Production (see Appendix Tables 10 and 11) with base 100 in 1950 rose to 313 in 1967. Within the industrial sector, electric power rose to 430 index points. Government intervention here was paramount. The State owned only 5.5 per cent of the electric power companies in 1940; by 1955, it owned 41 per cent, and in 1960, the entire electrical energy industry was nationalized. Between 1950 and 1965, generating capacity rose from 1.2 to 5.3 million kilowatts and actual production from 4.4 to 17.3 billion kilowatts per hour.

The second fastest growing industrial subsector was manufacturing, which reached 326 index points in 1967 and increased its share of GNP from 20 to 25 per cent. Substantial diversification of manufacturing activities has taken place, improving the quality of occupational sources and enlarging the exports of manufactured products. The largest increases were in the manufacture of production goods, which expanded at an average 10 per cent per year, while consumer goods increased at 6 per cent per year. Steel ingot production increased from

300,000 tons in 1950 to 2.5 million tons in 1965.
Altos Hornos de México, a State enterprise, produced
about half the total amount. Cement production increased from 1.4 to 4.2 million tons; the chemical
industry grew the fastest, given its low beginning
level. Important advances were achieved in production of petrochemicals, sulphuric acid, caustic
soda, ammonium nitrate, and phosphate. Production
of durable consumer goods (electrical appliances,
automobiles) has received special attention in the
last years. For instance, although assembly plants
for motor vehicles were established in Mexico in
the 1920's, only 24 per cent of automobile parts
were made in Mexico as late as 1960. The government established quotas according to the degree of
Mexican-material integration in the various plants,
and, by 1965, Mexican-made parts formed 60 per cent
of the finished product. The automobile industry,
however, shows substantial excess capacity; less
than 120,000 cars, trucks, and buses were made by
more than ten companies in 1967. In other manufacturing activities, such as textiles, cigarettes,
and ceramics, growth has been slow.

     PEMEX, the only company exploiting and refin-
ing petroleum, has played a very important role in
national economic development, given that oil and
gas represent four fifths of all the energy consumed in Mexico. Petroleum and coal production increased 327 per cent between 1950 and 1967, making
Mexico virtually self-sufficient in hydrocarbons.
Through exploration, crude material and gas reserves
increased from 1.6 to 5 billion barrels; processed
crude oil increased from 56 to 135 million barrels;
and total consumption rose from 58 to 120 million
barrels.

     Construction also has shown a rapid, though
fluctuating, development, at a slightly faster rate
than the petroleum industry. Growth in this activity is largely determined by government investments
in irrigation, housing projects, and so on, as well
as by private-sector investments.

The only industry that has lagged behind
national development is mining, which has gone
through critical years (see Appendix Table 12).
At the beginning of the nineteenth century, mining
represented 50 per cent of the country's total production. Today it amounts to less than 2 per cent,
though it still accounts for 15 per cent of total
Mexican exports. World market conditions, among
other factors, have limited its expansion, except
for some nonmetallic products, such as sulphur.
Lead, copper, and zinc production have actually decreased relative to 1950. The government decision
to nationalize all foreign mining companies pro-
gressively has been another important factor limiting the expansion of mining. Today, two thirds of
the capital of a company must be Mexican to be allowed to exploit natural nonrenewable resources.
Foreign capital, as a result, has been directed
toward investment in manufacturing and trade.

An important problem affecting Mexican industry is the limited domestic market, resulting from
the low purchasing power of the majority of the
population and the unequal income distribution.
Also, industry has developed some waste, in the
form of high-priced, but poor quality products,
partly as a result of import-substitution policies
that did not respond to carefully studied priorities, but were motivated by balance-of-payment difficulties. Thus, in spite of the scarcity of investment capital, certain industrial activities
have overdeveloped, and others have not received
sufficient attention and lag behind in quantity and
quality of production.

Mexican industry also shows great geographical concentration.[18] In 1964, Mexico City and the
surrounding area (containing 14.2 per cent of the
population) contributed 41.3 per cent of the total
industrial product; and if one Northern and four
Central states are added, they cover 75 per cent of
total industrial production, indicating the strong
locational force of the market in the central part
of the country.

Another important national problem bearing on
the industrial sector is the large annual increase
in the labor force. Mexico must create new jobs
for 400,000 people per year, but agriculture is already overcrowded and industry has been unable to
absorb the additional workers fast enough, let
alone absorb the surplus rural labor force. Estimates indicate that about 25 per cent of the labor
force in urban centers is surplus, which means that
there are over one half million workers who are un-
employed or have marginal or unproductive jobs.[19]

Transportation and Communications

The development of transportation facilities
has received a great impetus in the last thirty-five
years, especially since 1950. It is noteworthy,
however, that practically all the expansion in the
transportation network has been in roads and air
transport.

Railroads were built prior to 1930. In that
year, Mexico had 23,345 kilometers of railtracks;
in 1950, it had 23,332 kilometers; and, in 1965,
23,672 kilometers. Although railroad facilities
have been somewhat improved in the last two decades,
no new ways have been opened.[20] The freight volume
transported has increased considerably, however,
from about 8,500 tons per kilometer in 1950 to
18,000 tons per kilometer in 1965.

The great improvement in transportation was in
roads. Although Mexico had only a total of 1,425
kilometers of improved and paved roads in 1930, by
1950, these amounted to 21,422 kilometers, of which
13,585 kilometers were paved.[21] In 1965, the national highway network had a total extension of 60,813
kilometers, of which 35,358 kilometers were paved.[22]
At the same time, the number of automotive vehicles
in circulation increased from about 300,000 in 1950
to over one million in 1965.

Air and maritime transports have also been
greatly expanded and improved. Commercial airlines

(passenger and freight) presently service all centers of some importance in the republic. Harbors
have been improved and are well connected with the
interior of the country by railroads and highways;
sea freight handled in Mexican harbors has more
than doubled between 1950 and 1964.

The great improvement in transportation facilities has been fundamental in promoting the economic
development of the country and, in particular, of
the agricultural sector. As shall be seen later,
the great expansion in cultivated land area and the
increased commercialization of agriculture would
not have been possible without a good transportation
network, to open up new regions and provide effective markets (domestic and foreign) for a larger
agricultural output.

Agricultural Activities

Mexican agriculture has been quite successful
in satisfying the growing domestic and foreign demand, particularly since 1950. Agriculture's contribution to the economy has been particularly important in the provision of needed foreign exchange:
Over one half of the country's export income in the
past seventeen years has derived from agricultural
and livestock products (see Table 18).

Presently, Mexico has become self-sufficient
in food and raw materials, except for rubber, wool,
and other minor commodities. Between 1950 and 1966,
wheat and bean production quadrupled; corn and
sugar cane tripled; cotton, coffee, and rice doubled.
Important increases were also experienced in tomatoes,
vegetables, oil crops, citrus fruits, etc. Livestock
production and fishing (especially for export) also
increased considerably, and forestry slowly expanded.
The factors that have made these increases possible
will be discussed at length in the following chapters.

From the standpoint of agriculture's position
in the total economy, however, it is noteworthy

that, despite the rapid growth experienced, agriculture has remained plagued by underemployment and
low incomes. The population dependent on agriculture increased by 4.5 million between 1950 and 1967,
though percentagewise it dropped from 57 to 43 per
cent in the same period (see Table 5). Agriculture's
contribution to GNP is currently only 16 per cent,
indicating a much lower labor productivity in this
sector as compared to industry, services, and other
sectors. An estimate indicates that as many as 2
million out of the 6 million farmers in Mexico may
be unneeded; for all farmers, working time averages
four to five months per year.[23]

A survey conducted in 1963 by the Bank of
Mexico[24] revealed that 9.3 per cent of the families
engaged in agriculture who had monthly incomes of
over 2,200 pesos received only 35.8 per cent of
their income from this activity; 26.4 per cent of
the farm families with incomes of less than 300
pesos per month obtained only 8.1 per cent of their
income from farming.

Thus, agriculture's fine performance in terms
of output contrasts sharply with the continued backwardness and poverty that affects large portions
of this sector. This represents probably the most
serious problem that Mexico will have to face in
the coming years.

Prices and Living Standards

The wholesale price index for Mexico City (see
Appendix Table 9), which perhaps represents the behavior of the price level for the entire country,
shows that inflationary pressures were still being
felt in the early 1950's. In fact, in 1951 and
1954-55, prices rose 50 per cent, probably as a
consequence of favorable export prices and hence
larger exports, low immediate returns of government
investments, and the 1954 devaluation. Tighter
money and credit control, plus other factors reviewed earlier, have contributed to holding price
increases down to a mere 3 per cent per year for

the last ten years.   Price rises have been higher
for popular consumer goods, such as food, even
though the State has set ceilings on some staple
foods.

It is often stated that living standards for
the majority of Mexicans have not improved, despite
increased productivity, minimum wages, and government social-benefit programs. Only 11 per cent of
the labor force is organized into unions, which are
very weak, although the percentage is much higher
for industrial and other workers in urban areas.
National policy has generally favored income concentration, but this fact alone has not necessarily
meant increased savings or their channeling toward
productive activities. It is apparent that in
Mexico part of these savings has gone into the construction of ostentatious homes and buildings,
luxury expenses, tourism abroad, capital flight,
and so on. This is doubly harmful because it also
limits domestic market expansion and generates
social dissatisfaction.[25]

The unequal distribution of income in Mexico
can be appreciated from the Industry and Trade Ministry estimates of June, 1964,[26] summarized in
Table 2. Out of 10.9 million economically active
inhabitants, 3.6 million (32.6 per cent) had a
monthly income of less than 300 pesos; 4.3 million
(39.3 per cent) had monthly incomes of 300 to 749
pesos. This means roughly that 72 per cent of the
active population had a monthly income of less than
750 pesos. And less than 1 per cent of the population had a monthly income of over 5,000 pesos.

This income is also poorly distributed region-
ally. The average income of workers located in the
Federal District was 494.52 pesos per month; that
of workers in the Northwestern states was slightly
lower. Some regions, such as the territory of
Quintana Roo, showed workers' monthly incomes (adjusted for living costs) of 145 pesos; in Oaxaca
the average was 152.44 pesos, and in Durango, 155.35
pesos.

TABLE 2

Distribution of Monthly Income
in Mexico in 1964

Monthly Income (pesos)	Economically Active Population	Percentages
Up to 299	3,557,511	32.6
From 300 to 749	4,280,417	39.3
From 750 to 999	907,960	8.3
From 1,000 to 1,500	975,169	8.9
From 1,501 to 2,000	256,630	2.3
From 2,001 to 3,000	212,362	2.0
From 3,001 to 5,000	129,459	1.2
From 5,001 to 10,000	70,544	0.6
From 10,000 and up	32,985	0.3
No income	486,649	4.5
Totals	10,891,686	100.0

Source: Nacional Financiera, S.A., El Mercado de Valores, No. 33, August 15, 1966.

Foreign Trade and Balance of Payments

At the beginning of the period under study, the Korean War stimulated foreign demand for Mexican exports at favorable prices, but by 1953 the terms of trade had started to deteriorate. Domestic business was slow in 1953, because neither

private nor public investment had increased, prices
and sales had dropped, unemployment had increased,
and there was a long period of drought that affected
agriculture. To stimulate the economy, the Mexican
peso was devalued in 1954 (for the last time) from
8.65 pesos per dollar to the present 12.50 pesos
per dollar. Exports continued to increase until
1956, but then remained more or less constant until
1962, when they picked up again. Sales of services
abroad (tourism) has become increasingly more important; during 1955-56, merchandise export represented 61 per cent of the total income in current
account, but in the last six years this has been
about 55 per cent. The terms of trade, based on
1950=100, dropped to 85 in 1955 and to 77.6 in
1963, and have improved slightly in the last years.[27]

In the seventeen-year period analyzed in this
section (see Appendix Tables 3-6), the performance
of Mexican exports has been satisfactory: Exports
have increased and have been diversified, and ship-
ment of manufactured goods has gained in importance.
In 1950, commodity exports amounted to $500 million;
in 1967, they reached $1,148 million. Agriculture
maintained its share of over 50 per cent, through
exports of cotton, coffee, sugar, tomatoes, cattle,
meat, fresh vegetables, and fruit. Mining products
have continued to decrease over the past years from
30 per cent in 1950 to about 15 per cent presently;
manufactured products such as processed foods,
chemicals, steel products (and excluding sugar) increased their share from 7 per cent of the export
market in 1950 to about 13 per cent during 1965-66.

In general, imports were more dynamic than exports, especially during 1950-55 and after 1960.
Strong government protection, through import permits that cover three fourths of all commodities
and through customs duties, were very effective
in promoting domestic substitutions for imported
items. Since earlier years, substitution of food
and of durable consumer goods has received priority,[28] so that today almost 80 per cent of imports
are represented by production goods: machinery

and other equipment, raw materials, and semifinished
products.

Two thirds of Mexican trade is carried out
with the United States. Some reasons for this are
geographical closeness, size of market, communication facilities, credit granted by the United
States, and investments and financing by North
American firms of some export activities in Mexico.
The danger of excessive dependency on a single market has prompted the government to widen the geographical areas of origin and destination of trade
with good results since 1950. Exports to the
United States have been reduced from 86.4 per cent
in 1950 to 62.3 per cent in 1965, and imports, from
84.4 to 65.8 per cent. Trade has been intensified
with Western Europe, especially the Common Market
countries, and with Japan, Mexico's second most important client. Mexico has also participated in
efforts to integrate Latin America into a common
market, by joining the Latin American Free Trade
Association (LAFTA) in 1960. Member countries had
reduced their tariffs by 30 per cent for more than
9,000 products by the end of 1965; Mexican exports
to member countries have increased from $6 million
in 1960 to $55 million in 1966-67. Mexican exports
to the Central American Common Market have also
been increasing in the past years and amounted to
$17.3 million in 1967.

Mexico's balance-of-trade deficit, which
amounted to a little over $100 million in the early
1950's, has increased to approximately $463 million
in 1967. This deficit has been partially covered
by the favorable net balance from tourism and border transactions. However, the remittance of profits of foreign investors has also increased (from
$66 million in 1950 to $240 million in 1965-66), as
have government foreign-debt payments. Therefore,
the most important element the country has depended
on to compensate for the current trade deficit has
been the inflow of foreign capital, mainly long-
term credits for government investment. This on
the whole favorable balance-of-payments situation

has contributed to the strengthening of monetary
reserves. It is noteworthy that the International
Monetary Fund (IMF) declared the Mexican peso a
hard currency in 1965.

Development Programming

In Mexico, discussion of development programming[29] has been going on since the 1930's. Between
1930 and 1950, a series of circumstances made selection of higher-profit projects easy, and no official
agency was needed to establish investment priorities
to maintain a high growth rate. In the early 1950's,
it became necessary to coordinate the activities
and expenditures of the numerous public agencies,
a duty carried out by the Investment Commission
(1953-58). This task was later taken over by the
Secretariat of the Presidency, but its planning
functions fell far short of the goals envisioned
by the law that created the office. Because of
low economic activity in 1961, the requirements of
World Bank loans, and commitments made under the
Alliance for Progress, a Joint Commission of the
Secretariat of the Presidency and the Secretariat
of the Treasury was set up in 1962 (with contributions from the Bank of Mexico and Nacional Financiera) to draft the Immediate Action Plan for
1962-64 and later the Plan for 1966-70, which included planning for the private sector.

Mexico's administrative stability, resulting
from its single-party system of government, has
given considerable continuity to national economic
and social policy, concentrating on industrial and
agricultural development, and construction of the
economic infrastructure. Mexico also has had substantial experience in sectoral and regional planning and in project preparation. However, many of
the public programs and plans formulated, which
may have been excellent in themselves, either did
not find necessary and timely support or were not
consistent with other programs; thus, they were
never fully implemented.

It appears then that presently there is little
organization of efforts in this area, that the economy has not utilized capacity in some lines of production, that occasional bottlenecks arise in the
government's own activities, and that there is
little coordination between public and private activities. This situation suggests the need for
greater communication and coordination in decision-
making to facilitate the mutual adjustment of the
various sectors and make possible a better evaluation of their performance.

CHAPTER **3** STRUCTURE AND
CHARACTERISTICS
OF AGRICULTURE

LAND USE

Mexico's mountainous topography and irregular
rainfall combine to limit the land area subject to
cultivation to an estimated 24 million hectares, or
about 12 per cent of its total area of 196.7 million hectares. In 1966, approximately 15 million
hectares were actually under cultivation, of which
approximately 4 million were irrigated, the rest
being seasonal or rainfall land (temporal). Within
this area, about 1.3 million hectares were planted
with permanent crops (fruit trees, coffee, etc.).

The most optimistic estimates made of potentially tillable land in Mexico indicate that approximately 37 million hectares could probably be
cultivated, including areas presently not covered
by the agricultural census (mostly in tropical and
semitropical regions), marginal lands, and arid
lands that would require artificial irrigation.
This estimate represents only about 20 per cent of
the total land area of the country.

Pasture lands cover another 79 million hectares, but about two thirds of these lands are located in the semi-arid regions of the north that
have a low grazing capacity. These lands must be
used for extensive exploitation with cattle, goats,
and sheep. The pasture lands in the central part
of the country are generally on hills and mountain-
sides, too steep to be cultivated, although grasses
are grown also on tillable land.

About 44 million hectares are considered to be forest. However, this includes areas in which grow the istle palm, candelilla, and other semidesert plants that yield products other than wood. An estimate of actual forest land puts the area at 33.5 million hectares, of which 14.5 million hectares consist of tropical and subtropical species, 10.5 million of coniferous species, and the remaining of other species. (For detailed data on land use in 1950 and 1960, see Appendix Table 13.)

In summary, the quantity and quality of agricultural resources in Mexico cannot be considered very favorable. The outlook for expansion of cropland is not bright either, because presently unutilized land is limited and its future use is heavily dependent on construction of costly irrigation works. Given the fast rate of population growth, this situation stresses the need for increased agricultural production on the existing land base, through development and adoption of new practices and inputs. This will be further discussed later.

AGRICULTURAL (CROPPING) REGIONS

As was discussed in Chapter 1, Mexico presents a great variety of climates and topographic conditions that define several distinct natural regions. Within these, many separate agricultural regions exist, depending on the slope of the land, soil quality, availability of irrigation water, access to markets, etc. These agricultural regions (see Map 5) form a mosaic of scattered areas throughout the country, presenting widely varying types of agriculture and methods of farming, commonly intermingled within each limited region.

In spite of these limitations, there has been considerable interest in Mexico in defining agricultural regions, independent of political subdivisions, as an aid in the study, development, and conduct of programs of assistance for agriculture. Thus, in a report published in 1936, the Secretariat of Agriculture divided the country into 37 agricultural

MAP 5

Agricultural Regions of Mexico

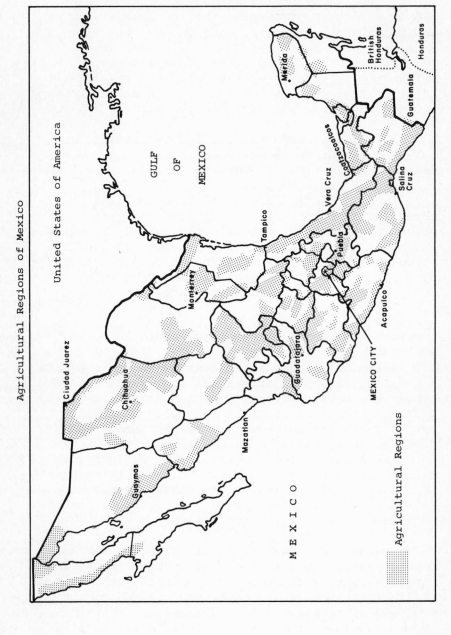

United States of America

GULF
OF
MEXICO

Ciudad Juarez

Chihuahua

Guaymas

Mazatlan

Guadalajara

Monterrey

Tampico

MEXICO CITY

Puebla

Vera Cruz

Coatzacoalcos

Acapulco

Salina
Cruz

Merida

British
Honduras

Guatemala

Honduras

M E X I C O

Agricultural Regions

economic regions, within the 5 major statistical
regions.[1] Another author has defined 44 economic
regions within 8 zones in the country.[2] The most
recent effort in this direction defines 52 agricultural economic regions in Mexico.[3]

Given such proliferation and diversity of agricultural regions, a thorough description would go
beyond the purposes of this study. In broad terms,
the agricultural regions in the semi-arid north of
Mexico are generally limited to the irrigated areas,
such as the Mexicali Valley, the Río Bravo Valley,
the Comarca Lagunera, the Delicias area, and the
coastal plains of Sonora and Sinaloa. These regions
present favorable conditions for agriculture: Farm
units are relatively large and are intensively
farmed (usually for cash crops only), modern technology is applied, there is heavy capital investment
in irrigation and machinery, and marketing facilities and government services are fairly well developed. Thus, these regions are characterized by commercial farming. Main crops are cotton, wheat,
rice, sesame, and vegetables such as tomatoes and
other high-value crops.

In the central part of the country, the agricultural regions correspond essentially to the various basins and valleys that receive enough rainfall
or are irrigated by means of smaller irrigation
projects. Some of the notable regions here are the
Bajio (basins of Jalisco and Guanajuato), the basins
of Mexico and Toluca, and the Valley of Morelos. In
these regions, farm units tend to be very small,
mechanization not widespread, and agricultural technology low. In general, these are regions of traditional agriculture, producing mostly corn, beans,
and potatoes, with mixed livestock-raising. In
some of these regions, however, the proximity of
large markets such as Mexico City has induced intensive forms of agriculture, for example, dairying
and vegetable production.

The lowlands along the Gulf coast include such
important agricultural regions as the Huasteca, Central Veracruz, and Tabasco. Sugar cane, bananas

and other tropical crops, and livestock are produced at the lower elevations, and corn and coffee predominate at higher elevations. Farms in these regions are generally geared to commercial production, although the level of technology and mechanization is still low.

Along the southwest coast, there is a wide variety of agricultural regions, dependent on either rainfall or irrigation. These include the coasts of Guerrero and Oaxaca, the Tierra Caliente region, the Mixtecas, Central Oaxaca, and so on. These regions present the poorest farming conditions of the country, are traditional to the point of still using the planting stick, and produce mainly corn and beans for subsistence purposes. Further inland, in Central Chiapas, are important coffee-producing valleys.

Finally, the Yucatán Peninsula constitutes an unimportant agricultural region, producing mainly henequen and corn and beans in isolated areas. Except for the henequen plantations, farming is practically all of a subsistence type and technology is quite primitive. An attempt is now being made to diversify the agriculture of the region with citrus and some vegetable crops.

LAND TENURE

The present land tenure structure of Mexico is an outgrowth of the Revolution of 1910. The fundamental concepts of the revolutionary movement in regard to land tenure are contained in Article 27 of the Political Constitution of 1917, which in essence states that: (1) Ownership of the land belongs to the nation, which has the right to transmit title of it to private parties; (2) land can be expropriated for reason of public benefit, with compensation; (3) the State has the right to impose controls and regulate the utilization of land in private hands for the public interest; (4) the State will take the necessary measures to break up

the large landholdings, develop small agricultural
properties, and create new agricultural population
centers with sufficient land and water. In addition,
the same article sets forth the limitations for ac-
quisition of land by foreigners, corporations, banking institutions, and religious organizations. Thus,
the Revolution's basic propositions on agrarian
structure are the proscription of latifundias as an
undesirable institution, the right of all rural
population centers to have lands (ejidos), and the
encouragement and protection of small holdings under
cultivation.

     The drastic reform of the land tenure system
of Mexico was the result of reaction against a long
historical process during which land property became
heavily concentrated in the hands of relatively few
families, while the vast masses of Indian peasants
were reduced to a semi-enslaved condition. The origins of this process date back to the early 1500's,
when the Spanish conquerors came to Mexico and found
the best agricultural lands already heavily settled
by various indigenous groups with fairly advanced
cultures. In preconquest times, the lands typically
belonged communally to the villages and were worked
communally, distinguishing three types of lands, depending on the destiny of the product: those to
support the expenditures of the community (altepet-
lalli), those to finance wars (mitchimalli), and
those to support religious activities (teotlalpan).
In addition, there were lands assigned to individual families or clans (calpulalli), which resembled
private property, though the land could not be sold
and was subject to regulations to protect the common
interest, such as the loss of rights to the land if
it was not tilled for two consecutive cropping sea-
sons.

     When the Spaniards subjugated the Indians, in
their efforts to impose Christianity and Spanish
civilization upon them, they developed the encomienda
system. Whole villages and their lands were given in
trust to individual conquerors or to religious orders
to administer and "civilize" the community, the

<u>encomenderos</u> being responsible for exacting work and
tributes from the Indians. Thus evolved the hacienda
with its typical class structure--the owners of essentially Spanish descent and the peasants, essentially Indian--which lasted until after the Revolution of 1910. Efforts made at the time of independence and in the 1850's, during the Reforma of
Benito Juárez, to restore the land to the Indians
were unsuccessful. By 1910, land ownership was so
concentrated that about 90 per cent of the rural
population owned no land at all. It was probably
the deep-rooted dissatisfaction with the social and
political implications of the hacienda, more than
its economic inefficiency, that gave rise to the
Revolution and subsequently to the agrarian reform.

Land expropriation and redistribution under the
reform proceeded slowly at first, but reached impressive proportions in the late 1930's under President Lázaro Cárdenas, and has continued at varying
speeds up to the present.

Redistribution of land under the reform has
been carried out mainly under two forms of tenure:
the <u>ejido</u> and the small private holding.

The <u>ejido</u> (from the Latin <u>exitus</u>, i.e., lands
situated at the point of exit from a village) system of tenure consists of a village and the lands
surrounding or close to it, the property rights on
these lands being vested in the community as a group
and not in individual members.* Each <u>ejidatario</u> is
entitled to receive a plot of arable land for his
lifetime use (a usufruct) and can pass it on to his
heirs, but cannot sell or rent it and must work it
himself. Should he leave the land idle for two consecutive years, his rights are forfeited. In a few
cases, the tillable land of <u>ejidos</u> has not been
divided into individual plots and is worked collectively, but the tendency in these cases too has been

---

*Legally, however, the lands belong to the
Federal Government.

toward subdivision. The pasture lands and woods
must remain permanently in common usufruct. Ejidos
and ejidatarios are not required to pay for the
lands they are granted. Within each ejido, an ejidal
agency is set up, composed of its members and elected
by popular vote, to administer and watch over affairs
of common interest.

Under the regulations of the reform law, individual ejidal parcels should have been 4 hectares of
irrigated land or 8 hectares of "seasonal" land;
however, throughout the period of application of the
law, there have been so many peasants entitled to
receive land, relative to the area available, that
often the units distributed have been of less than
2 hectares per family.* Even so, many peasants have
not received any land and have remained as "ejido
members with reserved agrarian rights," which en-
titles them to receive land in other than their villages of origin. In the process of fulfilling the
needs of these peasants, by relocating them and developing new population centers, an interior colonization scheme was developed. Furthermore, through
the process of land subdivision by inheritance,
there are presently many ejido units of less than
1 hectare of cropland, although the average size
for the country as a whole is about 7 hectares.

The land reform maintained and also created,
partly in an indirect way, numerous small private
land holdings. Originally, a small holding was
defined as one of 150 irrigated hectares or 300 hectares of seasonal land; later this limit was reduced
to 100 and 200 hectares, respectively. Properties
of up to these sizes are exempt from expropriation
and are protected by government certificates. The
new small holding resulted in part from the sale of
land in the irrigation districts, where the government put new land under irrigation. First priority

---

*Presently, units being distributed should be
of at least 10 hectares of irrigated land, or 20
hectares of seasonal land.

was given to settlement in the form of ejidos, but
the remaining land after ejido needs were fulfilled
was sold to farmers in units varying from 8 to 100
hectares. In some cases, the states were given
authority to subdivide the latifundias that fell
under their jurisdiction, and in the process small
farms were formed. In still other cases, some of
the colonization projects of the government were
conducted on a selling basis, and farmers who purchased the land were granted title to it. Finally,
the spontaneous subdivision of latifundias on the
part of landowners, who feared expropriation under
the agrarian reform, resulted in the formation of
many small holdings.

In spite of the substantial redistribution of
land effected under the agrarian reform, there still
exist very large holdings in Mexico. These are
located mainly in the semi-arid grazing lands of
the north, where the size limit is based on the
area needed to support 500 head of cattle. In addition, in the 1940's, the government granted temporary exemption certificates to the big ranchers,
whose lands would not be affected by the reform for
twenty-five years. Some of these certificates are
falling due at the present time, and the government
is proceeding to set up livestock ejidos in the
lands that become available. Other large holdings
exist in areas that are not heavily populated, such
as the Gulf Coast, but precise information on this
is unavailable, for the existence of these holdings
is illegal.

Another form of tenure that exists in Mexico,
especially in the states of Guerrero and Oaxaca,
though it is not widespread, is the agricultural
community. In this case, a group of people, generally very old Indian communities, have irrestricted
ownership of the land and may work it collectively,
or in individual units. However, many of these communities at present exist only in a legal sense, for
in practice the land parcels have become the property of those who work them. Thus, the government
is actually granting individual titles to these
farmers.

TABLE 3

Land Distribution by Tenure Groups, 1960

Tenure Group	Farm Units (thousands)	%	Land Area (thousands of ha) Total	Cropland	Crop-land, %	Average Size of Holdings (ha.) All Land	Cropland
Ejidos	1,523.8[a]	53.1	44,497.1	10,329.2	43.4	29.2	6.8
Private property, less than 5 ha.	899.1	31.3	1,328.1	1,259.0	5.3	1.5	1.4
Private property, more than 5 ha.	438.1	15.3	101,503.7			231.7	
Other[b] property, more than 5 ha.	9.2	0.3	21,755.3	12,218.6	51.3	2,364.7	27.3
Totals	2,870.2	100.0	169,084.2	23,816.9	100.0	589.1	8.3

[a]Number of ejidatarios that own land.

[b]Federal, state, municipal, and other property.

Source: Agricultural Census, 1960.

49

As a result of this long process of transformation of the land tenure structure of Mexico, a central feature of the country's agriculture today is
its dual system of tenure. Approximately one half
of the farm units consist of ejido parcels, controlling 43 per cent of the cropland of the nation,
the other half being mainly private properties (predominantly very small ones) that control the remaining 60 per cent of the cropland. Table 3 shows the
distribution of land by tenure groups according to
the 1960 census.

The various forms of tenure exist practically
in all regions of the country simultaneously, but
ejidos are relatively more important in the Central
and South Pacific regions in terms of the cropland
they encompass. Private properties are relatively
more important in the Gulf region. Other sub-
tenure forms, such as renting and sharecropping,
are insignificant in Mexico, at least as far as
published statistics reveal. Again, this is due to
the legal restriction of these arrangements, but
it appears that, in practice, renting of land occurs more often than can be documented.

The data in Table 3 point to another important
characteristic of Mexican agriculture: the predom-
inance of very small farm units (minifundia). In
fact, it can be estimated that 90 per cent of Mexican farms have less than 20 hectares of cropland,
and probably 50 per cent have less than 5 hectares
of cropland. When it is taken into consideration
that only about 60 per cent of the cropland of the
nation is tilled per year, this situation appears
even graver. Obviously, this is the result of the
scarcity of good agricultural land and of strong
population pressure, to which was added an agrarian
reform based on the postulate that every man who
works a piece of land has the right to own it; this
naturally led to the formation of minifundia. As
shall be discussed later, these very small farm
units pose a serious problem for the further modernization of Mexican agriculture and for the substantial improvement of farm incomes among the large
numbers of small producers.

CHAPTER **4** LONG-RUN EVOLUTION AND
SPECIAL FEATURES OF MEXICAN
AGRICULTURAL DEVELOPMENT

FROM 1900 TO 1930

Often the simple fact that the total agricultural output of a nation is growing is taken as an
indication of development; or with a little more
refinement, growth in agricultural output per capita is used as measurement of development. However, both total and per-capita agricultural output
could expand while the basic structure of production and/or incomes of the rural population remained at a low level. Or at least a significant
portion of the agricultural sector of an economy
might present this situation. This would be the
case if all the expansion in output could be
traced to increases in the cultivated land area
and in farm population, with the techniques of production remaining fundamentally unchanged. The
distinction between these two situations is important; for if output growth has come about in the
second manner, it would be hardly appropriate to
call this agricultural development. Hence, it becomes important in discussions of development to
examine what changes have occurred in the structure of production, distribution, and consumption
of agricultural commodities and in farm incomes.

In this study on Mexican agricultural development, special attention is focused on changes in
the structure of production: What new or improved
inputs have entered the production function, how
have the traditional inputs (land and labor) be-
haved, and what basic institutional modifications

51

have taken place that may have affected the factor
and product markets, in relation to the observed
behavior of agricultural output?

The present chapter is concerned with an over-
all view of long-run Mexican agricultural development, from the beginning of this century to the
present; the rest of the study concentrates on an
analysis of the period since 1950, during which important increases in agricultural productivity have
appeared. This approach will help dispel some of
the myths that have developed around the Mexican
experience and will bring to the fore the more important issues affecting its agriculture in recent
times and in the near future.

Figure 1 shows the evolution of agricultural
(crop) production since 1906 and the changes that
have occurred in land area harvested and in the
agricultural labor forces since 1925.* As was mentioned in Chapter 2, 1910 marks the end of the
Díaz dictatorship; it is significant that agricultural output rose from an average index value of
100 in 1900-02 to 160 in 1908-10, indicating that
"growth" was taking place, at least in agriculture,
during this period. Some of the negative aspects
of this growth, which were partly responsible for
the Revolution, were discussed earlier.

————————————

*Notice that the graph shows an index of the
volume of crop production. Although the source of
these data does not indicate how this index was
derived, it is apparent, by comparison with data
used in later chapters of this study, that this is
probably not an index of value of production, or
at least the index was not derived from the same
basic data, for the years after 1950, as used elsewhere in this study. It must be kept in mind,
therefore, that growth rates derived from the index are not directly comparable with the rates
used later.

FIGURE 1

Growth of Agricultural Production, Land, and Labor

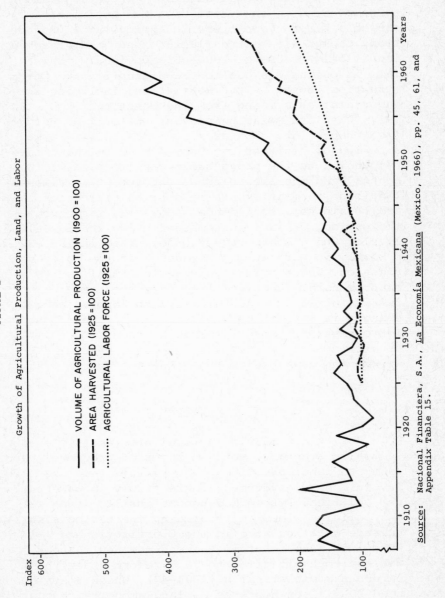

Source: Nacional Financiera, S.A., La Economía Mexicana (Mexico, 1966), pp. 45, 61, and Appendix Table 15.

53

During the next two decades, social and political events seem to have been the overriding influence on Mexican agriculture. The period 1910-21,
corresponding to the years of armed uprising,
showed a strong down trend in agricultural production, though with large fluctuations, that reached
levels below those of 1900-02. Obviously, this
fall in output was due to the disruption and destruction caused by the Revolution, including the
uncertainties arising from the Constitution of
1917, with its sweeping provisions for land reform
(see Chapter 3). The decade of the 1920's marked
a period of hesitant recovery of agriculture, corresponding to the progressive pacification of the
country and the slow pace of reforms, that allowed
landlords to maintain their control of the land
and regain some confidence. However, throughout
the period, production remained below the 1908-10
levels, and a sharp reduction occurred in 1929-30,
probably in part as a consequence of the world depression, which hit largely agricultural Mexico's
exports hard. The land area harvested and the agricultural labor force did not show appreciable
changes in quantities employed; thus, the slight
improvement in production may be considered simply
as a return toward earlier levels of productivity,
within the same basic structure of resource use.

LAND REFORM IN THE 1930'S

During the 1930's, agriculture remained essentially stagnant, both in terms of production and
land and labor use. However, by this time the
Revolutionary governments were firmly in power, the
new political system had become institutionalized,
and policies aimed at rebuilding the nation's agriculture as stipulated in the Constitution of 1917
were initiated. Foremost among the new changes
was the emphasis given to land reform under the
Cardenas administration (1934-40), which distributed 20 million hectares of land among three quar-
ters of a million peasants, or 65 per cent of all
the land distributed from 1917 to 1940 (see Table
30).

Much has been written in Mexico about the
land reform, and the most widely held belief in
the country is that this reform is to be credited
for the great advances that agriculture, as well
as the whole economy, have experienced in the last
quarter century. Unfortunately, this is a belief
that cannot be proved or disproved; at least,
there is presently not a single study that seriously analyzes this issue. Furthermore, it may be
impossible to determine a cause-effect relationship between land reform and economic (or agricultural) development because direct economic response
--if any--may lag considerably behind the institutional transformation. Most of the impact of these
reforms is social and/or psychological, and the
postreform period is seldom free of other (possibly
independent, but inseparable) events that affect
production. Indeed, all these factors are present
in the Mexican case, as shall be further analyzed
in this study. Therefore, the most that can be
done is to accept that land reform may have been
an important element leading to subsequent changes,
which in turn resulted in substantial agricultural
improvement. Whether this would have been possible
without the reform cannot be proved and is of only
historical interest at most.

Two facts associated with the land reform were
of immediate relevance, however. One is the redistribution of wealth and income that it effected,
simultaneously breaking the political power of
large landowners and changing the entrepreneurial
class in agriculture. The other fact is that land
reform did not result in rapid or appreciable
changes in resource use and agricultural output,
although by 1940 more than one half of all the
land distributed up to the present had been distributed. Furthermore, the reform affected the
best available lands prior to 1940, whereas subsequently more marginal lands have been subject to
the reform.

It would appear that the emphasis put on land
reform in the 1930's had much more to do with

national political and social interests than with
agricultural or economic development. At that
time, land represented by far the most important
form of wealth, and about 70 per cent of the population depended <u>directly</u> on it for their livelihood.
Naturally, the realization of all reforms proposed
by the Revolution hinged upon the redistribution
of wealth and power, which necessarily meant redistribution of land.

It would also appear that the Mexican leaders
quickly realized that land redistribution alone
would not solve the economic problems of the nation
and that it was at best a temporary solution. This
must have come to the fore when in the process of
land parcelization, units had to be formed that
averaged less than one half the minimum size required by law, which meant that farm family income
would likely never reach an acceptable level. In
point of fact, in the years after 1940, land redistribution was considerably slowed down and
played a very minor role among the government policies for agriculture. It was not until about
1960 that land redistribution regained momentum,
again in response to social and political unrest
among the peasants.

Gifts of land had a sedative effect on social
and political problems and were a means of retain-
ing population in the countryside; sectors of the
economy other than agriculture could expand and
provide new job opportunities. The organization
of agriculture which resulted from land redistribution was based on small family-type farms, and
was probably conducive to later output increases,
within a traditional pattern of production. It
also facilitated a "surplus" in agriculture, produced by price and wage differentials, although
this may not have been intended. The combined effect of this land policy permitted the government
to lower the social costs that would have been incurred had the underemployed rural people migrated
to the cities. The burden, however, was transferred to the same rural people, who had to support

themselves at near-subsistence levels, while at the
same time indirectly contributing to the economic
development of the nation.

With the realization that land reform alone
would probably not result in large output increases, a substantial impetus was given to agricultural credit during the 1930's, and investment
in irrigation was initiated. Under President
Cárdenas, the BNCE was founded specifically to
grant loans and promote agriculture among the
emerging ejidos set up by the reform program. In
the same decade, 144,000 hectares of land were put
under irrigation, and water distribution was improved on 103,000 hectares under government programs, thus initiating a process that was to become
probably the most significant element determining
Mexican agricultural development in subsequent
years.

The stress on land reform and irrigation during the 1930's required that agriculture receive
priority over other sectors in government policy,
although this was not reflected in the volume of
federal public investment. Only 16 per cent of
this investment was destined for agriculture, mainly for irrigation works, whereas 71.3 per cent of
federal investment was for transport and communications, the balance going to social benefit work,
industrial production, and others.[1] As mentioned
before, emphasis seems to have been placed on agriculture more for political and social reasons
than for economic ones. At least the policies
implemented did not result in significant increases in agricultural output during this period,
nor did these policies (e.g., irrigation) save
capital, as might have been expected at that stage
of Mexican economic development, if a rational effort toward development had been attempted. The
indications are that very few, if any, capital-
saving and output-raising techniques were introduced in agriculture at that time.

THE AGRICULTURAL DEVELOPMENT OF MEXICO

FROM 1940 TO 1950

The turning point in the development of Mexican agriculture came in the 1940's. About 1945, the production level of 1908-10 was finally reached again; from there on, further progress would have to come from use of more or better resources, new production techniques, better management, or any combination thereof. Starting about 1945, a rapid and sustained growth in the volume of agricultural output set in, paralleled by similar increases in the land area harvested and a somewhat slower increase in the agricultural labor force. Small gains were also made in land and labor productivity, as a result of increased use of capital inputs, which were minimal prior to 1940.[2] Some estimates indicate increases of six to eighteen times in capital inputs (machinery, equipment, fertilizer, and other working capital) used in agriculture, between 1940 and 1950.[3] On its part, the government continued large-scale investments in irrigation, incorporating an additional 529,000 hectares of irrigated lands and improving water distribution on another 391,000 hectares up to 1950. Crop credit granted by the government agricultural banks also doubled in real terms during the decade.[4]

In spite of this, agriculture fell behind industrialization in the government economic policy. For instance, by 1949-50, 27 per cent of public federal investment was being channeled for industrial promotion, whereas only 21 per cent was used for agriculture, and again mainly for irrigation; communications and transports were still receiving priority, with about 40 per cent of public investment. It is interesting, however, that agriculture should start expanding rapidly after the industrial sector initiated a vigorous development, the elements of which were examined in Chapter 2. This would indicate that agricultural development became possible only after the domestic market for agricultural products (especially for industrial crops, which increased nearly 40 per cent more than food crops between 1940 and 1950) grew stronger, when

industry could supply new inputs for agricultural
use and as the development of the economic infrastructure (mainly transportation) permitted the
opening up of new lands and better access to markets. It is to the credit of the agricultural sector that it was able to seize the opportunities
and contribute to the sustained growth of the over-
all economy, through greater provision of food and
raw materials, capital, and foreign exchange, as
well as labor. The contribution of capital needs
a further word of explanation.

The transfer of capital from agriculture to
other sectors was the principal source of financing the country's development from 1930 to at least
the late 1940's. During this period, Mexico had
no other major producing sectors and had little
access to foreign capital, the result of government
policies that penalized foreign investors. The
agricultural "surplus" seems to have been made possible mainly through the price system and export
taxes, for direct taxation of agriculture has always been very moderate. Unfortunately, there are
no studies available that have thoroughly analyzed
this aspect of Mexican development and the existing price data are incomplete and inadequate.*
But it appears that this must have been true, for
there are no other visible explanations of how the
country's development could have been financed.
Even extraction of forced savings through inflation
probably hit agriculture hardest, given the two
thirds of the population depending on this sector
at the time.

DEVELOPMENT SINCE 1950

The process of agricultural development accelerated after 1950. The period from 1950 to the
present is analyzed in greater detail in the following chapters; however, some general remarks will
be made here.

---

*See "Marketing and Prices," in Chapter 6.

In the first place, it is noteworthy that
Mexican agricultural development has been the
fastest among all Latin American countries since
1940, and few other developing countries in the
world surpass the Mexican record.[5] The growth of
agriculture in Mexico has allowed the country to
reach virtual self-sufficiency in food and even
enjoy a continued net food surplus, and at the
same time agricultural exports have been expanding
regularly.

On the other hand, in spite of the remarkable
growth in agricultural production, the present
level of Mexican agricultural productivity is not
high when compared with other developing nations.
Crop output at present is only about $100 per
hectare, a value exceeded by sixteen of the twenty-
six countries studied by the U.S. Department of
Agriculture and output per agricultural worker is
$420, lower, for example, than that of Argentina,
Colombia, Venezuela, and Chile.[6]

The discrepancy between Mexico's fast rate of
growth in total agricultural output and its low
and slowly improving level of productivity is explained by the large contribution that land and
labor, the traditional agricultural inputs, have
made to the productive process in agriculture.
Changes in these two inputs, as well as other ones,
are explored in Chapter 6; one estimate considers
land and labor increases responsible for about
70 per cent of Mexico's total growth in agricultural production in the last twenty-five years.[7]
Productivity increases, though, have become more
rapid since 1950, especially in certain regions
and for certain crops. On the average, crop yields
have risen more than 50 per cent in the last fifteen years. Also, as can be seen in Figure 1, although farm labor has continued to expand steadily,
its growth rate has fallen in the last decade.
The land area harvested, on the other hand, has
increased more rapidly, but the much faster growth
rate of output since 1950 clearly shows that important gains in productivity have been made from
that year on.

The most important factors accounting for productivity increases in the last seventeen years
have been irrigation, fertilizers, and improved
seed varieties (see Chapter 6). As has been mentioned before, the government has invested millions
of dollars in irrigation works since the 1930's,
and the cost of irrigation water is heavily sub-
sidized by it. The impact of irrigation on agricultural production and productivity can be seen
by observing that in 1950, only 13 per cent of
total agricultural production came from the irrigated lands, which represented 12 per cent of the
cropland area. By 1960, 26 per cent of production
came from irrigated lands, and these had increased
to about 18 per cent of the cropland area.

Fertilizer use, on the other hand, increased
more than 2,000 per cent, in terms of nutrient
elements, from 1950 to the present, and development of new plant varieties, especially for certain crops such as wheat, has also made tremendous
advances. In both cases, as in irrigation, government participation and promotion have been fundamental in achieving these dramatic changes, although no plans or well-stated long-run policies
were followed, nor have these developments received the propaganda and quasi-religious backing
that land reform has.

To summarize, then, it appears that since the
mid-1940's, when Mexican agriculture began to show
signs of substantial development, the main influ-
ences have been expansion of the transportation
network, which allowed a substantial increase in
the land area cultivated; expansion of irrigation,
which increased the tillable land area as well as
yields; increased use of fertilizers; crop research, which resulted in higher-yielding vari-
ties; and expansion of the agricultural labor
force. To this should be added the "pull" effect
of domestic industrialization and, in some cases
(e.g., cotton production), of the work market that
created larger markets for agriculture's produce.

As a concluding remark, it is important to
stress the present dualism that characterizes Mexican agriculture. This dualism cuts across different sections, but roughly it may be represented
as follows. On the one hand, there are some regions (typically the Pacific Northwest, parts of
the North, and circumscribed areas elsewhere in
the country) where farms are primarily private and
where farm units are larger than average, have a
greater proportion of irrigated lands, and show a
more advanced level of technology and capitalization. Farms (and livestock ranches) in these regions can be classified as commercial and are frequently or largely oriented to the export market.
Productivity and income levels among these farms
are much higher than the national average. This
group represents probably no more than one fifth
of Mexican farms.

On the other hand, there are the more traditional farming regions, where a larger percentage
of the land is operated in the form of ejidos,
farm units are typically quite small, land they
control is mostly "temporal" and hence more subject
to weather vagaries, and levels of capitalization
and technology are generally low. Agriculture in
these regions tends to be, in varying degrees, of
a subsistence type, largely oriented toward production of the traditional crops (mainly corn and
beans) for home use and the domestic market, or
sometimes also for the foreign market, as in the
case of coffee and henequen. This group, representing the majority of Mexican farmers, includes
many farm units that are marginal in terms of their
level of production and income and that must necessarily disappear in the long run if Mexican agriculture is to be fully modernized and rural misery
is to be eliminated. The process of farm consolidation and rural migration that this entails is
one of the great problems that will confront the
country in the future. The other is the process
of modernization and economic and social better-
ment of the rest of the farmers who will remain in
agriculture.

CHAPTER **5** GROWTH OF AGRICULTURAL
OUTPUT AND EXPORTS
SINCE 1950

AGRICULTURAL GNP AND POPULATION GROWTH

Gross agricultural output (expressed in constant 1950 prices) increased approximately 96 per
cent from 1950 to 1967, or at an average compound
rate of slightly above 4.0 per cent per year (see
Table 4). The increase from 1960 to 1965 was
slower, at an average rate of 3.8 per cent per year
and it further slowed down to 2.5 per cent between
1965 and 1967. Although the long-term rate of increase is well above the 3.3 per cent annual rate
of population growth, the decreasing momentum of
agricultural growth must be seriously considered.
Furthermore, the growth rate of agriculture is not
sufficient to keep up with the growth of internal
demand for agricultural products. The latter is
estimated to have expanded at a rate of about 4.9
per cent per year from 1950 to 1967,[1] which has
resulted in a slower rate of increase in the real
net balance of agricultural foreign trade, probably on the order of 3 per cent per year.* The

----

*Notice that domestic consumption of agricul-
tural products represents about 80 per cent of domestic production; hence a higher rate of growth
of demand does not preclude a continued expansion
of agricultural exports, as has in fact occurred
in Mexico. See section on foreign trade at the
end of this chapter.

63

TABLE 4

Agricultural and Gross National Product
(millions of pesos, 1950)

Activity	1950	1960	1965	1967[a]	Average Annual Rate of Change		
					1950-60	1960-67	1950-67
Crops	5,999	9,178	11,579	11,999	4.3	3.9	4.2
Livestock	2,903	4,450	5,267	5,669	4.3	3.5	4.0
Forestry	263	254	279	298	0.3	2.3	0.7
Fishing	77	136	147	162	7.0	2.5	4.5
Total agriculture	9,242	14,018	17,272	18,128	4.3	3.8	4.0
Total GNP	40,577	73,482	98,200	112,358	6.2	6.2	6.2
Agriculture as % of GNP	22.8	19.1	17.6	16.1	--	--	--

[a]Preliminary.

Source: Nacional Financiera, S.A., La Economía Mexicana en Cifras (Mexico: Nacional Financiera, 1965, 1966); and Banco de Mexico, Informe Anual 1967 (Mexico: Banco de Mexico, 1968).

FIGURE 2

Mexico: Growth of Total GNP, Agricultural GNP and Population

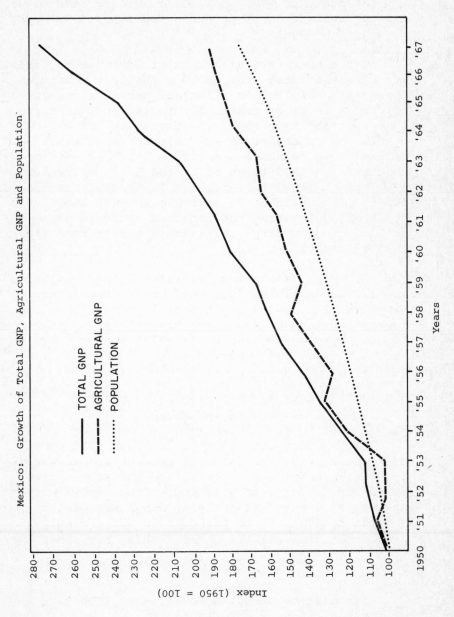

65

internal demand for agricultural products is projected to grow at an average rate of approximately
4.5 per cent per year until 1975, with a rate of
4.2 per cent for crop products and 5.0 per cent for
livestock products.[2]

The slower rate of growth of agriculture, relative to the total economy over the past seventeen
years, has resulted in a further decrease in agriculture's share of total GNP, to 16.1 per cent in
1967. At the same time, the percentage of the
population dependent on agriculture (rural) has
decreased in relative terms from 57.4 per cent of
the total in 1950 to an estimated 43.0 per cent in
1967, as is shown in Table 5. In absolute terms,
though, it continues to increase in ever larger
numbers, aggravating the problems of rural unemployment and poverty, as is further discussed later
in this study.

In terms of the economically active population,
agriculture employed 54.2 per cent of the labor
force in 1960 and 58.3 per cent in 1950, according
to the censuses of the respective years. A more
recent estimate indicates that 51.1 per cent of
the work force was employed in agriculture in 1965.[3]

AGRICULTURAL PRODUCTION BY
SECTORS AND REGIONS

Crop production constitutes about 67 per cent
of Mexican gross agricultural product and livestock
production about 31 per cent, and the rest corre-
sponds to forestry and fishing. Crops increased
at about 4.2 per cent per year and livestock at
4.0 per cent* over the period 1950-67. Forestry
production grew slightly, and fishing has shown the

---

*It must be noted, however, that livestock
statistics are very unreliable.

TABLE 5

Change in Rural and Urban Population, 1950-65

Population	1950		1960		1965		1967		Annual Rate of Growth 1950-67
	Thousand Persons	%	Thousand Persons	%	Thousand Persons	%	Thousand Persons	%	
Urban	11,262	42.6	18,254	50.7	23,602	55.3	26,028	57.0	5.0
Rural	15,174	57.4	17,749	49.3	19,087	44.7	19,643	43.0	1.6
Total	26,436	100.0	36,003	100.0	42,689	100.0	45,671	100.0	3.3

Source: Censo General de Población, 1950 and 1960, as adjusted in Secretaría de
Agricultura y Ganadería, et al., Proyecciones de la Oferta y la Demanda de Productos
Agropecuarios en México, a 1970 y a 1975 (Mexico: Banco de México, S.A., 1965), p. 42;
Dirección General de Estadística, Anuario 1965; and "El Día," January 17, 1968.

greatest average rate of growth, about 4.5 per cent
per year, although widely fluctuating from year to
year. The growth of all these sectors, except forestry, has been slower in the past seven years than
in the previous ten. The relative contribution of
each to agricultural GNP, however, has changed very
little since 1950.

An outstanding feature of this high average
rate of growth of agricultural production is the
strong difference in rates among various regions,
which indicates an uneven process of development
within the country. The regional pattern of growth
of crop production is presented in Table 6; the
regions indicated are the same as those used by the
census and described in Chapter 1. Although the
period analyzed covers only up to 1962, other
available data indicate that the trend has not
varied in more recent years.

TABLE 6

Changes in Value of Agricultural Production, 1949-51
to 1960-62, by Regions (weighted by 1960 prices)[a]
(millions of pesos)

Region	1949-51	1960-62	Average Annual Rate of Growth
North	1,961.7	2,713.5	2.7
Gulf	1,281.1	2,151.3	4.3
North Pacific	1,149.8	2.873.0	7.9
South Pacific	1,209.6	2,057.0	4.5
Central	2,387.9	3,197.7	2.4
Republic total	7,990.1	12,992.5	4.1

[a]Includes the value of thirty-seven crops;
excludes livestock.

Source: Derived from data of the Dirección
General de Economía Agrícola (volume of production
and prices) and the 1950 and 1960 agricultural
censuses.

Agricultural production has grown the most in the North Pacific region, with a 7.9 per cent average rate of growth per year over the period 1949-51 to 1960-62. The slowest growth of production has been in the Central region, with a 2.4 per cent rate; this is the oldest settled region of the country, where the traditional crops are mostly cultivated. The other fastest-growing areas have been the South Pacific and Gulf regions. These differences, of course, reflect changes in physical production as well as in the relative prices of commodities predominant in each region.

As will become apparent from the subsequent discussion, the differential rates of growth among these regions can be attributed to various factors. First, the amount and quality of the additional land put under cultivation is of great importance. Although the increases in land area have been relatively larger in the Gulf and South Pacific regions (see the following section), the positive change in the proportion of irrigated lands to new lands has been greatest in the North Pacific region. Therefore, although irrigation may have been a particularly strong factor in the North Pacific, the sheer increase in land area has accounted for the relatively high growth rates in the other two regions mentioned, which have not otherwise shown striking development features. Second, technological developments related to the main crops grown in each region, including better varieties, fertilization, etc. (e.g., wheat in the North Pacific), have also determined different average rates of growth. Third, shifts in the pattern of crops raised in each region--with greater response on higher-value crops, especially in the North Pacific --have resulted in a relatively larger growth in the value of production in some regions, although increases in physical production might have shown a lesser difference.* Finally, other factors, such

----

*If the value of agricultural production in Table 6 had been calculated on the basis of 1950 prices, even larger differences in the rates of growth would have resulted.

as the degree of commercialization of production
and greater capitalization, help explain differences in the regional rates of growth.

GROWTH OF INDIVIDUAL CROPS

Further insight into the process of agricultural development can be gained by examining the evolution of production of the main crops grown in the
country. Among the six major crops (corn, beans,
cotton, wheat, sugar cane, and coffee) that comprise 83 per cent of the total harvested area and
about 63 per cent of the total value of crop production, the fastest expanding ones since 1950 in
terms of total volume of production have been wheat
and beans (Table 7). Wheat had the fastest growth
until 1962-64, but the mounting surpluses of this
crop determined policy measures that resulted in a
substantial reduction in the area cultivated and
in a relative stabilization of the volume of production since 1964. The production of corn, coffee, cotton, and sugar cane has also in each case
more than doubled since 1949-51 to 1964-66. Among
other crops, rice is rapidly gaining in importance,
with a three-fold increase in the volume of production over the same period.

These increases in volume of production have
been due both to expansion in the area planted and
to increases in average yields, as will be discussed later. Production of the major crops increased in all regions of the country, though in
some to an insignificant degree. The larger production of corn, beans, and cotton, the traditional
crops of Mexico, originated mostly in the Central
region; the North Pacific region contributed over
four fifths of the increased wheat production and
one third of the larger cotton crop. The increase
in sugarcane production came mostly from the Gulf
and North regions, whereas coffee was produced
primarily in the South Pacific and Gulf regions.
These developments obviously follow the regional
pattern of crop production in Mexico, which is

TABLE 7

Increase in Production (Tonnage) of Important Crops

	Per Cent Increase		Annual Rate of Increase	Per Cent of Total Increase by Regions[a]				
Crops	1949–51 to 1962–64	1949–51 to 1964–66	1949–51 to 1964–66	North Gulf	North Pacific	South Pacific	Central
Corn	108.7	178.6	7.1	12.0 18.6	4.9	11.0	53.5
Beans	202.5	282.1	9.4	36.0 14.6	7.6	8.8	33.0
Cotton fiber	99.2	131.0	5.8	5.9 0.3	33.1	4.7	56.0
Wheat	205.7	181.8	7.2	3.0 0.0	85.3	0.0	11.7
Sugar cane	104.3	147.5	6.2	22.3 36.3	13.2	8.7	19.5
Coffee	117.1	154.7	6.4	0.9 28.1	0.5	56.9	13.6
Tomatoes	26.6	51.1	2.8	— —	—	—	—
Henequen	60.0	76.0	3.9	— —	—	—	—
Rice	150.9	206.1	7.7	— —	—	—	—
Sesame	110.1	122.8	5.5	— —	—	—	—

[a]Refers only to the period up to 1962–64.

Source: Dirección General de Economía Agrícola and Appendix Table 15.

71

basically determined by the nature of production
possibilities, but to the extent that some of these
crops can be grown in several regions, differences
in the rates of growth denote a move toward further
specialization in those crops that enjoy an advantage in particular regions.

The relatively slow growth of the value product of the Central region, as contrasted with its
substantial contribution to the greater volume of
production of some of the basic crops, is an indication of the more favorable prices enjoyed lately
by the other major crops, as well as by some of
the lesser crops grown elsewhere.

EXPANSION OF CULTIVATED LAND AREA

Mexico's total cropland area is approximately
24 million hectares, of which more than 14 million
are harvested annually. The area harvested expanded from about 8.3 million hectares in 1949-51
to 14.5 million in 1964-66, making an increase of
about 75 per cent. The increases in cropland area
by regions have been approximately as follows:
North, 40 per cent; Gulf, 85 per cent; North Pacific, 46 per cent; South Pacific, 68 per cent;
Central, 48 per cent. Table 8 shows the absolute
and relative increase in area harvested for the
major crops and the whole country during this
period.

Among the major crops, beans, sugar, corn,
and coffee had the largest relative acreage expansion, whereas cotton and wheat acreage expanded
little and were actually reduced after 1964. The
largest absolute increases were for corn and beans,
the basic staple foods of the Mexican people, with
almost half the expansion being in the Central region. The area devoted to cotton grew mostly in
the North Pacific and was substantially reduced in
the North region, where the area devoted to other
crops such as oranges, alfalfa, and chickpeas, in
addition to those shown in the table, was expanded.

TABLE 8

Increase in Area of Major Crops Harvested

	Total Per Cent Increase in Area		Per Cent of Total Area Increase by Regions[a]				
	1949-51 to 1962-64	1949-51 to 1964-66	North	Gulf	North Pacific	South Pacific	Central
Corn	60.2	92.4	13.1	19.7	1.8	13.6	51.8
Beans	96.3	128.4	37.1	5.6	0.8	10.8	45.1
Cotton fiber	7.8	2.7	-138.3	-2.4	146.0	43.7	51.0
Wheat	29.5	13.0	- 37.2	-0.5	187.3	- 2.2	-47.4
Sugar cane	84.5	109.8	22.6	55.8	5.6	9.6	6.4
Coffee	95.6	90.6	2.3	21.5	5.2	53.3	17.7
Tomatoes	13.0	- 11.1	--	--	--	--	--
Henequen	36.4	38.6	--	--	--	--	--
Rice	26.4	38.7	--	--	--	--	--
Sesame	53.4	66.9	--	--	--	--	--
Total Mexico	57.0	75.0	--	--	--	--	--

[a]Refers to the period 1949-51 to 1962-64.

Source: Dirección General de Economía Agrícola and Appendix Table 15.

Wheat production has concentrated also in the North
Pacific region; in all other parts of the country,
the area devoted to wheat has been reduced. The
lands planted in sugar cane and coffee expanded
mainly in the Gulf and South Pacific regions, respectively. These changes thus denote a further
regional specialization in the production of the
major crops grown in the country.

INCREASES IN CROP YIELDS

     Long-term crop-yield changes are due to numer-
ous factors that cannot be separated from each
other. These refer to shifts in the location of
production, use of irrigation water, quality of the
new land put under crops, use of new or improved
inputs (e.g., crop varieties, fertilizer, chemicals
for pest control), and so on. Although these various factors are examined in greater detail in the
following chapter, in this section a broad view of
changes in crop yields in Mexico is presented.
The evolution of yields of important crops in the
period 1949-51 to 1964-66 is shown in Table 9.
The most striking results have been obtained with
wheat and cotton fiber among the major crops,
whereas coffee and particularly sugar cane have
shown little improvement. Among other crops, the
best results have been obtained with potatoes.

     With most crops, there is a clear tendency of
a sustained increase of average yields throughout
the period up to the most recent years. As with
the increase in value of agricultural production,
changes in the average yields of crops hide substantial differences existing among regions. Table
10 presents the average yields of the six major
crops in 1962-64 and the increases experienced
since 1949-51, in the five regions of the country.
Yields tend to be higher in the North Pacific region and show fast rates of improvement, because
the state of agricultural technology in this part
of the country is more advanced. The rate of
improvement in yields of some crops has been

noteworthy also in other regions, such as the
Gulf, for beans, and the Central region, for cotton
and wheat. This further indicates the uneven pattern of development in agriculture, not only for
regions, but also for individual crops.

TABLE 9

Average Yields of Important Crops
(100 kg/ha.)

Crop	1949-51	1959-61	1964-66	Total % Increase 1949-51 to 1964-66
Corn	7.5	9.0	11.5	53.3
Beans	2.6	4.3	4.1	57.7
Cotton fiber	3.5	5.2	7.8	122.9
Wheat	9.1	14.8	22.9	151.6
Sugar cane	509.0	--	601.5	18.2
Coffee	4.0	4.2	5.4	35.0
Potatoes	45.0	56.5	82.5	83.3
Rice	17.3	21.3	23.6	36.4
Tobacco	10.0	13.5	13.2	32.0
Sesame	4.8	--	6.3	31.2

Source: Dirección General de Economía Agrícola,
for the periods 1949-51 and 1964-66; and United
Nations, Statistical Bulletin for Latin America,
Vol. II, No. 1, March, 1965, for 1959-61.

TABLE 10

Yield Increases of the Major Crops by Regions

Crop	North		Gulf		No. Pacific		So. Pacific		Central	
	Avg. Yield[a] 1962-64	Per Cent Inc.[b]	Avg. Yield[a] 1962-64	Per Cent Inc.[b]	Avg. Yield[a] 1962-64	Per Cent Inc.[b]	Avg. Yield[a] 1962-64	Per Cent Inc.[b]	Avg. Yield[a] 1962-64	Dollar Inc.[b]
Corn	8.2	29.8	11.6	26.4	14.7	53.0	10.0	15.4	9.5	28.4
Beans	4.2	57.8	7.8	110.5	8.1	100.7	3.8	48.4	3.0	49.5
Cotton	4.8	39.1	6.8	93.2	7.5	114.3	8.0	218.3	7.3	220.0
Wheat	14.7	72.1	4.5	-35.6	28.2	133.0	7.8	25.5	15.9	105.2
Sugar	583.5	31.7	469.4	- 8.4	770.5	57.4	528.1	26.8	89.6	44.7
Coffee	3.0	-19.9	4.7	16.1	4.1	5.3	4.4	6.3	3.5	- 8.4

[a]Yield expressed in 100 kg per hectare.

[b]Total per cent increase in yield from 1949-51 to 1962-64. For wheat and beans, the starting period is 1950-51; for cotton, sugar, and coffee, the ending period is 1962-63.

Source: Dirección General de Economía Agrícola.

AGRICULTURAL PRODUCTION AND YIELDS
BY TENURE GROUPS

The number of farm units and land area they controlled in 1960 by tenure groups was presented in
Chapter 3.   Corresponding data for the year 1950
are shown in Appendix Table 13.   In spite of the
expansion in the cultivated land area, the average
size of the farm unit had not changed appreciably
since 1950.   (The average size of ejido parcels was
28.7 hectares in 1950 and in 1960 it was 29.2 hectares.)   In terms of cropland, the average size was
6.5 hectares in 1950 and 6.8 in 1960.   As for private and other properties, their average size increased from 78.1 to 92.5 hectares between 1950 and
1960; in terms of cropland, however, there was almost no change.   In fact, the average size of the
nearly 1 million farms of less than 5 hectares
stayed at about 1.3 to 1.4 hectares of tillable
land; the average size of farms larger than 5 hectares remained at exactly 27.3 hectares of tillable
land in the two census years.   Hence the proportion
of the cropland exploited under ejidos, small private units, and larger private units, remained
about the same between 1950 and 1960.   The relative
stability of the tenure structure throughout this
period suggests that this factor is of little importance in explaining the rapid development of
Mexican agriculture since 1950.

However, the level of productivity and the rate
of growth of production among the various tenure
groups differ importantly.   Therefore, a further
examination of these aspects will throw light on
significant features of Mexican agriculture that
have great relevance for its future development.

The value of production by tenure groups in
1960 is shown in Table 11.   About 58 per cent of
the total value of production originated in the
larger private farms, which encompass only 15.6 per
cent of the total number of farm units of the country.   The small private farms, representing 31.3
per cent of the farm units, produced only 6.5 per

TABLE 11

Value of Agricultural Production by Tenure Groups, 1960

Tenure Group	Family Units (%)	Value of Production (million pesos)			Average Value of Production ($)[a]	
		Total[b]	Total Value of Production (%)	Crops	Whole Farm Unit	Crop Value per ha. Cropland[c]
Ejidos	53.1	7,221.4	35.7	5,869.9	4,739.1	568.3
Private and other property	46.9	13,011.9	64.3	8,525.7	--	--
Less than 5 ha. priv.	31.3	1,308.5	6.5	823.1	1,455.3	653.8
More than 5 ha. priv. and other	15.6	11,703.4	57.8	7,702.6	26,164.5	630.4
Totals	100.0	20,233.3	100.0	14,395.6	7,049.4	604.4

[a]Number of farm units given in Table 3, Chapter 3.

[b]Includes crops, forestry, and livestock products; excludes production in urban areas (poblaciones).

[c]These figures represent averages over all farm units (or over all the cropland of the nation) although not all farm units reported crop production in 1960.

Source: Agricultural Census, 1960.

cent of the total value of production. The rest
came from ejidos. To the extent that value of agricultural production may be taken roughly to represent farm income, the figures on value of production per farm unit indicate that important differences exist in income among these tenure groups.
Larger farmers enjoy gross incomes that on the average may be six times as large as those of ejidatarios
and eighteen times as large as those of the small
farmers. Therefore, the minifundio and its associated low income problem, affecting a large number
of Mexican farmers, represents a very serious problem that the rapid growth of agriculture output
has not been able to correct.

Although comparisons of changes in agricultural production between two single years are ana-
lytically not very satisfactory, some insight can
be gained into the relative rates of growth of production in each tenure group by looking at the census data for 1950 and 1960. The value of total
production, in current pesos,* increased approximately 180 per cent in the ejidos, 123 per cent in
the small private farms, and 238 per cent in the
larger farms. Again, given the relative stability
of the tenure structure during the period, these
rates of growth indicate that progress in Mexican
agriculture has come mostly from the larger private
farms, followed by the ejidos, and the smaller private farms have contributed the least to output
growth. This is in conformity with theoretical
knowledge about agricultural development and has
interesting implications for policy, oriented toward
the economic growth of agriculture, policy that may
be in conflict with the agrarian-reform doctrine
still partially being pursued in Mexico.

----

*The percentages indicated obviously include
price inflation; however, assuming that this has
affected all farmers more or less evenly, differences in the rates of growth may be taken to represent differences in real output growth.

A rough indication of productivity per unit of land area can be obtained from the figures on average value of crops per hectare of cropland in Table 11. Small private farms show the highest productivity, which is to be expected given the very small size of many of these farms, on which substantial labor inputs are applied in what may be a garden-type cultivation. Obviously, though, marginal returns to labor are close to zero in these situations. Ejidos show the lowest productivity of the three groups, which probably is due to the organizational inefficiency and other problems associated with this form of tenure, which obstruct better utilization of the land and other resources. Also, differences in the quality of cropland controlled by each of these groups may be of some significance, but, unfortunately, no data on this are available. It may be true, however, that population pressure in the ejidos has induced the cultivation of very marginal lands (former pastures of the ejidos), whereas similar action is less likely to have occurred among the private farms.

Very few research studies have been conducted in Mexico to compare productivity among farms of different sizes and tenure arrangements. One such study by Carlos Castillo[4] in the Bajio region, an important but traditional farming area, concluded that yields and productivity were generally higher in the private farms than in the ejidos. Table 12 summarizes his findings.

Another study, by Donald Freebairn,[5] analyzed comparative production efficiency among three tenure types of farms in the Yaqui Valley in 1963. This valley is representative of the most progressive farming in Mexico. The conclusions drawn from this study are that private farms were the most productive ones, followed by collective ejidal farms, whereas individual ejidal parcels had the lowest productivity. For instance, average wheat yields were 2.56, 2.26, and 2.23 metric tons per hectare for each type of farm, respectively; estimated residual labor earnings were U.S. $3,400,

TABLE 12

Productivity of Private Farms and Ejidos in El Bajio, 1954

	Wheat-Intensive Farms		Wheat-Extensive Farms		Wheat-Corn Farms	
	Private	Ejidos	Private	Ejidos	Private	Ejidos
Index of yields	152.6	121.9	110.3	99.8	116.4	106.7
Value of agric. prod. per ha. (pesos)	1,388	1,033	705	633	795	632
Gross annual income per worker (pesos)	9,087	7,818	4,775	4,820	8,802	5,863

Source: Carlos Castillo, "La Productividad de los Recursos en el Bajio," Problemas Agrícolas e Industriales de México, Vol. VII, 1956, pp. 127-54.

$295, and $303 for each group, respectively; and
the estimated rates earned on investment were 14,
9, and 4 per cent, respectively.

In summary, these studies as well as the census data, lead to the general conclusion that private farms are more productive than the ejidos.
Given that about one half of Mexico's cropland is
controlled by ejidos, this difference in productivity has a large impact on total agricultural output
and points to an important area for study and policy
action, directed at remedying those deficiencies in
ejido organization that are keeping its productive
efficiency low.

As should be expected, a considerable proportion of the agricultural product is consumed on the
farm in the smaller units, as well as in the ejidos.
This is shown in Table 13; the larger private farms
reporting sales market approximately 75 per cent of
their total production, whereas the smaller farms
market only about 46 per cent, with the ejidos in
an intermediate position. As a consequence, the
larger farms (representing only 15.6 per cent of
all farm units) contribute more than 60 per cent of
the total marketed product, the ejidos about one
third, and the smaller units, the rest.

Furthermore, it should be noted that a considerable number of farm units did not report any crop
sales, the difference being greatest for small private units, where only 36.3 per cent reported crop
sales. Comparable data for ejido parcels are not
available, but probably they present a similar situation.

Grouping the farm units according to their
volume of sales, as in Table 14, it can be seen
that the greater part of the marketed product is
produced by a very small percentage of the farms.
Assuming that each ejido parcel had sales of less
than $15,000 (not an unreasonable assumption given
the maximum size of 20 ha. of land for ejido parcels, and the average volume of sales of about

TABLE 13

Value of Sales by Tenure Groups, 1960

Tenure Group	Value of Total Sales as % of Total Value of Production	Value of Sales (million pesos)		Total Sales (%)	No. of Farm Units (thous.)[a] with Crop Sales	Avg. Value of Crop Sales per Unit (pesos)
		Total	Crops			
Ejidos	66.2	4,777.6	4,542.7	33.9	1,374.6[b]	3,304.7
Less than 5 ha. private lands	46.0	602.5	550.8	4.3	326.4	1,687.5
More than 5 ha. private and other lands	74.5	8,722.1	6,724.7	61.8	268.8	25,017.5
Total	69.7	14,102.2	11,818.2	100.0	1,969.8	5,999.7

[a]Notice that the number of units reporting crop sales is much smaller than the total number of farm units in each category existing in the country in 1960.

[b]Only 16,869 ejidos reported crop sales, or 90.2 per cent of all ejidos in 1960. Applying this same proportion to the total number of ejido parcels, the figure of 1,374.6 is obtained.

Source: Agricultural Census, 1960.

TABLE 14

Farm Groups by Volume of Crop Sales, 1960

Group by Value of Sales (pesos)	Private Farms				Ejidos			
	No. of Farms[a] (thous.)	(%)	Value of Crop Sales (million pesos)	(%)	No. Whole Ejidos[b] (thous.)	(%)	Value of Crop Sales (million pesos)	(%)
Less than 3,000	421.2	70.8	475.4	6.5	0.4	2.4	0.8	--
3,000-15,000	105.7	17.8	764.9	10.5	1.3	7.7	13.8	0.3
15,000-100,000	57.2	9.6	1,995.8	27.4	7.4	44.1	372.1	8.2
Over 100,000	11.0	1.8	4,039.0	55.5	7.7	45.8	4,156.0	91.5
Totals	595.2	100.0	7,275.5	100.0	16.8	100.0	4,542.7	100.0

[a] Farm units reporting crop sales.

[b] Ejidos reporting crop sales.

Source: Agricultural Census, 1960.

84

$3,300 for ejidal units), it can be concluded that
3.5 per cent of all farm units produced 51.1 per
cent of the value of crop sales, and 96.5 per cent
of all units produced only 48.9 per cent of the
value of crop sales. If detailed data were available for sale of livestock products, given that
these come mostly from very large ranches, the distribution would appear even more skewed.

The preceding data lead to the conclusion that
a large number of farms and farmers in Mexico are
of a subsistence type and represent a drag on the
development of agriculture. The existence of this
group of farmers points to the necessity of formu-
lating special programs and policies to solve their
problems, which represent an important social, as
well as economic, issue. This will be discussed
further in a later chapter.

An indication of differences in crop yields in
different types of farms can be obtained from the
census data for 1960. Table 15 shows the national
average yields for some of the major crops.

TABLE 15

Yields of Major Crops by Tenure Groups,
1960 (kg/ha.)

Crops	Ejidos	Private Farms less than 5 ha.	Private Farms more than 5 ha.
Corn	842	846	839
Beans	554	830[a]	559
Cotton	1,380	1,473	1,378
Wheat	1,066	1,137	1,522
Sugar cane	48,630	48,271	44,879
Coffee (cereza)	1,375	1,348	1,588
Potatoes	4,472	4,807	5,029
Rice	2,206	3,829	1,930
Tobacco	1,151	920	954

[a]Beans grown mixed with corn; yields adjusted
to a per hectare basis.

Source: Agricultural Census, 1960.

There is not a uniform pattern for crop yields
in the three types of farms. For wheat, potatoes,
and coffee, the large private farms show the highest yields; ejidos had the highest yields for sugar
cane and tobacco; for the other crops, the small
private farms showed the highest yields. It is significant, however, that the prices received for
these crops were generally higher for the larger
farms, which thus helps to account for the relatively greater value of production indicated earlier
for these farms.

EVOLUTION OF LIVESTOCK PRODUCTION

The unreliability of livestock statistics in
Mexico does not allow a thorough analysis of the
changes in production over the last decade and a
half. The following partial information will, however, give some understanding of the evolution of
livestock activity in Mexico.

Pasture land (natural and seeded) devoted to
livestock-raising comprise about 79 million hectares, according to the 1960 agricultural census.
Of these, 33 million are plains pastures and 46
million are foothill pastures. In addition, livestock is raised on arable lands left fallow or in
between plantings. Most of the pasture lands are
in arid and semi-arid regions that have a very low
carrying capacity.* In 1950, pasture lands were
reported at 67.4 million hectares,[6] indicating a
17.2 per cent expansion in the area devoted to livestock production between 1950 and 1960.

Table 16 shows the estimated numbers of livestock existing in the country in 1950 and 1964.
Looking at the most important species, cattle,
there was a substantial increase of about 70 per
cent from 1950 to 1964. This sharp increase is

---

*On the average, 10 hectares of land are
needed per head of cattle.

partly due to the recuperation of the livestock industry after a serious outbreak of foot and mouth disease (<u>aftosa</u>) in 1948, when more than 2 million head of cattle had to be sacrificed to control and eliminate the disease.

TABLE 16

Mexico: Livestock Numbers, 1950-64

Species	Number of Head (1,000)			Per Cent Change 1950-64
	1950	1960[a]	1964[b]	
Cattle[c]	15,713	17,668	26,838	70.8
Sheep	5,086	5,169	6,513	28.0
Goats	8,522	9,732	9,190	7.8
Pigs	6,896	5,988	9,325	35.2
Horses	3,581	2,489	5,785	61.5
Mules and asses	4,307	2,875	6,818	58.3
Poultry and fowl	56,994	57,668	75,479	32.4

[a]The 1960 Census considerably underestimated livestock numbers, because of "evident omissions in the answers of farmers, ranchers, etc.," <u>Agricultural Census</u>, 1960, p. 527.

[b]The figures for 1964 are estimates calculated by the Secretaría de Agricultura y Ganadería, <u>Dirección General de Ganadería</u>, adjusting and projecting the figures reported by the <u>Dirección de Economía Agrícola</u> "which are, on the contrary, exaggeratedly high." Secretaría de Agricultura y Ganadería, <u>Informe</u>, 1964, p. 393. For instance, the <u>Dirección General de Economía Agrícola</u> reported 35 million head of cattle for 1961. See Secretaría de Industria y Comercio, <u>Anuario estadistico de los Estados Unidos Mexicanos, 1962-63</u> (Mexico, 1965).

[c]Including working animals.

<u>Source</u>: <u>Agricultural Census</u>, 1950, 1960; for 1964, Secretaría de Agricultura y Ganadería, <u>Resumen del informe de labores</u>, 1964, p. 393.

Hog numbers fluctuated from a maximum of 11 million head in 1956 to about 6 million in 1960, because of the extremely unfavorable prices in 1957 and 1958. This induced the government to introduce controlled prices for hogs, which have been in effect since 1960, helping to foster hog-raising.[7]

The larger increases in livestock numbers, in general, as compared with the expansion in pasture lands, indicate a better or more intensive use of land. In fact, a sizable investment has gone into seeding pasture lands, improving the water supply, controlling grass pests, and similar measures, over the last fifteen years, especially in the northern regions; also supplementary feeding has become a frequent practice in the arid lands of the North. However, cattle-raising in Mexico is still mostly of an extension type, based on grazing. In limited areas, such as Queretaro and the Mexico Valley, dairying is conducted on an intensive basis. Pork and poultry production are mostly conducted on a modern intensive basis.

To the extent that undercounting the livestock numbers in the 1960 Census was even throughout the country, the data in Table 17 show the regional pattern of livestock-raising in Mexico, according to the statistical regions described earlier. It is noteworthy that the highest quality cattle for beef production are in the North and North Pacific regions, where the predominant breeds are Hereford, Angus, and Shorthorn, whereas in the rest of the country, the quality of the cattle is much poorer. Cebu cattle and crosses from them are becoming more important, especially in the Gulf region (Veracruz).

Current livestock production can be estimated from the figures for livestock-slaughtering. For cattle, which are an important export, the number of animals exported alive must also be included (see Appendix Table 16). There has been an increasing trend in the production of all kinds of livestock except goats* in the period 1956-65, for which

---

*A large number of goats are slaughtered on the farms and thus probably are not registered.

data are available. The sharpest increases were for
sheep, followed by beef cattle, with annual rates of
12.5 and 4.0 per cent, respectively. After a period
of very rapid increases up to 1961, there followed
one of relative stagnation during 1961-65.

TABLE 17

Regional Distribution of Livestock, 1960

Region	Pasture Land Area (mill. ha.)	Number of Head (thousand) Cattle[a]	Sheep	Goats	Pigs
North	26.1	5,101	2,226	6,280	1,129
Gulf	4.6	2,922	161	152	912
North Pacific	14.1	2,416	74	266	506
South Pacific	6.1	2,016	520	885	1,140
Central	8.2	3,733	2,188	2,149	2,301

[a]Excludes working animals.

Source: Agricultural Census, 1960.

AGRICULTURAL EXPORTS AND IMPORTS

Agricultural exports in the last five years
have constituted approximately 57 per cent of total
Mexican exports. In 1966, agriculture contributed
$669 million of foreign-exchange earnings, as com-
pared with $253 million in 1950; throughout the
period, therefore, agricultural exports (in current
dollar terms) expanded at an average rate of 6.3
per cent per year (Table 18). The most striking
change has been the twenty-fold increase in the
value of livestock exports. While export earnings
from agriculture have risen rapidly, imports of

TABLE 18

Mexico: Value of Exports (millions of current U.S. dollars)

Economic Sector	1950		1960		1965		1966		Total Per Cent Change 1950-66
	Dollars	Per Cent of Total	Dollars	Per Cent of Total	Dollars	Per Cent of Total	Dollars	Per Cent of Total	
Agriculture	253.1	51.3	442.1	59.8	655.9	58.9	668.9	56.1	164.3
Crops[a]	231.4	46.9	360.4	48.8	551.2	49.5	539.5	45.2	133.1
Livestock	2.5	0.5	45.4	6.1	60.1	5.4	73.8	6.2	1,952.0
Fish	19.2	3.9	36.3	4.9	44.6	4.0	55.6	4.7	189.6
Mining	147.2	29.8	157.6	21.3	185.0	16.6	185.4	15.5	26.0
Manuf.[a]	33.3	6.7	81.9	11.1	118.3	10.6	149.2	12.5	348.0
Other[b]	59.7	12.2	57.2	7.8	154.7	13.9	188.9	15.9	216.4
Total	493.4	100.0	738.7	100.0	1,113.9	100.0	1,192.4	100.0	141.7

[a]Sugar and molasses included under agriculture rather than manufacturing.

[b]Includes some agricultural and forest products.

Source: Nacional Financiera, S.A., La Economía Mexicana en Cifras (Mexico: Nacional Financiera, 1965); and Banco de México, Informe Anual, 1960, 1966.

agricultural products have been falling, resulting
in an increasingly more favorable balance of trade
for agriculture. This balance averaged 2.5 billion
current pesos in 1958-60, and it increased to 6.7
billion current pesos in 1963-65.[8]

The principal agricultural products exported
are listed in Appendix Table 17. Six basic products,
cotton (fiber, seeds, and waste), cattle livestock
(and meats), sugar (and molasses), coffee, henequen,
and tomatoes made up 80 per cent of the total value
of agricultural exports in 1964-66. Livestock and
sugar can be considered as "new" products for export in Mexico, for they were relatively unimportant
in 1950, when cotton, coffee, and henequen alone
made up 90 per cent of total exports. Other important exports are melons, rosin, strawberries, canned
pineapples, and, since 1964, corn and wheat. Moreover, shrimps are also a major export amounting to
an average $50.5 million annually in 1963-66. It
is noteworthy that about 70 per cent of exports go
to the United States.

As noted earlier, imports of agricultural products have shown a slowly decreasing trend, though
with considerable fluctuations in some years. The
main agricultural imports in the last five years
have been wool, rubber, forages, and breeding cattle,
but during 1963, corn was the single major agricultural import. On the other hand, around 1950, the
major agricultural imports were wheat, rubber, wool,
corn, beans, and various livestock products. That
is, the structure of the agricultural foreign trade
of Mexico has changed significantly in the past fifteen years, with the country becoming virtually
self-sufficient in the basic food products, while
enlarging and diversifying the volume of exports.
This reveals the substantial development achieved
by the agricultural sector.

CHAPTER **6** FACTORS INFLUENCING
MEXICAN AGRICULTURAL
DEVELOPMENT

The discussions in Chapters 2 and 4 highlighted
some of the basic factors at work in Mexican agriculture since the 1930's that have had a direct or indirect impact on its development. Continued political stability, consistent long-term economic policies, land reform, expansion of the transportation
network and of the economic infrastructure in general, the stimulus provided by industrialization,
an expanding world market, and population pressure,
all have brought about a vigorous demand for agricultural products and favorable supply conditions
that have made possible the remarkable growth in
Mexican agricultural production, especially in the
post-1950 period.

In this chapter, a more detailed analysis is
made of the changes that have occurred since 1950
in agricultural inputs, including some nontradi-
tional inputs as well as institutional changes
affecting this sector of the economy. First, an
effort is made to determine how much of the production increase may have been due to the expansion of
the land area under cultivation and how much to
yield increases (which, in turn, depend on a host
of factors). The growth of the agricultural labor
force and the greater use of capital inputs that
made possible the cultivation of the larger land
area and the attainment of higher yields are described and discussed in relation to the observed
growth in agricultural output, and each particular
input or factor is examined individually. No attempt is made to establish direct cause-effect

relationships or the percentage contribution of each
input to yield increases, for this would require a
more careful analysis than has been achieved for
Mexican agriculture. No rough approximations are
possible either, for most of the inputs are highly
complementary. Irrigation water, fertilization,
and improved seeds, for instance, would not be likely to produce striking yield increments unless used
jointly. In fact, the data presented in the following sections show that all these factors have been
expanding simultaneously throughout the period under
consideration here.

The data in Table 19 (derived from the formula
presented below*) give the relative contributions
of land expansion and yield increments to the growth
of total volume of production, for the six major
crops of Mexico, in the period 1949-51 to 1964-66.

Expansion of the land area accounts for about
half of the total increases in corn and bean production (using half the total harvested area of the
country); yield improvements account for about one
quarter of the increase, the higher yields on new
land area for the other. Conversely, in cotton and
wheat, yield improvement has accounted for most of

---

*For any one crop, the volume of production,
P_2 in 1964-66, may be broken down as follows:

$$P_2 = A_1 \cdot Y_1 + (Y_1 [A_2 - A_1]) + (A_1 [Y_2 - Y_1])$$
$$+ ([A_2 - A_1] [Y_2 - Y_1])$$

where A_1 and A_2 are the areas harvested in 1949-51
and 1964-66, respectively, and Y_1 and Y_2 are the
average yields over the same two periods; thus, the
first term in the equation gives the volume of production in 1949-51, the second term may be called
the "area effect," the third the "yield effect,"
and the fourth term is a combination of the area
and yield effects (that is, the result of the
yield increases in the new land area and of the
changing locational pattern of crop production).

TABLE 19

Contribution of Area and Yield Increments to Agricultural
Output, 1949-51 to 1964-66

Crop	Relative Per Cent Due to Area Expansion	Relative Per Cent Due to Yield Increment	Relative Per Cent Due to Yield and Area Combined	Total Per Cent Increase in Volume of Production
Corn	51.7	29.8	18.5	100
Beans	45.5	20.5	34.0	100
Cotton	2.1	93.8	4.1	100
Wheat	7.2	83.4	9.4	100
Sugar cane	74.4	12.4	13.2	100
Coffee	58.6	22.6	18.8	100

the increase in total volume of production, with
very little expansion in the land area harvested,
the rest being due to higher yields and such factors as differences in average yield of land, changing crop mixes, relative prices, etc. For sugar
cane and coffee, more than half the increase in production has been due to the expansion in area harvested. For the total crop production of the country,* it can be estimated that about 40 per cent
of the increase shown in the period has been due to
expansion of the land area harvested, the rest being due to higher yields and such factors as differences in average yields of land, changing crop
mixes, relative prices, etc.

EXPANSION OF THE AREA UNDER CULTIVATION

More than 6 million hectares of new lands were
put under cultivation between 1949-51 and 1964-66,
or about a 75 per cent increase.[1] The relative increases in cropland area by regions was presented
in the previous chapter. Assuming that on the average the new lands had the same yield potential as
those currently under production, expansion of the
area cultivated would account for about 40 per cent
of the growth of agricultural production in the
past seventeen years.

The single major factor in this expansion is
investment in irrigation. Approximately 1.5 million
hectares of new land were put under irrigation during this period, thus accounting for about 30 per
cent of the expanded area. This expansion was concentrated mostly in the northwest part of the country, where irrigation is especially important because some double-cropping is done on irrigated
lands (see Table 21).

For the rest, cropland area expansion has

------

*This increased approximately 190 per cent at
constant 1950 prices over the period considered.

spread throughout the country, motivated by factors
such as population pressure, new roads, redistribution of lands under the agrarian reform program,
and favorable prices. In general, the new cultivated lands were those previously untilled or in-
frequently tilled (en descanso); cleared lands (especially in the Southeast or Gulf region); or former
pastures.

The crop area expansion and yield increments,
however, cannot be wholly separated; a very important factor affecting both is irrigation, which has
allowed large areas of new land to be put under cultivation, while at the same time contributing substantially to higher yields.

AGRICULTURAL LABOR FORCE

The labor force in agriculture was estimated
at 6.9 million persons in 1965, having increased at
an annual rate of 2.6 per cent since 1950, when it
was approximately 4.8 million persons.[2] Given the
slower rate of growth of rural population, the proportion of the labor force increased from about 32
to 36 per cent of the rural population during this
period.

These figures represent only a crude estimate
of the labor input, for there is substantial underemployment and seasonal unemployment in Mexican
agriculture, but it is clear nonetheless that a
substantial increase in agricultural labor has
taken place.

This increase in rural population (and labor)
with no effective alternative job opportunities has
probably been the most important factor influencing
the opening up of new lands for cultivation. In
this sense, much of the growth in agricultural output in Mexico (especially in the more traditional
areas) has been of a "horizontal" type, that is,
more labor has been applied to more land, under an
essentially constant production function, thus

resulting in greater output with no great change in factor returns. An estimate was mentioned in Chapter 4 that would put the labor contribution at about 20 per cent of the growth in total agricultural output in the last twenty-five years.

The fastest growth in the agricultural labor force occurred in the South Pacific region, followed by the North Pacific and Gulf regions; the Central and North regions had the slowest rates of increase.[3] It is interesting to notice that the Gulf and South Pacific regions also experienced the fastest rates of cropland expansion, and the North had the smallest area expansion (see Chapter 5).

As should be expected, given the small size of most farming units in Mexico, the majority of the agricultural labor force consists of family labor. In 1960, only 24.1 per cent of the labor force consisted of wage earners, the rest being nonsalaried workers. The proportion of wage laborers was highest in the North Pacific region and lowest in the South Pacific and Central regions. On the average, two thirds of the wage laborers were employed by private farms larger than 5 hectares, the balance being employed in ejidos. In contrast, about one half of the family-supplied labor works on ejidos, slightly over one third works on the private farms of less than 5 hectares, and the balance, on the larger private farms.[4] It can be seen that this pattern of labor employment reflects the earlier descriptions of relative degrees of commercialization and traditionalism of agriculture in the various regions of Mexico.

An important characteristic of the agricultural labor market in Mexico is the bracero program, that is, the annual migration of laborers to the United States during the harvest season in that country. This program was initiated during World War II; an agreement was formalized between the two countries in 1951. In that year, 192,000 Mexican braceros went to the United States. A peak figure was reached in 1956, when over 445,000 braceros

migrated; by 1964, migration had dwindled to about
178,000.[5] The program was officially terminated in
1965, but in spite of this, 103,563 braceros were
employed in the United States that year.[6] This program has resulted in an annual increment to the
Mexican balance of payments that fluctuated between
$25 and $38 million per year, throughout the period
1951-64.[7]

     In addition to the braceros, there are illegal
migrants to the United States who engage in agricultural work. Counting only those that were appre-
hended and returned to Mexico, they amounted to
over 500,000 in 1951, reached a peak figure of over
1 million in 1954, and have diminished to a few
thousands since then.[8]

     The possibility for underemployed Mexican agri-
cultural laborers to work during part of the year
in the United States has represented an important
source of supplementary income for the rural population. The increasing pressure in the United States
to terminate the importation of foreign agricultural
labor will force Mexico to develop its agricultural
economy and domestic job opportunities at a faster
pace yet. This challenge is being met, as is indicated by the current expansion of labor-intensive
vegetable production in the Northern part of the
country, which is oriented to the U.S. export market.

                    IRRIGATION WATER

     Irrigation has probably been the most signifi-
cant factor behind the agricultural development of
Mexico, particularly since the early 1950's.[9]
Table 20 shows the expansion in irrigated acreage
since 1926, when a National Irrigation Commission
was established (later transformed into the Secretariat of Hydraulic Resources), and Table 21 indicates the regional pattern of irrigation development. From 1950 to 1967, 1 million hectares of new
lands were put into production through government
irrigation projects; on more than 400,000 hectares,

TABLE 20

Mexico: Expansion of Irrigation, 1926-67[a] (1,000 hectares)

Period	New Irrigation by Private Individuals	New Irrigation by Government		Improved Irrigation by Government	
		In Period	Cumulative	In Period	Cumulative
Before 1926	900[b]	--	--	--	--
1926-34	--	83.9	83.9	64.7	64.7
1936-40	--	63.5	147.4	55.0	119.7
1941-46	--	272.5	419.9	276.7	396.4
1947-52	--	386.7*	806.6	238.8	635.2
1953-58	--	551.1	1,357.7	196.6	831.8
1959-64	--	174.4	1,522.1	76.3	908.1
1965-67	--	142.7	1,674.8	16.9	925.0
1926-67	1,200[b]	--	1,674.8	--	925.0
Average per year 1926-67	29.3	40.1		22.6	

[a]Total irrigated area of the country, according to figures shown here would be 900 + 1,200 + 1,674.8 = 3,774.8 thousand hectares. Area of improved irrigation is not added, for presumably it does not imply expansion of irrigated areas.

[b]Figures are rough approximations.

Source: Nacional Financiera, S.A. La Nacional Financiera en el Desarrollo Económico de México, 1934-64 (Mexico: Nacional Financiera, 1964), p. 20; and Secretaría de Recursos Hidráulicos, Sinopsis del Informe de Labores, various years.

irrigation was improved by similar projects. In
addition, probably one half million more hectares
were irrigated by private individuals or ejidos in
smaller projects, including pump irrigation. This
implies about a 90 per cent increase in the irrigated area of the country over this period, from
approximately 2.0 million to 3.8 million hectares.*
Nearly half of the newly irrigated lands are located
in the North Pacific region, and in total, more than
70 per cent of these lands have been developed in
the semi-arid northern part of the country. As was
shown previously, it is in the North Pacific region
that Mexican agriculture has experienced the greatest rate of development.

TABLE 21

Expansion of Irrigation, by Regions

| | New Land Area Put Under Irrigation by the Government (1,000 ha.) | | |
Region	Before 1946	1947-52	1953-60	Total 1947-60
Pacific North	150.5	129.1	333.9	463.0
North	154.2	126.2	140.9	267.1
Central	113.4	98.3	102.0	200.3
Pacific South	1.4	28.0	10.4	38.4
Gulf	0.4	4.9	22.5	27.4

Source: Adapted from Secretaría de Recursos
Hidráulicos, Informe de Labores, 1960-61 (Mexico,
1962).

----

*Estimates of irrigated land area of Mexico
vary widely among published sources. For instance,
the Census reported a total of 4.2 million hectares
in 1960; the sources quoted here indicate about 3.8
million hectares for 1964. The difference seems to
be due mainly to variation in annual availability
of irrigation water; the highest figures would indicate the "area subject to irrigation" and the
lower ones the "area actually irrigated."

Irrigated lands are devoted principally to corn, cotton, and wheat, which occupy 77 per cent of the total irrigated crop area of the country, as shown in Table 22. Cotton, wheat, and alfalfa, however, are the major crops most dependent on irrigation. Thus, improved irrigation would seem to be a very significant factor explaining the increased yields of these crops, although it is considered that the full yield potential on irrigated lands is far from being realized, mainly because of the limited use of fertilizers and improved seeds.[10]

TABLE 22

Main Crops Grown Under Irrigation, 1960

Crop	Area Under Irrigation (1,000 ha.)	Per Cent of Total Crop Area	Per Cent of Total Irrigated Area
Corn	629.4	9.2	26.9
Cotton	603.7	80.3	25.8
Wheat	578.1	68.3	24.7
Sugar cane	106.1	35.2	4.5
Beans[a]	76.0	10.3	3.2
Alfalfa	57.6	70.2	2.5
Rice	53.6	55.7	2.3
Other	236.1	--	10.1
Total	2,350.6[b]	--	100.0

[a]Excludes beans planted together with corn.
[b]Irrigated area of harvested crops.
Source: Agricultural Census, 1960.

The higher yields on irrigated lands, plus the stability of production under these conditions, are largely responsible for the sustained increase in total agricultural production in Mexico.

FERTILIZER USE

Fertilizer consumption has been growing at a rapid pace since 1950, constituting the other major factor accounting for the significant increases in agricultural production in Mexico. Total fertilizer applications per hectare, however, are still well below the amounts used in the developed countries, as demonstrated in the following tabulation.[11]

Country	Fertilizer Consumption (in Tons of Nutrient Elements) per 1,000 Hectares of Arable Land
Mexico	8.6
United States	36.2
Japan	248.7
Western Europe	78.5

The data presented in Table 23 indicate that nitrogen consumption increased twenty-four-fold between 1948-52 and 1966; phosphate consumption increased ten-fold, and potassium, five-fold. Total consumption of this last element, however, is still fairly low. In terms of total nutrients per hectare of harvested land, fertilizer use increased from 2.6 kilograms per hectare in 1948-52, to 14.9 in 1960, and to 25.4 in 1966. Fertilizers are being adopted by Mexican farmers at a rapidly increasing rate, total consumption of nutrients having more than trebled since 1960.

The area receiving fertilizer applications increased from 504,000 hectares in 1950 (about 5 per cent of the harvested area), to 1,782,500 hectares in 1960. This is still only about 15 per cent of the total area harvested.[12] This would indicate that, although fertilizer use has increased greatly, it is only a beginning, and a tremendous potential remains for higher crop yields through greater fertilizer use.

The principal crops receiving fertilizer applications during the past few years have been

cotton, wheat, and, more recently, corn. By regions,
the greatest increase in fertilizer use has occurred
in the North Pacific region, where over one third of
the harvested area is presently fertilized; the Central and North regions follow in importance, with a
proportion of their fertilized area similar to the
national average; the Gulf and the South Pacific
regions show the lowest use of fertilizers, as well
as lower rates of increase in use, with less than
10 per cent of their harvested area receiving fertilizer applications.[13]

TABLE 23

Consumption of Fertilizers, 1948-66
(1,000 tons of nutrient elements)

Fertilizer Element	1948-52	1956	1960	1964	1966	Total Per Cent Increase
Nitrogen	10.4	69.5	118.2	228.5	261.1	2,410.5
Phosphate	8.9	28.6	43.6	59.5	103.7	1,065.1
Potassium	2.2	6.7	17.0	12.5	14.2	545.4

Sources: For 1948-52, Food and Agriculture
Organization, Production Yearbook (Rome, Italy,
1960); 1956-64, Nacional Financiera, S.A.; 1966,
Secretaría de Agricultura y Ganadería, Programa
Nacional de Fertilizantes.

The greater use of fertilizers in the North
Pacific region is again easily explained by the
greater degree of commercialization of agriculture,
the availability of irrigation water, the predomin-
ance of the wheat crop (for which excellent improved
varieties have been developed), and the better economic position of farmers in this area, who do not
need to depend on government credit for the purchase

of inputs. However, the increased use of fertilizers in the Central region must be attributed to
government promotion, through extension services,
propaganda, and supply of credit, concentrated on
the high-rainfall areas of Jalisco, Michoacán, and
México, as well as in Veracruz in the Gulf region.[14]

More difficult to explain is the still relatively low use of fertilizers in Mexico. This must
be attributed to a combination of factors: the
scarce and variable rainfall in many of the agricultural areas, inadequate supply of improved seed
varieties and other complementary inputs that would
allow better crop yield response, low incomes of a
majority of farmers and very limited availability
of credit, and the usual lag in adoption of new
practices by farmers, more acute in the case of
traditional, illiterate, and poorer ones, as are
many of the Mexican agricultural producers.

The increased yield potentials to be realized
from greater fertilizer (and complementary inputs)
use in Mexico, however, are quite good, as has been
demonstrated in various experiments. For instance,
in most areas where corn is presently planted,
yields could be increased to 4 tons per hectare,
against the usual 1 ton now obtained.[15] The additional cost incurred would be about 940 pesos per
hectare, equal to the cost of 1 ton of corn. Therefore, a doubling of the present yield would be sufficient to cover the additional investment needed.[16]
Experiments conducted with potatoes also indicate
good response to fertilizers, both in physical and
economic terms.[17] In general, fertilizer applications are recommended for practically all crops by
the National Agricultural Research Institute.[18]

It is to be expected, therefore, that a much
greater use of fertilizers in Mexican agriculture
will be made in coming years. The government is
promoting its use through a variety of means, including price ceilings, as well as greater domestic
production of fertilizers. Presently, there exist
more than thirty plants that supply about one half

of the domestic needs, the rest being imported,
mostly from the United States. Government protection of the industry, through an import-licensing
system and import duties, is expected to result in
self-sufficiency in fertilizer production by 1970,
although importation of phosphoric and potassic raw
materials will expand. It is important to observe,
however, that the domestic price of fertilizers may
be 10 to 50 per cent higher than the equivalent imported product, depending on the type of fertilizer
and other factors, which represents a penalty on
Mexican farmers and an obstacle to pushing fertilizer applications to higher levels.[19]

IMPROVED SEEDS

Production of improved seeds in Mexico dates
back to the mid-1940's with the first results of
the research undertaken by the Rockefeller Foundation in cooperation with government agencies. Today,
the major agency in charge of producing improved
seeds on a commercial scale is the Productora
Nacional de Semillas (PNS), which utilizes the
varieties developed by the agricultural research
institutions. In fact, this agency has a monopoly
in the production of certain improved seeds, notably
hybrid corn and beans, and no production by private
companies or farmers is allowed. Table 24 gives
the production of improved seeds by PNS for the
main crops over the past few years.

PNS indicates that it supplies 20 per cent of
the total corn seed planted annually in Mexico, and
25 per cent of the wheat seed, the rest being produced directly by farmers. Nearly all wheat seed
is in improved varieties, largely produced by the
farmers from earlier acquisitions of PNS seeds.
According to the 1960 Census, only 308,700 hectares,
or 4.5 per cent of the total area in corn, were
planted with hybrid seeds. Other sources,[20] however, indicate that 625,000 hectares (about 10 per
cent of total corn area) were planted to improved
corn seed in 1961. For industrial crops, such as

cotton and sugar cane, the development and distribution of new varieties is mostly in the hands of
large private concerns; reportedly, most or all of
the cotton crop is in improved varieties.

TABLE 24

Production of Improved Seeds for
Selected Crops (metric tons)

Crop	1949-50	1955-56	1959-60	1960-61	1961-62	1965-66
Corn[a]	2,250	5,200	6,840	b	7,360	3,920
Wheat	--	--	20	409	6,508	27,886
Beans	--	--	93	90	--	1,480
Sorghum	--	--	166	79	153	5,445
Rice	--	--	--	--	--	4,275
Potatoes[a]	--	--	--	--	--	13,052
Oilseeds	--	--	--	--	--	2,590

[a]For corn and potatoes, figures shown are average production for the two years indicated; for
other crops, the periods correspond to the cropping
year.

[b]Not applicable, given explanation in note a.

Sources: Productora Nacional de Semillas,
Quince Años de Producción de Semillas de Alta
Calidad (Mexico, 1962); Secretaría de Agricultura y
Ganadería, Memoria de Labores 1965-1966 (Mexico,
1966).

Production and adoption of improved seed varieties thus seem to have been important in raising agricultural production in Mexico, especially for wheat and cotton. It is interesting, however, to speculate why adoption of improved corn seed has been so much lower than for these other crops. Several reasons account for this. In the first place, corn is grown mostly in the traditional agricultural regions, where farm size and income problems, weather vagaries, cultural levels, etc. produce a less progressive attitude on the part of farmers than in the more commercialized and advanced regions of the North. Secondly, successful use of hybrid corn seeds necessitates a "package" of inputs and practices. This has not been well developed, extended, or otherwise made available to Mexican farmers to any large extent; also, the need for a "package" makes adoption more complicated, and hence retards its widespread appearance on the scene. Thirdly, given the great variation in agricultural regions or areas in Mexico and the high specific adaptability of hybrid corns, a great number of varieties must be developed (unless non-photo-period-sensitive varieties of wide adaptability are bred) and this has not been done to a sufficient degree. Also, the monopolistic character of the seed industry has caused mass reproduction of seeds to be insufficient for the needs of the country. Finally, other factors such as scarcity of credit and a corn quality problem (in Mexico, corn is used mostly for human consumption) have also resulted in a slower rate of adoption of hybrid corn.

The former reference to corn yield potentials, however, when improved seeds are used along with fertilizers and other inputs, indicate that there is available technical knowledge and inputs for increased yields and production of corn in Mexico. Hence, if an appropriate program is put into effect, corn production on the presently cultivated area could increase tremendously.

PLANT PROTECTION

The government agency responsible for plant
protection programs is the Dirección General de
Defensa Agrícola, which operates quarantines and
campaigns against specific pests and diseases with
both biological and chemical control methods. In
1963, the Dirección employed 1,426 persons and had
a budget of 25 million pesos ($2 million) but its
principal activities were concerned with control of
insects and diseases attacking cotton, beans, fruit
trees (citrus), and grasses.[21]

Farmers have increased their use of pesticides
almost nine-fold between 1950 and 1964, from 14,100
to 121,000 tons of ready-mix products, at an average rate of 18.1 per cent per year.[22] The principal
crop thus treated is cotton. Approximately 2.2 million hectares per year (18 per cent of the total
harvested cropland) were treated with insecticides
from 1959 to 1961.[23] However, the spotty and limited scope of these measures suggests that they
were not a vital factor in the remarkable increase
in agricultural production.

AGRICULTURAL CAPITAL AND CREDIT

Technological changes in agriculture, such as
mechanization and use of fertilizers, improved
seeds, and pest controls, require greater capital
investment at the farm level. Table 25 shows some
of the changes in the capital structure of Mexican
agriculture between 1950 and 1960. Private investment in mechanical equipment and irrigation facilities grew very rapidly, as did public investment in
irrigation. The capital value of livestock, which
constitutes more than two thirds of the total agricultural capital, also increased substantially but
is not included in the table because of the under-
estimation mentioned earlier.

In terms of the regional distribution of agricultural capital, investments per hectare of harvested

land or per worker employed are highest in the
North Pacific and North regions, which utilize two
to three times as much capital as the next highest
region, the Central region.[24]

TABLE 25

Amount and Composition of Capital in
Agriculture, 1950 and 1960[a]
(millions of 1960 pesos)

Type of Assets	1950	1960	Average Annual Rate of Growth
Fixed capital			
Construction	1,347	1,691	2.3
Rail tracks and roads	57	71	2.2
Hydraulic works	1,255	1,922	4.4
Semifixed			
Machinery, equipment, and vehicles	2,564	4,317	5.4
Tools and appliances	426	287	-3.9
Total	5,649	8,288	3.9

[a]Excludes livestock.

Source: Secretaría de Agricultura y Ganadería,
Proyecciones de la Oferta y la Demanda de Productos
Agropecuarios de Mexico, a 1970 y a 1975 (Mexico:
Banco de México, S.A., 1965).

Most capital investment, especially in mechanical equipment, is concentrated in the non-ejido
sector. During the decade 1950-60, mechanization
of Mexican agriculture was rapid, with an increase
in tractor numbers from 2.6 to 5.1 per 1,000 hectares of cultivated land.[25] Mechanization is growing slowly in the ejidos too, for though they had

only 16 per cent of all tractors in 1950, by 1960 they had 20 per cent of the total.

In Mexico, most of the farms or ejido parcels are very small. Quality agricultural soils are scarce, and many farmers live close to the traditional socio-economic subsistence level. Consequently, savings and capital accumulation within the farms are almost nonexistent. Under these conditions, credit is an essential factor for agricultural improvement, a fact that was recognized long ago in Mexico.

The three major government banks providing credit to agriculture up to 1965--the BNCA, the BNCE, and the Banco Nacional de Comercio Exterior-- were created in 1926, 1936, and 1937, respectively. The annual volume of loans granted by these banks from 1950 to 1963-66 is shown in Table 26. The credit granted by these institutions has increased steadily, with the BNCE maintaining its share of about 50 per cent of the total government credit granted per year. In terms of 1950 purchasing power, the increase in volume of government credit to agriculture from 1950-51 to 1962-63 has been 146 per cent, which is almost twice as large as agricultural GNP over the same period. Nevertheless, the BNCE estimates that it is able to serve only about 18 per cent of the ejidos of the country, encompassing some 250,000 ejidatarios in 1964;[26] the BNCA served only a little over 31,000 persons in 1963.[27] Also, in spite of the increase in agricultural credit granted, the percentage of bank credit received by agriculture in relation to the total for the country decreased from 38 per cent in 1942 to 20 per cent in 1960.[28]

In 1955, the Guarantee and Development Fund for Agriculture was set up under the trusteeship of government and directed by the Bank of Mexico to provide credit to farmers through private banks. The volume of loans advanced under this fund is shown in Table 26. Although the figures are not always available, private banks, encouraged by the government, extend agricultural loans by several

means, the fund being one. Private bank credit to
agriculture is now estimated to be equal to or to
surpass government credit. Table 27 shows the volume of agricultural credit outstanding at the end
of each year up to 1964, separating private commercial institutions and government finance agencies.
The absolute and relative importance of government
finance to agriculture is overestimated in this
table, for the balance shown accumulates the past-
due loans of government banks, although many are
probably uncollectable, but not those of private
banks.

TABLE 26

Agricultural and Livestock Loans Granted
by Mexican Government Banks, 1950 to 1963,
at Current Prices (millions of pesos)

Year	Ejido Bank	Agricul- tural Bank	Foreign Commerce Bank	Bank of Mexico[a]	Total	Total in 1950 Pesos[b]
1950	204.1	184.0	48.0		436.1	436.1
1955	604.6	357.1	154.3		1,116.0	699.7
1960	1,249.4	526.4	191.2	212.2	2,179.2	1,028.7
1961	968.4	598.8	204.9	187.8	1,959.9	909.9
1962	1,150.0	725.9	213.0	189.6	2,278.5	1,022.7
1963	1,200.0	914.5	191.0	226.1	2,531.6	1,115.7
1964	1,198.5	962.6		365.5		
1965	989.0	1,073.2		520.5		
1966	1,142.7			618.4		

[a]Fondo de Garantía y Fomento para la Agricultura,
Ganadería y Avicultura, established in 1955.

[b]Value in terms of 1950 pesos, as deduced from
the current and real value of total GNP.

Source: Adapted from Foreign Agricultural Service, The Agricultural Policies and Programs of
Mexico, 1964 (mimeographed) (Washington, D.C.: U.S.
Department of Agriculture). For 1962 and 1963, the
figures were modified according to the latest annual
reports of the corresponding banks; 1964- 66, direct
information.

TABLE 27

Volume of Agricultural Credit Outstanding at End of Year
(millions of pesos)

Type of Institution	1950	1959	1960	1961	1962	1963	1964
Commercial institutions							
Deposit and savings banks	--	1,201	1,235	1,241	1,275	1,561	1,979
Other finance companies	--	534	382	604	682	706	842
Other private finance	--	15	13	17	19	16	20
Total private	338.6	1,750	1,630	1,862	1,976	2,283	2,841
Government finance agencies	723.5	3,174	3,930	4,458	4,950	5,661	6,140
Total	1,062.1	4,924	5,560	6,320	6,926	7,944	8,981
Per cent of government agencies	68.1	74.6	70.7	70.5	71.5	71.3	68

Source: Banco de México, S.A., Informe Anual, 1960-64.

Within the last five years, a number of factors, from the relative slow-down in agricultural
production to social unrest in some rural areas,
have made it clear that more vigorous policies in
support of agriculture should be established.
Credit appears to have been selected as one of the
chief means to achieve this. To coordinate and improve the operations of the two existing agricultural banks, the Banco Nacional Agropecuario was
founded in 1965, at the same time the Banco Nacional
de Comercio Exterior discontinued its operations in
agriculture. The government is also applying increasingly greater "moral persuasion" on the private
banking system to expand its operation in the agricultural sector. In addition, foreign financing
has been sought to step up agricultural credit operations. In 1962 and 1965, the United States
loaned Mexico $20 million for this purpose, and so
did the International Bank for Reconstruction and
Development, which extended a $25 million loan in
1965. These facts indicate the tremendous importance currently being given to credit as a means of
promoting agricultural development in Mexico.

It is difficult to document the use of agricultural credit in Mexico by length of term and purpose
of loans. Some partial data are presented in Table
28.

These data indicate that more than half of the
credit granted by government institutions is short
term, for direct production (avio); a smaller proportion is for mortgage, marketing, or other purposes; and the rest is intermediate term, mainly
for plantations, irrigation, and livestock. The
production credit is used mainly for cotton, wheat,
corn, and beans.

An important noticeable trend in the past four
or five years has been the increase in loans for
livestock, both by the BNCA and the Banco de
Comercio Exterior, and particularly by the Guaranty
Fund through the private banks. More than 65 per
cent of the loans granted under the fund auspices

TABLE 28

Agricultural Credit Granted by Term and Purpose (millions of pesos)

Purpose	Banco Nacional de Crédito Ejidal				Banco Nacional de Crédito Agrícola				Banco Nacional de Comercio Exterior		
	1958	1959	1963a	1965a	1958	1959	1963a	1965a	1961	1962	1963
Production (avio)	585.1	805.6	871.6	491.5	257.4	254.9	713.3	834.2	90.3	107.7	101.1
Cotton	248.0	332.7	288.0	101.3	85.0	68.5	195.0	209.2	31.1	34.6	21.1
Wheat	102.3	147.4	111.8	99.7	60.7	64.6	150.0	164.2	3.5	4.3	4.9
Corn and beans	93.6	154.0	198.2	178.7	84.7	79.2	190.0	170.9	10.3	12.8	11.5
Henequen	65.3	65.3	83.0	--	--	--	--	--	--	--	--
Rice	25.6	35.4	25.8	22.8	--	--	15.0	14.8	10.6	8.0	3.2
Sugar cane	8.3	8.9	--	5.6	--	--	--	--	--	5.3	9.2
Coffee	11.3	12.5	--	8.7	--	--	--	--	--	0.2	0.1
Other c	30.8	49.3	164.6	74.7	27.0	42.6	158.3	275.1	34.8b	42.5b	51.1b
Equipment, livestock, etc. (refaccionario)	75.4	131.4	157.6	55.6	33.9	115.0	99.6	71.8	67.3	90.2	59.6
Permanent crops	21.8	24.3	66.8	15.7	8.0	39.2	3.0	1.3	--	--	--
Irrigation	24.8	73.6	32.1	2.8	7.2	5.9	7.0	33.3	--	--	--
Machinery	8.0	7.8	24.9	10.9	4.4	6.3	10.0	2.9	1.7	8.3	2.5
Land clearing	15.6	7.9	10.5	7.3	0.8	1.6	--	2.3	1.3	1.1	0.3
Livestock	--	--	13.3	--	7.4	61.7	75.0	21.4	54.1	69.4	51.5
Other c	5.3	17.7	10.0	18.9	6.1	0.3	4.6	10.6	10.2	11.4	5.3
Mortgages, direct and other	161.5	142.9	171.0	144.9	78.4	98.7	101.6	167.2	47.3	15.1	30.3
Total	822.1	1,079.9	1,200.0	989.0	369.7	468.6	914.5	1,073.2	204.9	213.0	191.0

aApproximate breakdown.

bLargely for chicle.

cThis category may include some of the items listed when no detailed breakdown was available.

Source: Annual reports and unpublished statistics from each of the three banks for the years shown.

were for livestock in 1963. It is unfortunate that
no data are available on the loan activities of the
new Banco Nacional Agropecuario, for it is thought
that currently this has become the most important
government agency to deal with agricultural credit.

AGRICULTURAL EDUCATION, RESEARCH, AND EXTENSION SERVICES

Education, research, and extension services
are three activities closely interrelated and generally accepted to be of fundamental importance for
the development of agriculture. Because of this,
and because of the scope and growth of these activities in Mexico during the period analyzed in this
study, they are described in some detail in Chapter 8.

In terms of the role played by each in Mexican
agricultural development it is probably accurate to
say that research has had the strongest impact,
mainly through the breeding of improved varieties
of crops, as was shown earlier. Of course, education has also been generally improved among the
agricultural population, as shown in Table 29, but
the level and breadth attained are still too limited to be of much significance, except for the
"elite" of researchers and managers or administra-
tors. As for the role of extension services, the
scant numbers of technicians engaged in this activity over the past years also limited its effect on
development. Much more important would seem to be
the tremendous improvement in communications generally (roads, transport, radio, television, and
so on) that have allowed farmers to come in some
contact with new ideas and knowledge regardless of
their educational level.

MARKETING AND PRICES

The government intervenes in the marketing and
pricing of agricultural products. In 1961, Compañía
Nacional de Subsistencias Populares (CONASUPO) was

created, superseding a marketing agency in operation since 1938, to administer agricultural support
prices, maintain adequate reserves of basic food
crops, thereby regulating the domestic market, and
help to improve popular nutrition. CONASUPO is
currently supporting the prices of corn, wheat,
rice, beans, sorghum, and chile, generally at prices
well above the world market level.[29] In 1966,
safflower was added to the list.

TABLE 29

Education Level: Active Population in
Agriculture by Major Skills, 1950 and 1960

Type of Worker	1950		1960	
	Number	Per 1,000 of Total	Number	Per 1,000 of Total
Professionals and technicians	1,197	0.2	8,072	1.3
Managers, sales-men and other employees	26,868	5.6	83,215	13.5
Labor[a]	4,810,067	94.2	6,053,643	85.2
Total active agricultural population	4,838,132	100.0	6,144,930	100.0

[a]Labor is more than 50 per cent illiterate.

Source: Adapted from La Educación en el
Desarrollo Nacional (Mexico: Vo. Congreso Nacional
de Industrias, 1964). Based on seventh and eighth
population censuses, 1950 and 1960.

Data on agricultural prices in Mexico do not
lend themselves to a clear analysis of their effect
on the supply of agricultural products. Often the
prices reported are not those actually received by
farmers, but are "rural" prices, official prices,
or some average of these. Furthermore, data on
prices paid by farmers are not available. Some estimates, however, have been made of the trends in
agricultural prices. For instance, the BNCE[30] has
developed parity ratio indexes (prices received by
farmers divided by prices paid by farmers) that indicate the ratio was 103 in 1960 and 1961, 115 in
1950, and 100 in 1939, the base year. However,
these indexes are based on "rural" prices as indica-
tors of prices received, whereas prices paid are
based mostly on wholesale prices in Mexico City,
which obviously are not the prices actually paid by
farmers.[31] Therefore, the BNCE index most likely
is biased in favor of farmers; the true situation
may be that agriculture over a period of time has
suffered some price squeeze.

The data for the period since 1950,[32] though
suffering similar shortcomings, show that although
the general index of "rural" prices increased about
65 per cent between 1950 and 1960, prices of agricultural commodities relative to prices of manufac-
tures and services decreased by about 18 per cent
over the same period. In general, prices were more
favorable for agricultural products for the domestic market than for export. The general index is
not very meaningful, however, because important
differences exist among commodities.[33]

A rough indication of trends in price ratios
for various groups of commodities between 1950 and
1964 may be obtained from the data in Table 30.
These are indexes of wholesale prices in Mexico
City and therefore do not represent prices received
or paid by farmers; however, assuming rather constant marketing margins, they provide an indication
of trends over the period. It can be observed that,
except for grains, agricultural, and particularly
livestock, products seem to have enjoyed a favorable relationship when compared with the over-all
general index.

TABLE 30

Index of Wholesale Prices in Mexico City,
1951-66 (base 1954 = 100)

	1951	1960	1966	Per Cent Increase 1951-66
General index (210 items)	89.9	137.5	152.8	70.0
Unprocessed food	92.7	147.8	169.3	82.6
Grains	102.4	128.0	156.4	52.7
Vegetables	95.1	162.0	158.0	66.1
Fruits	84.7	119.1	129.4	52.8
Animal products	86.0	173.8	196.3	128.2
Nonfood consumer goods	92.6	132.8	152.9	65.1
Fuel and energy	91.4	159.4	183.3	100.5
Vehicles and parts	79.4	150.6	167.7	111.2

Source: Banco de México, Informe Anual, 1966,
(Mexico: Banco de México, 1966), p. 63.

Without a much more careful analysis, however,
it is very difficult to determine the role that
agricultural prices may have played in inducing
greater agricultural production. Probably the only
time this happened was with commodities enjoying
support prices, not because of a rising trend, but
because their price was above what the free market
might have determined at any time.

LAND REDISTRIBUTION

Agrarian reform has been a major factor in
Mexican agriculture since 1916, when the land

redistribution program was initiated, but it was particularly important in the 1930's, as was discussed in Chapter 4. From 1916 to 1967, more than 64 million hectares (about two fifths of the nation's total productive land) were distributed among over 2 million farm families.

The data in Table 31 show the pace of the land distribution program over the period indicated; it is important that almost 40 per cent of these lands were distributed from 1950 to 1967, and in particular, from 1958 to 1967. However, the quality of these lands (hillsides and pastures) is much inferior to that of lands distributed in the 1930's, which were the best in the country.

TABLE 31

Agrarian Reform: Land Redistribution, 1916-67

Period	Land Area Distributed (1,000 ha.)	Families Benefited
1916-34	10,618.2	938,701
1934-40	20,073.0	774,009
1940-46	5,327.9	112,447
1946-52	4,520.3	90,406
1952-58	2,282.0	38,739
1958-63	12,500.0	294,363
1963-67	9,470.0	131,460
Total: 1916-67	64,791.4	2,380,125

Source: Secretaría de Agricultura y Ganadería, Informe de Labores, 1963-1964; and for 1963-67, Informes Presidenciales al Congreso de la Unión, for each year.

As was mentioned earlier in this study, it would be nearly impossible to assess the contribution of the land reform program to Mexican agricultural development. However, it probably has played a significant role in the long run in providing incentives to the individual producers, in inducing the expansion and more intensive cultivation of land, and in effecting some income redistribution. In general, land reform, as a basic postulate and program of the Mexican Revolution, appears to have succeeded in transforming the political, social, and economic balance of the nation, thus helping to create conditions of internal peace and stability favorable to over-all economic development. The expanding economic activity has, in turn, provided markets and better opportunity for agricultural development.

On the other hand, it has had some unfavorable results also, such as creating a <u>minifundia</u> problem, some tenure insecurity, especially among the large livestock producers, as well as management problems, mainly in connection with operation of the <u>ejidos</u>. Some of these problems will be discussed further in Chapter 10.

CHAPTER **7** GOVERNMENT POLICIES
AND PROGRAMS FOR
AGRICULTURE

PUBLIC INVESTMENT AND PLANNING
IN AGRICULTURE

As has been repeatedly mentioned in this study,
Mexican Government participation, intervention, and
control in agriculture have been substantial ever
since the 1930's, when land reform received a big
push, large irrigation investments were initiated,
agricultural credit was expanded, and so on.
Whereas the history of this participation has been
explored in earlier chapters, government policy for,
and promotion of, agriculture in the recent past
and at the present time is now considered. Attention is centered on those aspects of public policy
that have a direct bearing on agriculture; however,
the indirect benefits accruing to agriculture from
other government action, such as development of the
transportation network and of the economic infrastructure, as well as industrial promotion, should
not be forgotten.

A good indicator of government interest in
agricultural promotion is probably the federal budget, including the transfers made to decentralized
government agencies. By showing government investment and expenditure for agriculture over the years,
it indicates the degree to which stated policies
may in fact be implemented. In Table 32, all budget
expenditure items that go to agriculture have been
classified under "agricultural development." This
consistently constituted about 10 per cent of government expenditures, and most of this expenditure

TABLE 32

Agriculture's Share in the Federal Budget

	Average 1949-50		1961		1963		1965		1967	
	Mill. $	%	Mill. $	%	Mill. $	%	Mill. $	%	Mill. $	%
Agricultural development[a]	310	9.2	1,218	11.0	1,289	9.3	1,926	10.8	2,636	11.9
Secretaría de Agricultura y Ganadería	41	1.2	252	2.3	271	2.0	390	1.9	418	1.9
Total federal government	3,602	100.0	11,041	100.0	13,801	100.0	17,854	100.0	22,108	100.0

[a]Agricultural development includes mainly the Secretariats of Hydraulic Resources, Agriculture and Livestock, and Agrarian Affairs, and also small portions of budgets of other Secretariats.

Source: Nacional Financiera, Nacional Financiera en el Desarrollo de México, 1964, p. 28 and Table 28.

was for irrigation projects. Table 33 gives a detailed breakdown of the budget for 1965 and 1967,
as compared with 1949-50. It is apparent that agriculture's share has not varied radically and that
the major shift in government policy, as reflected
by the budget, has been toward the expansion of education at all levels. It should be noticed, however, that the figures shown in the two tables correspond to the "authorized" expenditures of the
Federal Government; in fact, actual or effective
expenditures under the federal budget tend to be
twice as large, thus generating substantial budgetary deficits.[1] For instance, in 1965, total actual
budgetary expenditures of the Federal Government
were 36.7 billion pesos; expenditures of the three
secretariats concerned with agriculture were only
1.6 billion pesos. This would mean that agriculture was allocated only about 4.5 per cent of the
realized Federal budgetary expenditures.

The budget of the decentralized agencies and
government enterprises has been rapidly increasing
in the last years, from 19.2 billion pesos in 1965
to 33.4 billion in 1967. This, however, is mostly
financed with revenues of the same agencies and enterprises; the deficits are covered through government transfers or subsidies. These agencies also
suffer the same deficit problem as the Federal Government; in 1965, actual expenditures of these agencies were 8.1 billion pesos more than their authorized budget.

Four agencies dealing with agriculture have
received very large government subsidies in the
last few years, as shown in Table 34. The most important of these, the marketing agency CONASUPO,
has been second only to the National Railroads as
recipient of government transfer payments.

Government subsidies for agriculture through
decentralized agencies amount therefore to slightly
above 1 billion pesos per year in the last few
years, or almost two thirds of the direct allocations in the federal budget. The social welfare

TABLE 33

Distribution of the Federal Budget (millions of pesos)

Rank 1965-67	Ministry	Average 1949-50 Amount	%	1965 Amount	%	1967 Amount	%
1	Education	298	8.3	4,563	25.5	5,775	26.1
2	Hydraulic Resources	254	7.0	1,477	8.3	2,103	9.5
3	Public Works	453[a]	12.6	1,280	7.2	1,573	7.1
4	Defense	523	14.5	1,230	6.9	1,386	6.3
5	Communications	[a]	--	1,124	6.3	1,186	5.4
9	Agriculture	41	1.2	340	1.9	418	1.9
14	Agrarian Affairs	15	0.4	109	0.6	115	0.5
	All others	2,018	56.0	7,731	43.3	9,552	43.2
	Total	2,602	100.0	17,854	100.0	22,108	100.0

[a]In 1949-50, Public Works and Communications were a single ministry.

Source: Dirección General de Estadística, Anuario Estadístico 1951-52, and Excelsior, December 13, 1965 and 1967.

124

nature of these expenditures is strongly indicative
of the particular orientation of current government
policy for agriculture.

TABLE 34

Transfers of the Federal Government to
Consumption and Social Aid by National
Agricultural Agencies and Enterprises
(million current pesos)

Agency	1960	1963	1965	1966
CONASUPO	--	400	634	500
Ejidal Bank	50	417	375	415
Agricultural Bank	30	30	30	30
Agricultural Insurance Corp.	86	33	100	100
Subtotal agriculture	166	880	1,139	1,045
Total all agencies	1,641	3,036	3,803	4,226

Source: Secretaría de Hacienda.

Mexico does not have a national planning commission and has not formulated national development plans from which a clear picture of its agricultural policies could be formed. Nevertheless,
the considerable degree of government decision-
making for agriculture, involving goals, projections, and comprehensive policy measures, is sometimes considered to be equivalent to planning,[2]
although this is not well integrated with the development of other sectors. Occasionally, partial
(for example, for such crops as cotton, sugar, and

coffee) or sectorial plans are formulated, but these
are seldom fully implemented and thus are of limited
use. In addition, there are many government agencies, concerned especially with investment and
credit activities (Ministry of Finance, government
banks, etc.) whose planning and intervention cuts
across various sectors, including agriculture. It
is often considered that a much greater coordination than now exists should be achieved among the
several agencies directly or indirectly concerned
with agricultural development.[3] Finally, it should
be noted, as is shown subsequently, that the government sometimes appears to have a "development plan"
for agriculture, but the widespread opinion in the
country is that no well-integrated plan really exists.[4] Indeed, these government plans are more in
the nature of broad statements of objectives, needed
changes, etc., but do not contain precise projections of investments and expected output of crops,
by regions or nationally. In general, they are not
plans in the strict sense of the word, as are those
of India, for instance.

At the end of 1965, a five-year National Agricultural Plan was submitted to the President, with
the following basic objectives:

(a) To produce the basic foodstuffs necessary
    to satisfy the increasing internal demand,
    improving also the quality of the products.

(b) To supply agricultural raw materials for
    industry.

(c) To produce surpluses for export and in-
    crease foreign-exchange earnings.

More specifically, the plan would aim at: reducing the current grain surpluses; seeking new
markets for coffee exports; expanding cacao production and processing; producing import-substitution
crops; and in general raising incomes of rural
people. Subsequently, annual stages of the agricultural plan have been formulated, redefining the

objectives and quantifying targets;[5] nevertheless,
this still remains essentially a statement of desired goals. This plan probably stemmed from the
critical findings of the research undertaken to study
the future supply and demand of agricultural products, the Projections study referred to several
times in this book. This analysis of supply and
demand may be what has come closest to a serious
effort at planning although it represents only the
first, or "diagnostic," stage. In fact, the ad hoc
committee that was set up to conduct this study was
made permanent in 1966, with the objective of pur-
suing further the over-all analysis and projection
of agricultural activities, which may bring it close
to being an agricultural planning office.

At the end of 1962, Mexico had formulated an
Immediate Action Plan for 1962-64, under the requirements of the Alliance for Progress agreements,
which had as one of its important objectives to
stimulate agricultural production. This was to be
achieved by allocating about 18 per cent of public
investment for farm improvement, mostly irrigation;
in addition, it was hoped that about 14 per cent of
private investment would also go to agriculture.
No follow-up or evaluation of the achievements of
this plan are available, and in fact, all indications are that it was never really put into effect.

Other important partial development plans are
the following: The Río Lerma-Chapala-Santiago Plan;
the corn plans of Jalisco, Veracruz, Michoacán, etc.;
the sugar plan; and the various plans in connection
with irrigation development, which will be discussed
subsequently.

In 1966, a National Livestock Program also was
formulated to serve as the basis for developing livestock over the 1966-70 period.[6] The formation of
this program also was prompted by the finding of
the Projections study that the greatest shortages
in the next ten years would be in livestock products,
especially beef. This program contains a long list
of goals and means to achieve them, all with the

fundamental objective of raising livestock production. Again, however, "economic planning" is
notably absent from this program.

Aside from the statements in the most recent
plans just mentioned, Mexican agricultural policy
is concerned fundamentally with expanding agricultural and livestock production, both for the domestic and export markets, and with improving the incomes and living conditions of the rural people.
Within these general objectives, it is also seeking
to diversify agriculture and to increase the processing of farm products in the country. The major
means by which the government attempts to achieve
these goals are reviewed in the following sections.

LAND DISTRIBUTION

It is the stated policy of the government to
continue the land redistribution program until all
the "affectable" lands have been passed on to small
farmers or ejidatarios.[7] Estimates of the area
available for distribution vary widely, and unsatis-
fied peasant requests for land exceed 2 million.[8]
It is apparent, however, that most of the better
lands for distribution have been disposed of, if
the present limits of inaffectability are maintained.[9] Furthermore, it is the minifundia (farms
of less than 5 hectares) that are becoming increasingly more of a problem.[10]

As most federal lands are in tropical or arid
zones, their distribution and settlement require
the expansion of existing population centers or the
creation of new ones. Present policy is not favorable to the creation of new centers as part of the
land distribution scheme. Small-scale resettlement
programs have been continued in the past few years,
moving farmers from arid or more populated areas to
the tropical and largely unpopulated Southeast. As
these programs are expensive and risky, no large-
scale movement of farmers is expected, but resettlement will be continued.

Since the repeal of the Colonization Law in 1962, all settlement of land sponsored by the government is to be carried out in the form of ejidos, thus not granting full ownership rights to the beneficiaries.* The government has reasserted also its policy of not extending the inaffectability clause for grazing lands when the original twenty-five-year exemption from distribution falls due. Therefore, all grazing lands that become available for distribution will be turned into livestock ejidos. In fact, it appears that future land policy will have to concentrate on the formation of livestock and forestry ejidos, in the more marginal lands of the north and south, including eventually the exploitation of the deserts.[11] This will require large investments and greatly expanded credit services.

A major task of the land policy at the present time is the correct definition of farm property and ejido boundaries and the legalization of land rights of present owners or holders of land (parcelamientos legales). The present lack of a good cadastral survey represents a serious obstacle to land policy.

In general, Mexican land policy is still aimed at eliminating the last remains of latifundia and supporting the ejidos and small private holdings, as two basic postulates of the Revolution. Although the efficiency of agriculture under these forms of land tenure now seems dubious, no basic changes in land policy are contemplated, with improvement to be achieved through other means, mostly through credit and extension programs. At this stage of Mexican development, land reform is more a policy goal in itself, with strong rural welfare characteristics, than a means of achieving greater productivity in agriculture.

---

*However, in the old communities, where over time the land has been subdivided into individual units and the "community" has ceased to be, government is granting ownership titles to individuals, since these have refused to adopt the ejidal system of tenure.

LAND RECLAMATION AND IMPROVEMENT

Land reclamation through irrigation has been
the most important single policy tool of the Mexican Government in promoting agriculture. Irrigation
development accelerated since the late 1940's, after
the Secretariat of Hydraulic Resources (SHR) was
created in 1946, and was stepped up during the
1950's and up to the present. This can be clearly
appreciated from the Federal budget data in Table
32. The SHR has responsibility for the planning,
construction, control, and administration of irrigation and flood-control works, as well as supplying
potable water and sewage disposal.

Irrigation investments are effected under four
major programs: the Large Irrigation Program, concerned with the development of major structures on
rivers for irrigation of areas larger than 5,000
hectares; the Small Irrigation Program, concerned
with development of irrigation schemes for areas of
less than 5,000 hectares, considered to be of great
social importance because it benefits the groups of
smaller and poorer farmers; the Commissions, largely autonomous and concerned with studying, developing, and operating irrigation projects in the areas
under their jurisdiction; and the Irrigation Rehabilitation Program, concerned with rehabilitation of
irrigation areas where, because of hasty or faulty
planning and maintenance, distribution systems and
soils deteriorated (mainly because of salinity
problems).

The SHR exercises a heavy control on much of
the irrigated land of the nation, especially
through the Irrigation Districts. In 1964-65,
these covered over 2 million hectares of irrigated
lands, or more than one half the total of the nation.[12] In these areas, water allocation among the
various crops, and among farms, is determined by
the Irrigation District authorities, in consulta-
tion with the Secretariat of Agriculture. This control over water, which is indispensable in these
areas, becomes a powerful policy tool to guide

production according to government objectives, and
is in fact extensively used. At various times, cotton, wheat, safflower, and other commercial crops
have been favored, whereas others, such as corn and
beans, have been discouraged through water allocation.

Irrigation work in Mexico has been criticized
because it was estimated that return on investment
was too low.[13] This was attributed to insufficient
attention given to the improvement of farming methods in the areas put under irrigation, inadequate
complementary water distribution systems and drainage works, construction of some poorly located dams,
etc. However, no exhaustive analysis has been made
yet on this matter, and it is recognized that it is
very difficult to determine the real returns obtained from irrigation projects in Mexico.[14]

Expansion of the crop area through irrigation
will likely continue to be the single most important
government measure to increase agricultural production. The current federal budget allocations for
the Secretariat of Hydraulic Resources and the number of irrigation projects under way indicate that
the traditional rapid pace in this area is being
continued. In 1964-65, three major dams were completed and nine were under construction, irrigation
canals were under construction in four zones. Close
to 500 small irrigation systems were completed or
under way. Land reclamation also includes drainage,
antisalinity, and other restoration projects in existing irrigation areas.[15]

Plans drawn up by the SHR for 1965-70 indicate
that an additional 623,000 hectares will go into
production in the period, 74 per cent of which will
be in the Northern and Central regions.[16] A long-
range plan considers increasing the total irrigated
area of the country to 5.9 million hectares by 1985.[17]

In addition to irrigation with surface water,
over 800,000 hectares are irrigated with subterranean
water by private farmers and _ejidos_, but with author-
ization and under the surveillance of the SHR, which

often regulates the amount of water that each farmer
can pump. Further increases in deep-well irrigation
at present rest on private enterprise, with the aid
of credit programs from official banks and assistance from the SHR. The potential for this type of
irrigation, however, is not well known because of
the lack of an inventory of subterranean waters.[18]

Limited land improvement in the form of soil
conservation measures is also conducted or encouraged by the government. Forest protection has received much attention recently, and programs (mostly
through livestock credit) for pasture improvement
have also expanded.

MARKET REGULATIONS AND PRICE CONTROLS

As stated earlier, the government has supported
the prices paid to farmers for certain crops.
CONASUPO is responsible for the administration of
these prices and is authorized to buy and sell in
the local market, to import certain products when a
shortage threatens, and to transport and store agricultural products. Through subsidiary agencies it
operates over 400 retail stores, of which 274 are
in the Federal District area, to help maintain retail ceiling prices on the basic foods. In addition, it operates a system of 51 "mobile stores"
and 56 dairy stores in the lower-income areas of
the Federal District.[19]

In 1965, CONASUPO was made into a decentralized
agency of the government to give it more flexibil-
ity in its services and permit it to act as an ad-
visory, planning, and executive organization.[20]

Presently, Mexico is facing the problem of having produced surpluses of corn, wheat, and beans,
and government policy is making important changes
to adjust to the new situation. In 1965 and again
in 1966, the support price for wheat was lowered,
and subsidies for freight, storage, and milling
were eliminated. CONASUPO will buy corn at the

support price only in the nonirrigated areas, where
almost nothing else can be grown.[21]   Thus, the government exercises control over the production of
various commodities through its price policy, and
it also partly regulates the location of production,
both through its price and water allocation policies.
In the case of corn, these policies clearly favor
the smaller, traditional producers, rather than the
cause of increased crop production. The reason for
this is obviously social and political.

In addition, corn and wheat have been sold in
the world market at prices below the support level.
Grain storage capacity of Almacenes Nacionales de
Depósito also was expanded by 40 per cent in 1964-65,
surpassing the present capacity of 4 million tons.

Although there are no direct acreage or production controls in Mexico, there is some regulation
of agricultural production through the credit policies of the government agricultural banks and through
allocation of water in the Federal Irrigation Districts. As already mentioned, this latter measure
at present definitely favors production of cotton
and other export crops and penalizes corn and bean
production.

The government also has intervened in other
areas than land and water. In labor, it has set
minimum wages for agricultural workers, which in
1966-67 averaged 15.72 pesos per day (against 18.69
pesos for city workers). However, it is not known
to what extent these wages are actually paid. The
government also has set ceiling prices on fertilizers, as was mentioned earlier, and prices of agricultural machinery are also controlled. Furthermore, through allocation of official bank credit,
considerable control is exercised over the purchase
of agricultural machinery, supplies, and so on. In
spite of all this, however, there has not been any
major integrated program specifically concerned
with the availability and distribution of inputs
in the agricultural areas. This is largely left
to private enterprise.

FOREIGN TRADE REGULATION

Foreign trade of agricultural commodities is extensively regulated in Mexico.[22] The purpose of this regulation is to restrict imports and encourage exports. Imports are discouraged by high taxes and a severe licensing system, and exports are encouraged by selective, low export taxes, credit facilities, and barter arrangements.

All imports of agricultural products are subject to permits either from the Ministry of Industry and Commerce or from the Minister of Agriculture. As mentioned before, certain basic food commodities are imported exclusively through CONASUPO, as was edible oil during 1965. CONASUPO has also imported corn, sorghum, and nonfat dry milk, but only when domestic production has been insufficient to meet demand at the desired prices. Among the agricultural imports subject to high import taxes are the following: cheese; fresh, dried, and preserved fruits; fruit juices; nuts; canned fish; fresh and canned vegetables; tobacco; and animal fats.

A compensatory foreign-exchange system has also been set up to encourage exports of certain agricultural products, such as cotton and coffee. Under this system, import permits for a list of commodities are granted subject to the exportation of an equal value of agricultural products, approved by the government. Export taxes on many agricultural commodities (wheat, corn, rice, beans, strawberries, etc.) were lowered in 1964 in order to promote larger exports and to help the farmers meet the increased costs of production.

Mexico is not a member of the General Agreement on Tariffs and Trade (GATT); it has bilateral agreements with several countries, especially soft-currency areas. It is a member of three international commodity agreements for wheat, sugar, and coffee. Mexico is a member of the Latin America Free Trade Association (LAFTA); agricultural products, however, represent only a small proportion of Mexico's trade with LAFTA countries.

AGRICULTURAL CREDIT

The substantial government action in this area
was discussed in Chapter 6. Credit control may be
regarded as one of the important tools of the Mexican Government's agricultural policy. Agricultural
credit as a policy tool is used to help increase
output, to encourage production of specific crops
or products, and to provide relief to small farmers
and ejidatarios, although these objectives are usually not clearly separable.

Selective credit controls by the Bank of Mexico
(central bank) induce private banks to make agricultural loans; private credit is directed to production purposes. Through the same controls, private
banks are encouraged to lend for certain purposes,
such as livestock-raising; thus, indirectly the government can encourage particular lines of production.

Promotion, orientation, and/or control of agricultural production is achieved more directly through
the national banks. By heavy concentration of loans,
the government hopes to increase the output of
selected commodities. In the past four or five
years, for example, the BNCA and the Guarantee Fund
have been giving decisive importance to livestock
promotion in all its aspects, which includes not
only granting substantial loans, but also establishing centers for sheep-breeding and for livestock-
fattening.

Both the BNCE and the BNCA perform functions
for ejido and small private farmers. In this respect, the government recognizes the need to help
the lowest-income sectors of the rural population
and conducts an "incomes program" through credit
operations that are in fact equivalent to family
subsidies.

Efforts are being made, however, to rescue
these farmers from their present situation. The
large AID and IBRD loans to Mexico for agricultural
credit to small farmers, which is administered

through private banks, includes the provision of technical assistance to the farmers so that this credit can be used productively.

CROP AND LIVESTOCK INSURANCE

Mexico is one of the few Latin American countries that has developed an effective agricultural insurance system under government auspices.[23] Started in 1946, it first covered only damage by hail, but later was expanded to provide comprehensive agricultural and livestock insurance. Insurance was operated partly by private companies grouped in a consortium and partly by a federation of mutual insurance companies. This insurance system operated consistently at a loss that by 1959-60 had reached the figure of $143.1 million.

To remedy this situation, in 1963, a new agricultural insurance law was passed that created the Aseguradora Nacional Agrícola y Ganadera, S.A., combining the various mutual companies and the consortium under a single semigovernmental entity. This agency issues insurance directly in some regions, and in others it reinsures mutual companies against risks of droughts, hail, frost, hurricanes, fires, diseases and pests, water damage, and death of animals. This insurance is compulsory for borrowers from the national agricultural banks, a requirement that has helped to spread the system and improve its operation.

EDUCATION, RESEARCH, AND EXTENSION SERVICES

Long-range government policy for agricultural development includes the support of agricultural education, research, and extension services.

Nine of the eleven higher agricultural schools of the country are either state or federal institutions; only two of them are private. The Ministry of Agriculture operates the National School of

Agriculture,Chapingo, which is the largest and best-
equipped institution for higher agricultural education in Mexico. It also provides partial financial
support for the provincial schools and lends its
personnel and research facilities to help their program. These provincial schools are becoming increasingly more important in terms of quantity and quality of students trained.

Because all other programs of assistance to
agriculture (such as credit, extension services,
research, disease control) increasingly require
more technically trained personnel, efforts are
being made to expand and upgrade agricultural education. The most significant effort is the Plan
Chapingo, which is discussed in Chapter 8.

A very important aid to agricultural development is the work of the National Institute of Agricultural Research, which evolved out of cooperative
work with the Rockefeller Foundation and which carries out a systematic and successful program of
crop improvement. The new techniques and varieties
are demonstrated on individual farms in cooperation
with the extension service; a government agency,
Productora Nacional de Semillas, produces seeds of
these improved varieties on a commercial scale. Research in the livestock industry, on the other hand,
is quite deficient, because of lack of support for
the institutions responsible for it. Specialized
agencies for sugar and coffee research receive better support and have been more successful.

The Extension Service operates in every state,
but with an extremely inadequate staff. The personnel of the Extension Department of the Secretariat of Agriculture has not been expanded substantially in the recent years, and earlier plans
to increase the number of extension agents from
about 400 to 2,000 by 1970 appear to have little
chance for fulfillment.

OTHER

The government is also engaged in a program
for the improvement of the livestock industry by establishing livestock-breeding centers, pasture improvement, research in animal nutrition, and importation of breeding stock, in addition to providing
credit for livestock production.

Other policy measures for agriculture include
plant protection programs, animal disease control,
and establishment of processing plants for agricultural products. These as well as many other projects, often conducted by semi-autonomous government
agencies, are not sizable programs and currently do
not play a major role in Mexican agricultural policy.

The foregoing brief review of past and current
government policies and programs for agriculture
shows that the government has intervened to a fair
degree, regulating and promoting agricultural development in the past seventeen years in Mexico. On
the whole, government policies have protected and
favored the agricultural sector; it is hard to consider any of the policies reviewed as discriminatory against agriculture. Hence, it can be concluded that the government has been successful in
providing the infrastructure, incentive, and stability necessary for farmers to invest in and adopt
new technologies, within the limits set by the
structure and average state of development of the
agricultural sector.

CHAPTER **8** AGRICULTURAL EDUCATION,
RESEARCH, AND
EXTENSION SERVICES

Broad and significant developments have taken
place in agricultural education, research, and extension services in Mexico since 1950. An economic
evaluation of the impact of these activities on the
growth of agricultural production is beyond the
scope of this study; however, a description of
these developments and of the present state of education, research, and extension services for agriculture will help to understand the role they are
playing in the improvement of the sector's performance.

The functions of agricultural education, research, and extension are carried out under the
general direction of the Ministry of Agriculture,
but interrelate in a system unique to Mexico. Under the Ministry of Agriculture there is a Sub-
Secretary for each of the program areas of agriculture, livestock, and forestry. However, the general trend is for more integration of the program
areas particularly in teaching institutions and in
agricultural extension. Figure 3 shows the organization of the Ministry of Agriculture.

The most significant effort to integrate education, research, and extension has been through
Plan Chapingo,[1] initiated in 1963. Under this program, the National Center for Agricultural Education, Research, and Extension was established at
Chapingo and inaugurated on February 22, 1967. The
physical plant of the National Agricultural School

FIGURE 3

Organization of the Secretariat of Agriculture and Livestock of Mexico

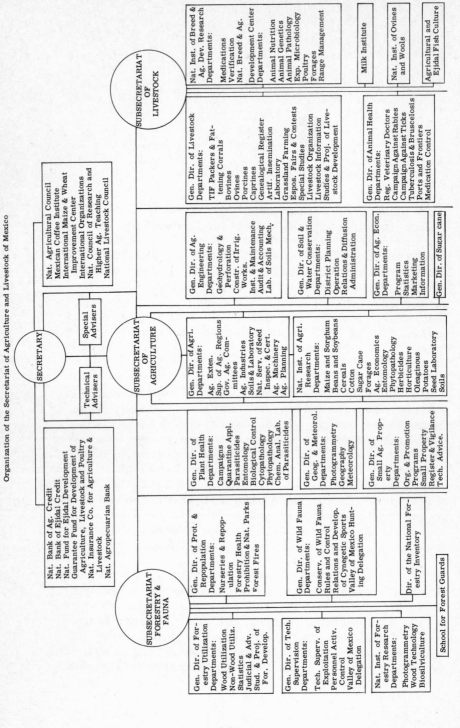

140

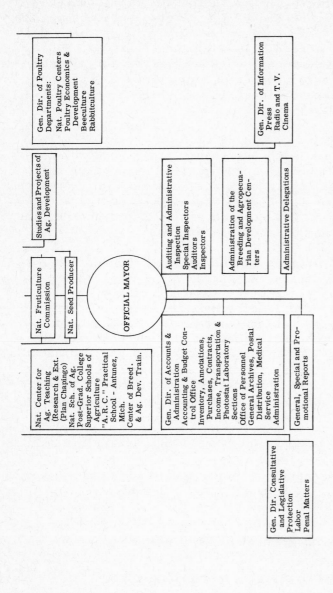

Gen. Dir. of Poultry
Departments:
Nat. Poultry Centers
Poultry Economics &
Development
Beeculture
Rabbitculture

Gen. Dir. of Information
Press
Radio and T. V.
Cinema

Studies and Projects of
Ag. Development

Nat. Fruticulture
Commission

Nat. Seed Producer

OFFICIAL MAYOR

Auditing and Administrative
Inspection
Special Inspectors
Auditors
Inspectors

Administration of the
Breeding and Agropecua-
rian Development Cen-
ters

Administrative Delegations

Nat. Center for
Ag. Teaching
(Research & Ext.
(Plan Chapingo)
Nat. Sch. of Ag.
Post-Grad. College
Superior Schools of
Agriculture
"A. R. C." Practical
School – Antunez,
Mich.
Center of Breed.
& Ag. Dev. Train.

Gen. Dir. of Accounts &
Administration
Accounting & Budget Con-
trol Office
Inventory, Annotations,
Purchases, Contracts,
Income, Transportation &
Photostat Laboratory
Sections
Office of Personnel
General Archives, Postal
Distribution, Medical
Service
Administration

General, Special and Pro-
motional Reports

Gen. Dir. Consultative
and Legislative
Protection
Labor
Penal Matters

Source: Secretariat of Agriculture and Livestock, "Estructura Organica y Directorio," 1963.

141

and Postgraduate College was enlarged to accommodate the headquarters of the National Agricultural Research Institute and of the Federal Agricultural Extension Service; facilities also were provided for an improved central library, meeting rooms, auditoriums, classrooms, and laboratories for all the institutions located at Chapingo. Livestock and forestry research is still maintained separately at locations other than Chapingo.

Plan Chapingo was carried out by the Government of Mexico with assistance from the Ford Foundation, the Rockefeller Foundation, the United Nations Special Fund, the Agency for International Development (AID) of the United States Government, and the Inter-American Development Bank. Assistance by the latter two was in the form of loans.

The objectives of the National Center for Agricultural Education, Research, and Extension are to provide a well-supported modern facility which will attract and hold leading Mexican agriculturists, and to provide national leadership in the three activities. The individuality of each activity is to be maintained, but the necessary and desired greater complementarity requires some administrative as well as physical integration. Administrative integration of the center is a slow and sometimes painful process, because some individual institutional autonomy must be sacrificed for more effective coordination. However, ultimate success of the concept of the National Center is highly dependent upon administrative integration as well as physical integration. The means for achieving this are presently under study by the Mexican agricultural leaders, but the organizational form that may evolve has not been determined yet.

AGRICULTURAL EDUCATION

Agricultural education in Mexico dates from 1832, when the Federal Government converted the orphanage of Saint Thomas into a school of agriculture. In its present form, agricultural education

is defined according to a specific law passed on
December 31, 1945. According to Chapter III of the
law, there are three levels of agricultural education: elementary, practical (vocational or subprofessional), and advanced (undergraduate and
graduate, university level). The responsibility
for all of these is shared by the Ministry of Education and the Ministry of Agriculture.

Elementary Agricultural Education

Elementary agricultural training is offered by
selected rural schools at the primary, secondary,
and "normal"* level. Table 35 shows the kinds and
numbers of schools offering this type of education,
with information on requirements and length of programs.

Education in rural areas of Mexico is still
very deficient and statistics show that only about
10 per cent[2] of the rural student population finish
sixth grade. There is a very high drop-out rate
after the third grade in the rural areas. In many
rural areas there are no school facilities beyond
sixth grade,** so students must go long distances
to complete their secondary education. For the
most part, there is no organized school transportation for students to reach these secondary schools,
nor are there boarding facilities at the schools,
except in rare cases.

Practical Agricultural Education

Practical agricultural training is offered in
programs from a few weeks up to four years in different schools throughout the republic and may be

---

*Schools for teacher's training.

**In fact, 1965 data of the Ministry of Public
Information and 1966 data of the Association of
Mexican Universities show only 11 per cent of the
rural schools provide six grades.

TABLE 35

Agricultural Education Institutions at the Elementary and Practical Levels

Type of Schools	Total Number	Number Offering Agriculture	Agric. Enrollment	Minimum Age of Students	School Years Required for Entrance	Length of Programs (years)	Administering Agency
Elementary							
Elementary-technical schools of regional technological institutes	--	5	375[a]	b	6	2	Ministry of Education
Rural normal schools	30	2	500[a]	--	9	3-4	Ministry of Education
Practical							
Training centers	15	15	6,000[a]	15	6	1	Ministry of Education
National School of Forestry and Game	1	1	125	--	--	3	Ministry of Agriculture
Practical Agric. School, Antúnez, Michoacán	1	1	138	18	3	1	Ministry of Agriculture
State and private practical schools of agriculture	14	14	2,300[a]	b		1-3	Various

[a]Estimated.

[b]Various ages.

Source: G. A. Hurt and John Holcomb, "A Study of Agricultural Education in Mexico at the Pre-professional Level," unpublished report, March, 1966; and personal information.

supported by federal, state, or local government
sources, or by private funding.

The practical agricultural schools are usually
terminal and provide boarding facilities. An example
is the Practical School of Agriculture at Antúnez,
Michoacán, which is administered by the Ministry of
Agriculture. The educational requirement for admission to this school is successful completion of the
third grade and a minimum age of eighteen. Further
admission requirements are that the student be a son
of a farmer and have access to 10 hectares of land.
A practical training program for one year is offered; its enrollment is limited, usually to about
125 students.

Of the thirty rural normal schools operated by
the Ministry of Education, only two (in El Roque,
Guanajuato, and Tonatan, Tamaulipas) offer an agricultural course. Several of these thirty schools
were formerly practical schools of agriculture operated by the Ministry of Agriculture.

The Ministry of Education also has regional
technological institutes (thirteen in 1966) which
operate at four levels: professional, vocational,
technical, and elementary. Of these, five include
agricultural courses at the elementary-technical
level.

The National Commission for Rural Progress,
which receives its support from private sources,
has five permanent centers for practical agricultural training and offers two four-month cycles per
year, with the two cycles considered terminal.

Advanced Agricultural Education

At the advanced or university level, there are
eleven schools that offer the ingeniero agrónomo
degree or its equivalent and two schools that offer
postgraduate education at the Master of Science
level. The data on these schools are presented in
Tables 36 and 37. It should be noted that only four

TABLE 36

Schools of Agriculture and Animal Husbandry

Name and Location	Year Founded	Enrollment 1966	Graduates by 1966	Professional Degrees Granted Through 1966
National School of Agriculture, Chapingo	1854	633[a]	1,997	1,283
Hermanos Escobar School of Agriculture--Cd. Juárez, Chihuahua	1906	588	2,498	1,106
Antonio Narro School of Agriculture--University of Coahuila, Saltillo, Coahuila	1923	411	1,272	769
School of Agriculture and Animal Husbandry, ITESM, Monterrey, N.L.	1948	331	410	400
School of Agriculture and Animal Husbandry, University of Sonora, Hermosillo, Sonora	1953	227	124	42

146

Faculty of Agriculture, University of Nuevo Leon, Monterrey, N.L.	1954	240	85	70
School of Agriculture, University of Sinaloa, Culiacán, Sinaloa	1960	380	56	0
School of Agrobiology, University of Michoacán, Uruapan, Mich.	1961	85	74	4
School of Agriculture, University of Jalisco, Guadalajara, Jalisco	1964	240	0	0
School of Agriculture, University of Chihuahua, Chihuahua, Chih.	1967	0	0	0
Escuela de Agricultura de la Universidad de Guerrero, Chilpancingo, Gro.	1967	0	0	0

[a]At professional studies level--additional students in secondary school (preparatory level).

Source: Personal communication with Directors of schools.

TABLE 37

Postgraduate Education

Schools and Specializations	Enrollment								Total Enrollment	Total Degrees Conferred
	1960	1961	1962	1963	1964	1965	1966	1967		
Postgraduate College, NSA[a]										
Agricultural economics	-	-	-	-	-	1	1	17	19	2
Botany	-	-	-	1	-	1	3	1	6	1
Entomology	3	1	3	3	5	2	1	3	21	7
Genetics	6	1	4	1	13	5	10	2	42	25
Plant Pathology	6	1	2	4	5	-	2	4	25	12
Soils	7	7	7	6	11	6	6	5	48	30
Statistics and computing	-	-	-	-	5	5	1	7	18	7
Total	22	10	16	15	39	20	24	39	179	84
Monterrey Institute of Technology										
Agricultural parasitology	NA	NA	NA	NA	NA	10	9	9	28	8
Water use and conservation	-	-	-	-	-	-	5	2	7	1
Plant improvement	-	-	-	-	-	-	5	4	9	1
Total						10	19	15	44	10

[a]In 1968, the Postgraduate School of the National School of Agriculture inaugurated courses in the fields of Irrigation and Drainage, and Information and Agricultural Extension.

Source: Personal communication with directors of the respective institutions, April, 1968.

148

of the eleven schools of agriculture at the university level existed before 1950, and there was no
postgraduate education in agriculture in Mexico until 1959.

The following is a brief description of the
programs of the schools of agriculture at the
ingeniero agrónomo degree level.

(1) The National School of Agriculture, Chapingo,
was formed in 1854 and receives its support directly
from the Ministry of Agriculture. The school offers
the professional degree in eight different speciali-
zations: forestry, agricultural economics, farm
crops, agricultural industries, irrigation, plant
pathology and entomology, soils, and animal husbandry.

(2) The School of Agriculture Hermanos Escobar,
Ciudad Juárez, Chihuahua, was founded in 1906 as a
private institution and for degree programs was incorporated into the University of Chihuahua in August, 1967. It is supported by fees and some grants
from the Federal Government. The school now offers
the ingeniero agrónomo degree; previously it offered only the agrónomo degree. Approximately one
half of the persons trained in agriculture at the
university level have studied at the Hermanos
Escobar school. A common curriculum is followed
by all students.

(3) The School of Agriculture Antonio Narro
is located in Saltillo, Coahuila, and was founded
in 1923 as a private institution, but it later became a dependency of the state of Coahuila and was
incorporated into the University of Coahuila in
1957. Presently, it receives its support through
the state university. A limited amount of specialization is offered in three areas: agriculture,
animal husbandry, and agricultural engineering.

(4) The School of Agriculture and Animal
Science of the Monterrey Institute of Technology
and Advanced Studies (ITESM), Monterrey, Nuevo Leon,

was founded in 1948. The ITESM is a private institution. The school offers degrees in two speciali-
zations: agronomy and animal sciences. In 1968,
an additional specialization in agricultural business was offered.

(5) The School of Agriculture and Animal Science of the University of Sonora, Hermosillo, Sonora,
was established in 1953, and is supported by the
state university. It offers the degree in two spe-
cializations: agronomy and animal science.

(6) The Faculty of Agronomy of the University
of Nuevo Leon, Monterrey, Nuevo Leon, was formed in
1956, and is supported by the state university. It
offers a single common curriculum, although recently it has instated some semispecializations of one
semester duration, in lieu of the thesis requirement.

(7) The School of Agriculture of the University
of Sinaloa, Culiacán, Sinaloa, was founded in 1960
and is supported by the state university. This is
the only school that offers two stages: After the
first four years it grants an agrónomo degree; if
the students go on another three years, they obtain
the ingeniero agrónomo degree.

(8) The School of Agrobiology of the University
of Michoacán, Uruapan, Michoacán, was founded in
1961 as a part of the state university. It offers
the degree of agrobiologist and all students follow
the same curriculum.

(9) The School of Agriculture of the University
of Jalisco, Guadalajara, Jalisco, was founded in
1964 as a part of the state university. The students follow the same curriculum and all students
are required to complete a thesis after their regu-
lar study program.

(10) The School of Agriculture of the University of Chihuahua, Chihuahua, Chih., was established
only in 1967 as a splinter from the Hermanos Escobar
school, and is supported by the state university.

Its present program leads to the <u>ingeniero agrónomo</u>
degree. Within the same university, there functions
an animal husbandry school, founded in 1957, for
study at the subprofessional level. Its curriculum
was changed in 1964 to a three-year university-level
program, with the title of <u>zootecnista</u> being awarded
after completion of the course and six months of
social-service work.

(11) The School of Agriculture of the University of Guerrero was established in 1967 and offers
a general agricultural curriculum. It is supported
by the state university.

As mentioned before, postgraduate studies in
agriculture in Mexico are available at only two institutions; they offer programs at the Master of
Science level in various fields, as shown in Table
37. These schools are the following:

(1) The Postgraduate College, National School
of Agriculture, Chapingo. The program was initiated
in 1959 and offers M.S. degrees in the following
fields: botany, agricultural economics, entomology,
statistics and computing, plant pathology, genetics
and soils, irrigation and communications. A postgraduate program in tropical agriculture was to be
initiated in 1968-69 as a part of the development
of the new tropical center at Cárdenas, Tabasco.

(2) The School of Agriculture and Animal Science, ITESM. The postgraduate program was established in 1960 with an M.S. degree program in plant
parasitology, to which there were later added programs in soils, irrigation, and genetics.

Several of the university-level programs in
veterinary medicine give a joint degree of Doctor
of Veterinary Medicine and Animal Husbandry (Doctor
de Medicina Veterinaria y Zootecnista). However,
emphasis is placed on the medical aspects of the
profession, with little attention to the animal production or husbandry techniques. The graduates go
into private veterinary practice or work in the

government livestock research programs; a few work
for the Extension Service. It should be noted that
of the eight schools (see Appendix Table 18) only
one existed before 1957.

Student numbers in agriculture and veterinary
medicine have been increasing in recent years with
the opening of new schools and some larger enrollment in existing schools. However, as a professional career, these fields are among the least important in Mexico. In 1966, they included only 3.4
per cent of the university student population. The
enrollment in these two fields as compared with
others is presented in Table 38.

The projected needs for trained agriculturists
at all levels[3] indicates a four-fold increase between 1960-80. The present rate of graduation will
fall far short of this goal.

Major problems in agricultural education include attracting and holding well-qualified professors, maintaining at least limited contact between
research and teaching, attracting sufficient numbers of good students, finding financial support,
and overcoming the lack of opportunities for rural
students to progress up the education ladder.

AGRICULTURAL RESEARCH

The National Agricultural Research Institute
(Instituto Nacional de Investigaciones Agrícolas,
INIA), established in 1961, forms the major crop
research arm of the Secretariat of Agriculture and
Livestock. It was the outgrowth of many years of
development and careful training of research scientists. The other two major research concerns of
the Secretariat, for forestry and livestock, are
managed through the National Forestry Research Institute (Instituto Nacional de Investigaciones
Forestales, INIF), established in 1952, and the
National Livestock Research Institute (Instituto
Nacional de Investigaciones Pecurias, INIP), which

TABLE 38

Higher Education: Enrollment in Agriculture and Other Careers

Career	1958		1962		1966	
	Number of Students	Per Cent	Number of Students	Per Cent	Number of Students	Per Cent
Agriculture and animal husbandry	1,470	2.3	1,332	1.3	2,375	1.7
Veterinary medicine	1,470	2.3	1,527	1.5	2,350	1.7
Engineering	13,802	21.6	24,575	24.3	33,501	24.1
Commerce and Accounting	10,032	15.7	18,067	17.9	29,803	21.4
Medicine	12,844	20.1	15,325	15.2	18,152	13.0
Law	8,431	13.2	13,572	13.4	17,972	12.9
Architecture	4,984	7.8	5,050	5.0	6,416	4.6
Pedagogy	a	--	7,051	6.9	6,577	4.7
Economics	1,598	2.5	3,368	3.3	4,850	3.5
All others	10,737	16.8	11,362	11.2	17,160	12.4
Total	63,899	100.0	101,229	100.0	139,156	100.0

aIncluded in others.

Source: For 1958, Centro de Estudios Educativos, S.A., Diagnóstico Educativo Nacional (Mexico: Textos Universitarios, S.A., 1964), p. 101; and personal communications with Mexican universities for 1962 and 1966.

dates from 1941. These plus other research institu-
tions--such as the Institute for the Improvement of
Sugar Production, the Mexican Coffee Institute, the
Mexican Institute of Technological Research, the Department of Hydraulic Resources--will be briefly described in this section. All major research institutions are listed in Table 39, with some additional information on the same.

Limited agricultural research was started before the Revolution of 1910-11, but it was interrupted and was not re-established until 1932-33,
when the Department of Experimental Fields was
created in the General Bureau of Agriculture. Under
that program, experiment stations were organized and
emphasis was placed on testing improved seeds as
well as other production factors.

The Government of Mexico and the Rockefeller
Foundation entered into an agreement in 1943 to establish a national agricultural research program on
Mexico's basic food crops. As part of this agreement, the Office of Special Studies was organized
in 1944, with the objective of increasing yields of
basic crops and training Mexican agricultural scientists. This program is a model of a successful cooperative effort and has led to revolutionary results in corn, wheat, potatoes, and other crop production; at the same time, it has equipped Mexican
agricultural scientists to continue the work. During the period 1945-64, 150 agronomists received
scholarships for studies leading to the M.S. degree
and 70 the Ph.D. under this program. In addition,
several hundred agronomists received practical on-
the-job training and gained first-hand field experience both on how to carry out agricultural research
effectively and on how to improve production techniques. From other sources, such as the Bank of
Mexico, FAO, and AID, additional scholarships for
study abroad were provided.

In 1947, the Department of Experiment Stations
was reorganized to form the Institute of Agricultural Research, and in 1961 this Institute was

TABLE 39

Agricultural Research: Institutions, Staff, and Fields, 1964-68

Institution	Professional and Technical Staff Numbers	Experiment Stations Operated	Fields of Research
National Institute of Agricultural Research (INIA)	250	32	Genetics, soils, entomology, phytopathology, weed control, economics, biometrics, communications
National Livestock Research Institute (INIP)	60[a]	4	Animal nutrition, reproductive physiology, range management, vaccines, animal breeding
National Forestry Research Institute (INIF)	32	4	All forestry research (forest management, soils technology, photogrammetry, etc.)
State Agricultural Research Programs	N.A.[b]	3[c]	Various; generally on crop research but occasionally also on livestock
Mexican Coffee Institute	55	3	Coffee culture, disease and pest control, coffee-producing areas, handling of coffee, beans, etc.
Hydraulic Resources	30[d]	9[e]	Irrigation engineering, salinity problems and drainage in relation to agricultural production
Sugar Production Improvement Institute	33[f]	6	Breeding new varieties, pest and disease control, soils and fertilizers, etc., for sugar cane
Schools of Agriculture and Animal Science	121[g]	9	Crop improvement (all major crops), soil management and fertility, entomology, plant pathology, agricultural engineering, agricultural economics, rural sociology, etc.
Center for Agrarian Research (CEA)	12	0	Land tenure and agrarian reform problems

(Cont'd)

| Mexican Institute of Technologi-cal Research | 50 | 0 |
| International Maize and Wheat Improvement Center (CIMMYT) | 23 | 0[h] |

[a]In 1968, eight of these researchers were studying abroad; but a few more staff are available through INIP's cooperative research program with the State of Mexico at its Santa Elena station.

[b]A number of the staff are on joint appointments with INIA.

[c]There are probably more, but the three best known are in the states of México, Sinaloa, and Hidalgo.

[d]A number of these are civil or other type engineers.

[e]In almost every Irrigation District, some research is conducted, but these stations have continuing research programs. See National Association of Directors, Agricultural Education, Investigation and Extension in Mexico, 1964, pp. 205-11.

[f]This number is distributed among research and extension workers who are working specifically on sugar production.

[g]Full-time professors employed by schools of agriculture, who presumably engage in research. Ibid., p. 53. Quality and amount of research varies a great deal among schools.

[h]operate through INIA stations at present, but may initiate selected stations under own direct management in future.

Source: Direct inquiry with respective institutions and National Association of Directors of Agricultural Schools, Agricultural Education, Investigation and Extension in Mexico, 1964.

incorporated with the Office of Special Studies to form the INIA. The objectives of INIA are the following:

> The abundant production per hectare that provides for the necessities of the producer must be the constant objective of technical assistance; to achieve this, the following research activities are required: (1) obtain improved seeds of the most important crops for each agricultural region of the country; (2) determine the best fertilizer practices; (3) establish the most efficient irrigation practices; (4) determine the best plant protection procedures for annual and perennial crops, as well as pastures; (5) determine the optimum planting time, seeding rate and methods; (6) establish the most effective cultivation practices; (7) determine the most efficient and economical harvesting and storage of crops; (8) carry out, by the most effective means, the transmittal of research results to the producers, either directly or through the agricultural extension service or credit agencies.[4]

In order to achieve these objectives, INIA operates seven regional and many auxiliary research stations (see Map 6). These are the following:

Northwest Region. Agricultural Research Center for the Northwest (CIANO), Ciudad Obregón, Sonora. This regional center has the following auxiliary stations: Mexicali, Baja California; Caborca, Sonora; Costa de Hermosillo, Sonora; and Valle de Mayo, Sonora.

State of Sinaloa. Agricultural Research Center for Sinaloa (CIAS), Culiacán, Sinaloa, which is operated in cooperation with the state government, and has one auxiliary station at Los Mochis, Sinaloa.

MAP 6

Agricultural Experiment Stations of INIA, State Governments, and Agricultural Schools

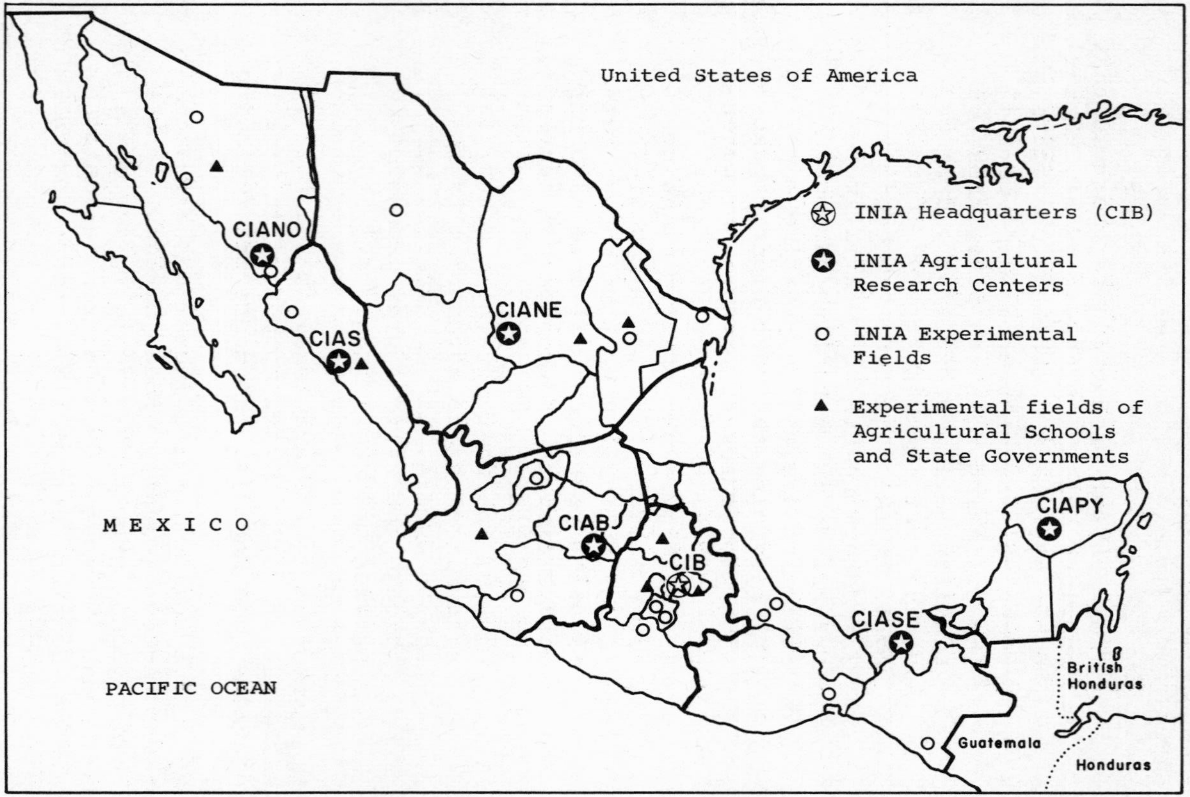

Northeast Region. Agricultural Research Center for
Northeast (CIANE), Matamoros, Coahuila, with auxil-
iary stations at Ciudad Delicias, Chihuahua; General
Terán, Nuevo León; and Río Bravo, Tamaulipas.

Bajío (Central Highland) Region. Agricultural Research Center for the Bajío (CIAB), El Roque, Guanajuato. This center has auxiliary stations at
Pabellón, Aguascalientes; León, Guanajuato; and
Antúnez, Michoacán.

Central Mesa Region. Basic Research Center (CIB),
Chapingo, Mexico. This center has the following
five auxiliary stations: Progreso, Morelos; Zacate-
pec, Morelos; Iguala, Guerrero; Santa Elena, Mexico
(in cooperation with the state of Mexico); and El
Mexe, Hidalgo (in cooperation with the state of
Hidalgo).

Tropical Region. Agricultural and Livestock Center
for the Southeast (CIASE), Cárdenas, Tabasco. This
center has the following four auxiliary stations:
Cotaxtla, Veracruz; El Palmar, Veracruz; Rosario
Izapa, Chiapas; Isthmus of Tehuantepec, Oaxaca.

Yucatán Peninsula. Agricultural Research Center
for the Yucatán Peninsula (CIAPY), Muna, Yucatán;
it has an auxiliary station at Santa Rosa, Maxcanú.

Of these stations, CIANO receives much of the
support from contributions by the producers of the
region. The others are practically fully supported
by the government and to date they have sought very
little private support.

As indicated earlier, crop research in Mexico
has led to significant production increases in the
basic food crops and the technology seems well im-
planted to maintain high levels of production.
This is particularly true in wheat and potatoes;
other crops, such as corn, beans, rice, and sorghum,
have the potential for further major production increases.

The INIP with headquarters at Palo Alto,
Mexico, dates from 1941, but the National Center
for Livestock Research (Centro Nacional de Investigaciones Pecurias, CNIP) only dates from 1962. The
latter program is the core research group and is an
outgrowth of animal science work carried out by
Mexican scientists and the Rockefeller Foundation.
There has also been close cooperation between Mexican animal scientists and United States Department
of Agriculture scientists on programs related to
hoof and mouth disease (aftosa), screw worm control,
and rabies control.

The research programs of INIP and CNIP are
really one and the areas of investigation include
nutrition studies, development and production of
vaccines and biological products, disease control,
and animal breeding.

Extensive nutrition studies have been carried
out for poultry (chickens and turkeys), swine, and
sheep. Research work on pastures and forages is
being conducted in both the semi-arid regions and
the subtropics for dairy and beef cattle.

The major diseases affecting livestock have received the attention of the veterinary medical personnel, and relevant work has been carried out on
the development and testing of vaccines and biological products essential for animal health.

In animal breeding and improvement, the main
effort has been on beef and dairy cattle in the
tropics and subtropics; less emphasis has been put
on swine breeding.

In addition to the research facility at Palo
Alto, the Institute has pasture and forage studies
at La Campana, Chihuahua, and Cotaxtla, Veracruz.
Animal breeding studies are conducted, for the most
part, at Palo Alto and Campo La Posta, Paso del
Toro, Veracruz. Poultry nutrition studies are conducted at Santa Elena, Mexico, in cooperation with
the state of Mexico experimental farm.

Many of the staff of the Institute have benefited from postgraduate study in veterinary medicine, animal science, or range management. However,
the number of staff members is so small that even
the well-trained staff cannot carry out a research
program on a national scale. This should be evident
when one considers that the sixty professional staff
members must cover research in all the diverse areas
of animal breeding, production, and disease control.

The INIF is an official body of the Mexican
Government and was founded in Mexico City in 1952.
Its antecedents date from approximately 1932, and
in 1960 INIF became a semi-autonomous research institution in order to develop its research program
with greater freedom. It has research sections
dealing with soils, mycology, entomology, seeds,
cytogenetics, chemistry, mechanical wood testing,
and botany.

The INIF has four research stations in operation which are located at San Juan Tetla, Puebla;
El Tormento, Campeche; Cupatitzio, Michoacán; and
La Sauceda, Coahuila. In addition to research activities at these stations and at the laboratories
in Mexico City, the Institute has carried out forestry inventory work in several states in cooperation with FAO and initiated projects in reclamation
of eroded forest lands. Again, as in the case of
other research agencies in Mexico, the number of
scientists engaged in research is extremely small.

The state agricultural programs differ widely
in quantity and quality of research. The two best-
established programs are in the states of Mexico
and Sinaloa. In both cases these programs cooper-
ate with INIA and both have recently constructed
excellent new physical facilities. A third program
in the state of Hidalgo also cooperates with INIA
on research activities.

The Mexican Coffee Institute participates in
the International Coffee Organization to represent
Mexico in the international market agreements as

well as act as a scientific organization. It operates a semi-autonomous agency under the Secretariat
of Agriculture and Livestock and was established in
1960 as an outgrowth of the National Coffee Commission established in 1949. The main experimental
station is at Garnica, Veracruz; additional experimental work is conducted at Rosario Izapa, Chiapas,
and El Palmar, Veracruz.

The Coffee Institute conducts both research
and extension and carries out its program with producers in forty-seven coffee-growing regions in
thirteen states. In 1968, the Institute employed
fifty-five agricultural specialists and forty-nine
agricultural technicians. The research and extension program emphasizes (1) increased production
per unit of area, (2) development and selection of
improved plants, (3) disease control, (4) total production control, (5) processing, and (6) diversification of regions that become unproductive. In the
latter, the Institute gives technical assistance,
particularly to farmers with scarce resources, in
the establishment of rubber tree or fruit tree plantations. With fruit tree plantings the emphasis
has been on citrus, avocados, and mangos.

The Department of Hydraulic Resources is under
the SHR. Earlier, it was noted that the Government
of Mexico has consistently given budget priority to
this Secretariat in support of construction of dams
and irrigation works. The department conducts research on soil drainage, soil salinity, soil mois-
ture management, and irrigation practices. There
is close cooperation between the department and the
personnel of the Federal Agricultural Extension Service. Increasing attention is being paid to the
more effective usage of irrigation water, but research in this area is still deficient.

The Sugar Production Improvement Institute is
involved in both research and extension work and
operates six experimental stations. It is concerned
with the development of improved cane varieties and
all aspects of production. There are six departments

or sections in the Institute--biometrics, genetics, soils, entomology and pathology, cultural practices, and extension. It receives most of its support from the Sugar Producers Association.

The schools of agriculture and animal science as well as the schools of veterinary medicine differ widely in quantity and quality of research. Most of the schools have some kind of research establishment and the National School of Agriculture at Chapingo and the ITESM have made significant contributions to agricultural technology through research. The research of the School of Veterinary Medicine of the National Autonomous University has also been noteworthy.

The Center for Agrarian Research (Centro de Estudios Agrarias, CEA) with its headquarters in Mexico City, has concentrated its research studies on land tenure and agrarian reform problems. Particular attention has been given to the ejidal sector in these studies. The Center is cooperating with the Inter-American Agricultural Development Committee on an important study of agrarian reform in Mexico, which should be completed in 1969.

The Mexican Institute of Technological Research (Instituto Mexicano de Investigaciones Tecnológicas, IMIT) was founded in 1950 by the Bank of Mexico, Nacional Financiera, and the National Bank of Foreign Trade. Its research is directed at studies on enrichment of foods, evaluation of commercial feeds for livestock, development of new products from agricultural and industrial by-products, and quality control. Its staff is located in Mexico City and the Institute receives support from public funds and from research contracts.

Located in Mexico is one of the international agricultural research centers. The International Maize and Wheat Improvement Center (Centro Internacional de Mejoramiento de Maiz y Trigo, CIMMYT) is supported by the Ford and Rockefeller Foundations.

This international center is backed by over twenty years of research work in Mexico on these two crops by Rockefeller Foundation and Mexican agricultural scientists.

The Center was founded in 1963 by the Mexican Secretariat for Agriculture and Livestock and the Rockefeller Foundation. In 1966, it was reorganized and established as a nonprofit scientific and educational institution to be governed by an international board. Since that time it has been financed jointly by the Rockefeller and Ford Foundations in cooperation with the Mexican Government.

The goal[5] of CIMMYT is to assist nations around the world to increase production of corn and wheat. In order to achieve this goal, the Center enters into cooperative programs of basic and applied research with other countries, but the majority of the basic research is conducted in Mexico. An integrated approach is taken to attack the problems and the scientists in the sections of genetics, physiology, soils, water utilization, fertilizers, and plant protection work closely together on the common objective. A communications program is included to help disseminate new technology, but to date research on the economics of the new production technology has been neglected.

In Mexico, CIMMYT cooperates closely with Mexican institutions and conducts practically all of its research on INIA research stations. Its staff represent many different nationalities and the majority are located in Mexico, but some are deployed in regional or cooperative national programs throughout the world.

AGRICULTURAL EXTENSION SERVICES

The Agricultural Extension Service has a strong central government control but is in the process of decentralizing a number of functions and strengthening its emphasis on agricultural production. The

Ford Foundation is cooperating with the Government of Mexico in its effort to make the Federal Agricultural Extension Service more effective in assisting farm families to increase agricultural production and levels of living. The FAO is also providing some assistance to extension training programs and other selected parts of the national program.

The Federal Agricultural Extension Service had its origins in a small group that established some agricultural service functions in 1911. However, this work was soon interrupted by the Revolution and work did not recommence until 1922. From 1922 until 1948, the program went through a number of re-organizations and always operated with a small staff and little support. When reorganized in 1948, the office was renamed the Agricultural Extension Service and has retained that name. However, this re-organization brought very little in the way of in-creased support, so by 1953 there were only forty agricultural technicians in the Service. In 1954, increased support was provided, and by 1956 there were about 230. Since that time there has been only a slight increase in the number of agricul-tural technicians in the Extension Service, but there has been a distinct rise in home extension agents. The data in Table 40 show the number of extension workers and sources of support.

The number of agricultural extension agents relative to farm families is about 1 to 10,000, as compared to the United States and Japan, where these ratios are 1 to 540 and 1 to 650, respective-ly. The agricultural extension agents and home demonstration agents have given priority attention to small farmers and ejidatarios. The small number of extension workers and the focus of their atten-tion leads one to the conclusion that the Agricul-tural Extension Service has not contributed sig-nificantly to Mexico's agricultural development. The big increase in production has come from the larger farmers in the better agricultural areas. It may be that the Agricultural Extension Service will be indispensable for further increases in

TABLE 40

Agricultural Extension: Personnel

Institution	Professional Agriculturists		Home Improvers		Agricultural Technicians		Total	
	1964	1967	1964	1967	1964	1967	1964	1967
Secretariat of Agriculture and Livestock--Department of Agricultural Extension	224	190	18	81	0	14	242	285
State governments	30	53	89	124			119	177
Committees (Banks, Secretariat of Hydraulic Resources, various agricultural organizations)	42	49	11	21			53	70
Totals	296	292	118	226	0	14	190	532

Source: Secretaría de Agricultura y Ganadería, Department of Agricultural Extension, personal communication.

166

agricultural production, if they are to come from
the small farmers,* who generally have not been
among the beneficiaries of the technological innovations introduced into Mexican agriculture.

The organizational structure of the Federal
Agricultural Extension Service remained practically
the same from 1948 until 1965 and is outlined in
Figure 4. In 1965-66 a four-year program was initiated to reorganize and improve the Federal Agricultural Extension Service with some support from
the Ford Foundation, creating five regional offices
as shown in Map 7 (corresponding to the same five
regions into which INIA research operations were
divided) and establishing closer ties with INIA.
This program appears to be progressing with good results, and two new regional offices are planned to
match with two new regional stations being established by INIA.

The first cooperative federal-state Extension
Service program was established in the state of
Mexico in 1955. This program still provides one of
the best examples of extension work in the Republic.
Since that time, cooperative programs have been implemented in the states of Baja California, Sinaloa,
Chihuahua, Campeche, Coahuila, Tamaulipas, Nuevo
León, Zacatecas, Jalisco, Guerrero, Tabasco, Guanajuato, and Yucatán, and in the Territory of Baja
California. The degree to which the programs are
cooperative varies from state to state, because
there is no fixed formula or legal long-term written agreement. Rather, in each case negotiation
takes place, usually between the Director of Extension and the Governor of a state, and the terms may
be changed with each change in administration.
Similar negotiation is carried out with other federal, state, or local institutions by the Director
of Extension to gain support for staff or programs.

---

*Particularly the ejidatarios, who control
about 50 per cent of the total cropland of the
country.

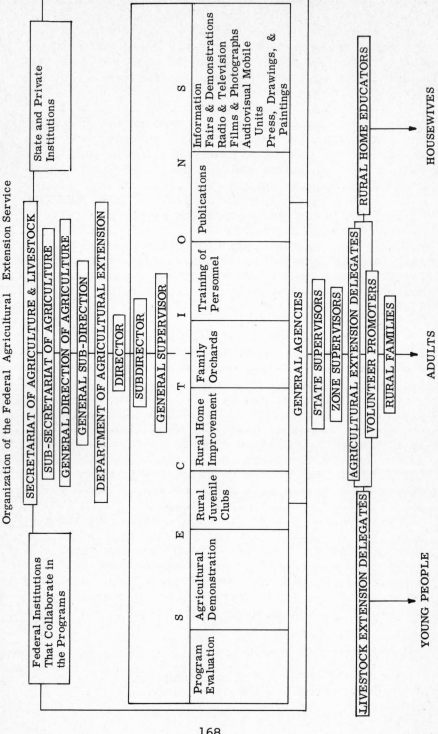

FIGURE 4

Organization of the Federal Agricultural Extension Service

MAP 7

Regions of Supervision of Agricultural Extension Service

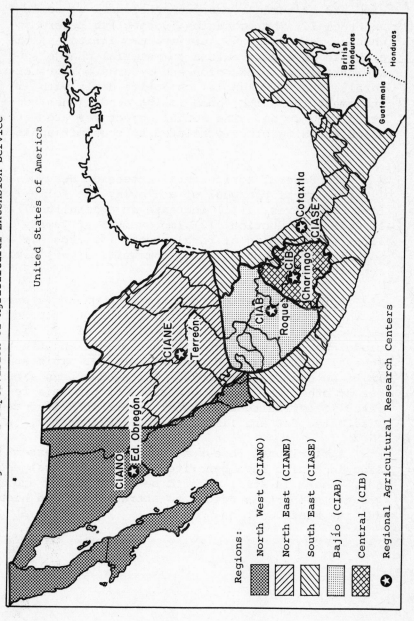

United States of America

CIANO
★ Ed. Obregón

CIANE
★ Terreón

CIAB
★ Roque

CIB
★ Charingo

★ Cotaxtla
CIASE

British
Honduras

Guatemala

Honduras

Regions:

North West (CIANO)

North East (CIANE)

South East (CIASE)

Bajío (CIAB)

Central (CIB)

★ Regional Agricultural Research Centers

The National Agricultural Plan for 1967-68[6]
states that the objectives of agricultural extension are of three types: educational, economic,
and social.   The educational objective refers to
changes in knowledge, ability, and attitudes; the
economic objective refers to material change, such
as increase in production and returns on agricultural crops.   The social objective deals with improvement in health, home living conditions, cooperation, and so on.   The social objectives are recognized as being closely related to economic achieve-
ment.

The Federal Agricultural Extension Service has
set for itself the goal of achieving the following
five objectives:[7]   (1) increase in agricultural and
livestock production, (2) improvement of family
life, (3) training of rural youth, (4) economic and
social improvement of rural communities, (5) civic
activities.

A four-year study to attempt to quantify some
of the effects of agricultural extension is being
conducted by the Postgraduate College of the National Agricultural School, in cooperation with the
Federal Agricultural Extension Service.   This study
is to be completed in 1970.   There have been a number of other studies on questions or programs related to agricultural extension work in Mexico and
a selected few are listed in the bibliography.

Agricultural research, education, and extension in Mexico have benefited the agricultural sector.   There is still much to be accomplished and
greater support is needed to attract and hold high-
quality staff.

CHAPTER **9** PROJECTED NEEDS
FOR AGRICULTURAL
PRODUCTION IN MEXICO

The discussion in the previous chapters was
concerned with the accomplishments of Mexican agriculture in the recent past. Attention is turned
now to the prospects for agricultural production
and to the needs for food and fiber in Mexico in
the years ahead. Forecasting future trends in
agricultural production is always a difficult and
uncertain venture. Nevertheless, it is an important one and quite necessary for determining long-
range policies for agriculture and investment priorities within the total economy, as well as within
the agricultural sector.

Fortunately, the recent study conducted in
Mexico on supply and demand projections of agricultural products[1] referred to earlier in this book
facilitates immensely the task of estimating future
trends of agricultural development in the country.
The contents of the present chapter are essentially
a summary of the Projections study,[2] except for com-
ments on its implications and limitations.

The objective of the Projections study was to
examine the prospects of supply and demand of agricultural products in 1970 and 1975, to evaluate
possible surpluses or shortages, given present conditions and trends. The study analyzed forty-four
crops and thirteen livestock products.

The projections are based on the hypothesis
that gross domestic product will grow at an average

rate of 6 per cent per year between 1961-70 and of
7 per cent per year between 1971-75. In order to
achieve these rates of growth, it is estimated that
the three major sectors of the economy will have to
grow as follows: agriculture, 4.0-4.5 per cent per
year between 1961-70 and 4.5-5.0 per cent in 1971-75;
industry, 6.7-6.9 per cent and 7.9-8.2 per cent in
each period, respectively; and services, 6.0 per
cent in 1961-70 and 6.9 per cent in 1971-75. Although the record for the period 1950-61 seems to
warrant the projected growth rates for industry and
services, those for agriculture are more difficult
to achieve. This difficulty was clearly recognized
in the study, which stressed the need to implement
policies to raise the level of technology and productivity in agriculture.[3]

The demand projections were based essentially
on past consumption trends, estimated future population growth, and the information obtained from an
extensive family-income and expenditure survey conducted in 1963, which made it possible to estimate
probable changes in the consumption of both urban
and rural people in response to income growth. In
addition, estimates were made of intermediate demand for industrial as well as agricultural purposes, and of external demand for the main agricultural exports of Mexico.

The supply projections were also based on extrapolation of past trends in volume of production,
cultivated land area, and yields, and were adjusted
to include information about the probable evolution
of the various inputs determining agricultural production.

It is important to notice that these projections assume an absolute and relative price level
as it existed in 1958-60; they exclude the possible
implementation of new programs that could alter
past trends or the assumptions of the study; and
possible abnormal changes in demand are not considered.

THE BALANCE OF PRODUCTION AND DEMAND
IN 1970 AND 1975

Under the assumptions of the study, agricultural production is projected to grow at 4.0 per
cent per year in the period 1961-70 and at 3.3 per
cent per year in 1971-75. Total demand, on the
other hand, is expected to grow at annual rates of
4.2 per cent during the first period and 4.3 per
cent during the second. Thus, by 1970 an agricultural deficit would appear that would be equivalent
to 3.3 per cent of the projected volume of demand,
and would increase to 8.0 per cent of total demand
by 1975. The deficits would be larger for livestock
products (10.9 and 15.1 per cent of demand for livestock products, in each year) than for crops (1.9
and 3.0 per cent of demand for crop products in each
year). The projected rates of growth for crop and
livestock products that give origin to these deficits are shown in Table 41.

TABLE 41

Projected Rates of Growth of Supply
and Demand of Crop and Livestock
Products (per cent per year)

	1961-70		1971-75	
	Supply	Demand	Supply	Demand
Crops	4.0	3.7	3.0	4.0
Livestock	4.0	5.1	3.8	4.8
Total	4.0	4.2	3.3	4.3

Source: Secretaría de Agricultura y Ganadería,
et al., Proyecciones de la Oferta y la Demanda de
Productos Agropecuarios en México, a 1970 y a 1975
(Mexico: Banco de México, S.A., 1965).

The over-all deficit in agricultural production is not uniformly distributed among the various
commodities; although for some the deficits are
serious, for others they are negligible, and for
other products there appear surpluses. The supply-
demand projections for selected crops and livestock
products are shown in Tables 42 and 43.

The main prospective shortages among crops are
in vegetables, fruits, oilseeds, sorghum, barley,
and tobacco, and important surpluses are expected
in wheat, rice, beans, and coffee. In the case of
livestock products, except for eggs, poultry, and
mutton, shortages are projected in all products.

This situation stems from the nature of demand
and supply for these commodities. Domestic demand
is expected to grow faster (because of higher income elasticities) for livestock products, in general, and for certain crops such as tobacco, sugar,
fruits, and coffee, whereas for other crops, such
as vegetables and oilseeds, demand is expected to
grow as in the past few years. In the case of most
cereals, pulses, and animal fats, demand is expected
to diminish relative to the past few years. Foreign
demand for the traditional exports of Mexico is estimated to grow slowly, at 1.9 per cent per year on
the average, reflecting the slow population growth
and near saturation of the major trading partners
of Mexico.

On the supply side, several difficulties determine the not too optimistic picture. Land area
expansion, which was an important impetus to the
rapid growth of output in the past decade, is considered to be approaching limits that will make
further increases in acreage difficult and slow.
Irrigation still offers a large potential, because
of the about 8 million hectares that are estimated
to be eventually subject to irrigation, only 44
per cent is presently realized--but the cost of
bringing in the additional land is very high.

TABLE 42

Balance of Supply and Demand of Agricultural
Products in 1970 and 1975 (tons)

Crop	Production 1970	Production 1975	Surplus (+) or Deficit (-) 1970	Surplus (+) or Deficit (-) 1975
Corn	8,839,827	10,226,978	+572,922	+394,376
Wheat	2,730,016	3,292,732	+734,589	+794,346
Rice	358,910	461,785	+ 32,469	+ 89,900
Sorghum	381,555	493,135	- 39,395	- 62,197
Potatoes	423,806	549,710	- 18,090	- 2,578
Beans	898,381	1,132,393	+ 77,937	+182,483
Tomatoes	518,644	570,020	- 67,969	-138,014
Onions	81,070	89,073	- 15,993	- 39,408
Alfalfa	6,469,518	7,410,780	- 99,656	-855,268
Oranges	864,830	950,378	-341,732	-589,336
Pineapple	236,660	269,259	- 71,990	-138,884
Bananas	388,375	448,511	- 72,972	-141,822
Cottonseed	1,073,628	1,145,203	- 18,595	-169,449
Sesame	194,905	214,142	- 37,537	- 87,272
Peanuts	114,466	130,907	- 25,510	- 51,159
Coffee beans	173,687	186,329	+ 25,336	+ 16,495
Tobacco	101,355	126,011	- 18,697	- 28,045
Sugar	1,911,546	2,349,252	- 58,333	- 88,991

Source: "Proyecciones de la Oferta y la
Demanda de Productos Agropecuarios en México a
1970 y 1975," Comercio Exterior, March, 1966.

TABLE 43

Balance of Supply and Demand of Animal
Products, 1970 and 1975 (tons)

Product	Production		Surplus (+) or Deficit (-)	
	1970	1975	1970	1975
Beef[a]	433,554	499,469	- 71,372	-133,534
Pork[b]	234,635	274,717	- 59,621	-113,163
Cattle on the hoof	43,970	43,970	- 22,630	- 33,330
Milk	5,427,485	6,645,312	-361,603	-639,162
Eggs	309,582	391,534	--	--
Animal fat	100,621	117,273	- 12,699	- 18,637
Clean wool	5,239	5,728	- 13,152	- 18,020

[a]Does not include suet.

[b]Does not include lard.

Source: Banco de México, Oficina de Estudios
Sobre Proyecciones Agrícolas.

Therefore, most of the larger output in the
years ahead will have to come from increased productivity: The Projections study estimated average
rates of yield improvement of 2.5 and 1.9 per cent
per year, between 1961-70 and 1971-75, respectively.
These estimates consider only the further adoption
by farmers of presently known technology. Therefore, those crops for which more research has been
done in the past (wheat, corn, beans, sorghum, etc.),
and for which improved varieties are available, show

relatively greater growth in future output; crops
such as vegetables, fruits, oilseeds, and feed
grains, for which little research and experimentation has been done, show a slower output expansion
and hence shortages.

The labor force in agriculture is projected to
increase by 1.5 million persons up to 1975 (but this
can hardly be considered a beneficial development in
Mexican agriculture). The tenure structure, however, is estimated to remain unchanged, which again
is not a favorable outlook, given the deficiencies
it now presents.

Capital investment in agriculture is projected
to increase at approximately the same rate experienced in 1950-60, that is, 1.8 per cent per year,
facilitated by continued public investment in infrastructure and greater government financing of
medium- and long-term farm investments. This, however, can hardly make up for the diminished rate of
cropland expansion.

Finally, given that a constant price level has
been assumed, those crops that have generally enjoyed relatively favorable prices in the past (corn,
wheat, beans, rice) show the development of surpluses, and those with less favorable prices (oilseeds, vegetables, feed grains) will be in short
supply.

In the case of livestock products, the insecurity of land tenure, diseases, and marketing ineffi-
ciencies, unless removed, will cause a very slow
expansion in output, in spite of the elastic demand,
and hence the projected general shortages in 1970
and 1975.

Leaving aside for the moment the limitations
(already apparent) of these projections of Mexican
agricultural production, some important implications arising from them are worth noting.

In the first place, the projected demand depends on the realization of a rate of growth for

the whole economy of 6-7 per cent per year; however, this rate may not be achieved if agricultural production grows at less than 4.0-4.5 per cent per year, as is the case after 1970 (see Table 41). Hence, the shortages after 1970 may be smaller than indicated, but the over-all growth rate of the economy also will have been slowed down.

Second, regardless of its degree, the mere existence of a shortage in agricultural products is of serious concern both for social and economic reasons. There is evidence that at the present time a segment of the population is undernourished, and without deep changes in income (or food) distribution in the years ahead, this problem will become graver, with all its serious social consequences. Even looking only at the average picture, it is likely that domestic demand will have priority; this will mean increasing food imports or cutting down some of the present exports (especially of beef cattle). In any case, the balance-of-payments position of the country may be weakened, with its various implications for the whole economy.

Third, to the extent that shortages and surpluses are not evenly distributed among products, the structure of agricultural production will have to be adjusted for prospective demand. If these adjustments can be made ahead of the development of imbalances, considerable waste in resources and products can be avoided.

In summary, the Projections study highlights the importance that sustained and possibly stepped-up agricultural development has for the over-all economic and social development of Mexico. It also points to the role that increases in agricultural productivity will have to play in the decade ahead, thus stressing the need for more research and for adoption of improved technology by farmers. All this will mean more carefully planned programs and policies for agriculture; that is, the role of government in promoting agricultural development may have to become yet greater than in the past.

LIMITATIONS OF THE PROJECTIONS STUDY

Probably, the preceding conclusions are valid even in the face of several limitations in the Projections study. Briefly, some of the most important of these appear to be the following:

The Data Problem

In spite of careful revisions of the available data, several errors or omissions were impossible to correct. Of particular importance are the data for livestock. The 1960 census data on cattle numbers were used, although it is accepted that these were undercounted (see the section on livestock in Chapter 5). Data on land-use capability, for instance, were unavailable. It is irrelevant, however, to stretch this point. Quantity and quality of data are always a problem; what is important is to be aware of the limitations of results arising from a particular set of data, and this study was no exception in this respect.

The Assumptions

Some of the assumptions were quite restrictive. One that affects both the demand and supply projections involves the relative prices. If prices were set in relation to market forces and if Mexican consumers and farmers reacted to prices (and there is evidence that they do), it is clear that many of the projected imbalances would correct themselves before they developed the magnitudes suggested in the study. In fact, the government moved to lower wheat prices in 1966, and wheat production this year is estimated to have diminished by 30 per cent relative to 1965.[4] Furthermore, the government set support prices and promoted the cultivation of safflower, and production increased 364 per cent from 1965 to 1966.[5]

The assumption of existing technological knowledge is also too restrictive. The chances are that continued agricultural research will yield new improved techniques, not only for those crops or products on which substantial research has been conducted in the past, but also for other crops that may become increasingly more important as the economy develops. Therefore, the supply of this last category of agricultural products need not be as inelastic as has been assumed in the study. With this assumption removed, the rate of yield increases may in fact turn out to be much higher than was estimated.

The Methodology

A shortcoming of the methodology employed is that agricultural demand was projected based on a certain assumed rate of growth of GDP, which in turn depended on a certain growth rate in the agricultural sector. If this will grow at a lower rate (as is projected), then GDP and hence agricultural demand will also grow more slowly. Surpluses and shortages will necessarily be of different magnitudes than projected. Here one or two more iterations to arrive at consistent results were clearly needed. Also, the supply projections were based on a very crude method, namely, simple extrapolation of trend with a few subjective adjustments, which can give only very rough approximations.

In general, one may say that the study was not aimed at obtaining balanced projections of supply and demand (for which prices of products and factors would have had to be included as variables) to determine needed resource reallocation, but it stopped one step short of this. By estimating prospective imbalances, the nature of needed price and resource adjustment becomes evident, though not the relative magnitude of changes.

In spite of the preceding limitations, the agricultural projections analyzed are indeed the best available for Mexico and they do seem to point correctly the general direction of adjustments that will have to be made in Mexican agricultural production in the years ahead.

CHAPTER **10** LIMITING FACTORS AND
ALTERNATIVE OPPORTUNITIES
IN MEXICAN AGRICULTURAL
DEVELOPMENT

In the early chapters of this study, it was
shown that Mexico is not richly endowed with
natural resources for agriculture. Most of
the country is either too mountainous or too dry
for a highly productive agriculture, and cropping
regions are scattered throughout the territory,
raising transportation difficulties. In spite of
these adverse factors, Mexico has succeeded in the
last two decades in increasing its agricultural
production at an extraordinary pace, although the
level of productivity is still below that of many
other developing as well as developed nations.

The characteristics of this agricultural growth
and the factors that have contributed to it were reviewed earlier. It was shown also that government
policies covering practically all aspects of agricultural activities have been fundamental in fostering agriculture. All the basic elements necessary
for development[1] have been present at least to a
minimum degree in Mexican agriculture: The country
has enjoyed substantial political stability and continuity in economic policy for a long period of
time; domestic and foreign markets for agricultural
products have been strong and rapidly expanding;
extensive and good transportation facilities have
connected all the major producing areas with the
domestic and foreign markets; substantial advance
has been achieved in the development and adoption
of improved agricultural technology; efforts have
been made to make inputs available in the producing

181

areas; and price and tenure conditions, in general, have provided the necessary incentives for farmers to increase production. Other complementary elements for agricultural development also have been present. Important advances have been made in agricultural education and in extension activities; production credit has been increased considerably; land expansion and improvement (especially irrigation) has been extraordinary; some degree of government planning for agriculture has taken place; and farmers have formed several associations and confederations aimed at collective action to protect or advance farming interests.

However, it is obvious that in spite of advances made in each of the preceding aspects, all of them still show deficiencies in quality, quantity, or rate of expansion that, therefore, represent the present obstacles or limiting factors for further agricultural development. It is probably true in any country at any one time that adjustments in institutions and factors of production do not occur as rapidly and efficiently as might be wished. Thus, the identification of some of the major problems facing Mexican agricultural development today is not meant as a criticism, but rather as an objective exploration aimed at pointing to the areas that need particular attention in the coming years to sustain or increase the past record of improvement. This point is stressed, because it is easy to criticize the shortcomings or deficiencies that a developing country may suffer; it is not so easy to appreciate the difficulties, pains, and efforts such a country must go through in order to break the bonds of traditionalism, poverty, and, sometimes, foreign domination that have kept it underdeveloped for generations.

The major factors that may be identified as presently constituting limitations for continued rapid development of agriculture are set forth in the following sections.

AGRARIAN PROBLEMS[2]

This refers generally to the land tenure
conditions prevailing in the country, including
legal-economic aspects that affect single farm
units as well as the complex institutional structure that these units constitute. In the broad-
est sense, and as has become apparent from previous
discussion, the agrarian problem in Mexico consists
mainly of the small size of the average farm unit,
which is a consequence of the small proportion of
high-quality land and the large and still-increasing
rural population. Furthermore, a large number of
units are of such small size that simply will never
be able to yield an acceptable minimum level of
family income. This problem is aggravated by the
long dry periods and poor-quality land in many
areas that contribute to the widespread underemployment of rural labor. However, it is reported that
there still exist some very large farms (latifundia)
that are illegal according to Mexican legislation.
The lack of a good cadastral survey represents a
serious obstacle to implementation of land policies
to remedy some of the tenure defects in Mexican
agriculture.

Though generally considered a model by many
persons in Latin America, the land reform that followed the Revolution of 1910-25 is not without its
problems. The coexistence of the ejido and the
private-property systems has tended to bring about
a dual agricultural policy, one for the ejido and
the other for private property, which is not easy
to formulate or to implement and which is inequit-
able and generates resentments. The ejido system,
without individual title to the land by those who
work it, has left the operators of these lands without definitive legal right to use the land as a
basis for credit; thus the ejidatarios are limited
to the Banco Ejidal as a credit source.

The ejidos tend to be broken into small individual units. This, plus the rapid population increase, has aggravated the problem of too many

small farm units, a condition that retards modernization of the agricultural techniques that would
substantially raise labor efficiency. Moreover,
the rigidity of land reform impedes the formation
of more economic farm units that could readily adopt
modern agricultural technology. Although some transfer of land in ejidos does occur, it is illegal; the
loss incurred by ejidatarios who move out and simply
forfeit their rights to the land represents a dis-
incentive to migrate and thus tends to perpetuate
or aggravate the minifundio problem and its associated underemployment and low-income problem.

    In addition to the inflexibility of tenure in
ejidos, there are also difficulties in the transfer
of private property. The absolute farm size limit
imposed by the Reform Law may also prevent in some
cases the formation of optimum-scale private farm
units. Because renting land is illegal--though it
is practiced somewhat anyway--this form of acquiring
control of land resources is not available to Mexican farmers.

    There is also considerable tenure insecurity
in Mexican agriculture. In the ejidos, this is due
to factors such as undefined boundaries, provisional
status, lack of legal parcelization, lack of the appropriate agrarian certificates, etc. Among private
properties, insecurity stems from lack of the appropriate land titles or inaffectability certificates,
farm size larger than the legal limit, invasion by
squatters, etc. The problem of excessive size and
expiration of inaffectability concessions is especially grave among cattle ranches at the present
time, which is preventing many improvements from
being made. Finally, the small group of ancient
communities presents an anarchic situation in their
organization.

    The agrarian-reform legislation that, in spite
of many positive accomplishments, gave rise to some
of the problems mentioned, has strong political and
social implications deeply imbedded in the Revolution and will not be overcome soon. Thus, the

government appears to be indirectly working to solve
agrarian problems by expanding land area through
irrigation, by improving the technological level of
agriculture through support for research and extension programs, and by its credit and price policies.
An eventual revision in the land-reform legislation,
however, is inevitable.

CAPITAL SHORTAGE

Closely linked to the previous problem is the
shortage of capital for agriculture, especially in
the Central and Southern regions of the country.
It is difficult to speed up the adoption of modern
equipment, because the present underemployment of
labor in small farms and ejidos would be increased.
Thus, the possibility of intensifying capital use
may be seriously limited by the size of land holdings, as long as land policy prevents this from
changing. Even if certain capital inputs, such as
fertilizers and chemicals, were used much more extensively in the smaller units and incomes were
doubled, they would still be frustratingly low.

In spite of these difficulties, government,
with the assistance of outside agencies, is attempt-
ing to extend larger amounts of credit to small
farmers and to thus lessen the capital shortage.
The present level of credit availability is still
quite low, as was mentioned previously, barely
reaching one quarter of Mexican farmers and often
excluding those with great need, but who may have
economic viability. There will remain a serious
lack of economic studies and research results in
the field of agricultural credit that could help
guide these programs. Also persisting will be the
shortage of trained manpower to supervise and ad-
vise farmers in the wise use of credit.

SCARCE EDUCATIONAL FACILITIES

Probably the most serious impediment to development of Mexican agriculture is the low level of

education of the rural population. In 1960, only
48 per cent of the rural population was reported to
be able to read and write, but the literacy rate
among the actual farm population is probably less
than this, because included in rural population are
the inhabitants of small towns, which usually contain schools. If farmers are to take advantage of
modern technology and to move into the commercial
agriculture stage, literacy must be substantially
increased.

Several reasons justify this need. In a general way, literacy helps raise the cultural level
of people, connecting them more effectively with the
more progressive sectors of a nation. This uncon-
sciously may make them desire higher consumption and
hence force them into greater productive efforts.
Where extension services have scant personnel, much
diffusion of knowledge can be achieved through the
printed word, both by government agencies and private enterprise. In a country like Mexico, with a
large ejido sector and many small farm units, cooperative action by farmers would seem a logical
solution for a wide range of problems; but experience shows that education, understanding, and sophis-
tication are needed for farm cooperatives to work.
Probably the scarcity of this type of organization
and the dismal results of many attempts at forming
them in Latin America are due primarily to the low
educational level of the Latin American rural inhabitants. Finally, if stepped-up migration out of
agriculture is one of the possible solutions to low
productivity and poverty in this sector, literacy
may diminish uncertainty and facilitate the movement of peasants to industrial jobs.

As previously noted, technically trained agriculturists are scarce in Mexico, and the current
output of agronomists and veterinarians from universities is not nearly sufficient to conduct the
work that would bring the whole agricultural community to a commercial and self-sustaining level.
The strong training in specialized fields within
agriculture that Mexico also needs is not being

adequately offered at present. In the short run,
a "technical elite" in agriculture may be even more
important than a general minimum level of literacy,
as T. W. Schultz has pointed out,[3] and hence the
present scarcity in Mexico may represent a serious
obstacle to faster rates of agricultural development.

TECHNICAL ASSISTANCE TO FARMERS

The extension services of the government and
of other agencies that also provide technical assistance to farmers in Mexico are presently insufficient for the needs of the farmers.

It can be argued that extension services are
particularly needed in countries like Mexico, where
the low educational and economic standards make
most of the farmers incapable of obtaining knowledge by themselves on such valuable topics as improved techniques, sources and use of credit, and
farm management methods. Therefore, one of the
most significant areas for increased government attention in the coming years is that of communication and spread of knowledge among farmers. An important objective of programs in this area should
be to shorten the time lag between obtaining research results and adopting the improved practices.

GAPS IN RESEARCH

Although much progress has been made in many
of the most valuable aspects of agriculture, several important areas remain in which little research
has been done. In the first place, livestock research had been neglected until recently, except in
relation to disease control. Animal breeding, nutrition, animal husbandry, dairy husbandry, and
range management are in great need of research and
experimentation. Progress in these fields may have
been handicapped by the dispute between veterinarians and agronomists as to exclusiveness of rights
to work in these subjects. If the government's

current efforts to stimulate livestock production
are to succeed, it will be necessary to investigate
several aspects of livestock-raising, including the
economic ones. For instance, it is practically impossible to find any studies concerned with costs
of production for the various livestock enterprises
or cost-return studies for alternative methods of
exploitation.

Another field in which little research has been
done in Mexico is irrigation-water management, from
the viewpoint of agronomy or crop production rather
than engineering. This is a serious matter, considering the vast irrigated land areas of Mexico and
the economic importance of the crops grown on such
lands. Some attention has been given to the salinity problems common in many irrigated areas, but
again the research has usually been conducted by engineers or chemists, rather than by agronomists concerned with crop production. It was mentioned
earlier that practically no sound cost-benefit
analyses of irrigation investment have been done in
Mexico. Given the continued government emphasis on
irrigation, this gap seems most serious.

Semidesert areas comprise nearly half of the
land area of Mexico. Although several million
people derive a livelihood from exploiting the vegetation of these arid zones, very little has been
done to survey the agricultural and forest resources
or to learn their proper management for sustained
exploitation and preservation. Lands are parceled
out under the agrarian reform laws, and extension
programs are initiated to help the inhabitants; yet
nobody really knows how much land is needed or what
practices should be followed for a farm family to
be able to live at a reasonable standard in these
arid regions. This is another field in need of
sound research.

By contrast, the tropical areas, vast and
largely unpopulated, constitute a great potential
resource for agricultural production. But little
is known about actual location of productive areas,

the crops suitable to them, adequate soil-management techniques, or their potential for livestock production. Government programs are under way to settle these areas; thus, further efforts should be made through research and pilot projects to ensure the success of the settlement programs and to allow their continuation and expansion. Past failures in colonization projects in southern Mexico also point to the need for sociological research.

Finally, one of the weakest aspects of research is in agricultural economics. Farm management and marketing, as well as land tenure and credit, are sorely in need of economic research. Much work will have to be conducted in all aspects of agricultural economics to provide basic information for policy and planning and for intelligent decision-making by farmers, government officials, and others concerned with agriculture, especially as commercialization increases.

SALARIES OF TECHNICAL PERSONNEL

Education, research, and extension programs in Mexico are primarily conducted by the government. These programs require highly trained technicians to operate at a reasonable level of quality and for continued improvement, especially in education. Great advances have been made in Mexico in training these technicians; in fact, reportedly, Mexico has the largest number of M.S.'s and Ph.D.'s in agricultural sciences of any Latin American country. It is vital that these individuals stay in government institutions engaged in education, research, and extension services, but unfortunately the budgets of these institutions generally are too low for them to offer salaries competitive with those of private commercial enterprise or other government agencies (mainly, the official banks). In the last few years, there has been a serious exodus of competent technicians from the agricultural and livestock research institutes as well as from agricultural colleges, because salaries have not been

sufficiently attractive. Given the great importance
of the maintaining of a first-rate technical elite,
especially in agricultural education and research,
in order to speed up Mexican agricultural development, budgets and salaries of these institutions
must receive top priority in the coming years.

MARKETING PROBLEMS

Mexico has a good network of roads that facilitate transportation of commodities in and out of
rural areas. The government has also improved the
marketing of the major crops. However, there remain
many smaller, isolated areas where marketing difficulties constitute a serious problem. The strong
price fluctuations and high spoilage losses of most
of the agricultural commodities that are marketed
privately must be diminished.

More attention must also be paid to the availability of inputs needed by farmers, so that these
can be purchased at the proper place and time. Expanded credit and extension programs would lose
much of their effectiveness if inept marketing of
seeds, fertilizers, and other materials were to cur-
tail their availability in the rural areas.

Further, there is a great need for national
and local market-news systems to provide reliable
and timely information on prices, crop conditions,
crop forecasts, official policies, and so on, to
aid the farmers in planning their production and
sale of crops and livestock. This type of service
is now practically nonexistent in Mexico.

A well functioning price system can be a powerful lever for inducing change in farming methods and
stimulating increased production and efficiency in
agriculture. Mexico could use advantageously an improved pricing mechanism and better distribution
facilities to bring large numbers of the subsistence
farmers thoroughly into the market system. Only
then will these farmers be in a better position to
help themselves to higher income and cultural levels.

AGRICULTURAL POLICY AND PLANNING

Policy formulation and planning for agriculture are handicapped in Mexico by the lack of reliable agricultural statistics and economic studies defining and analyzing the significant problems. Because crop forecasting is nonexistent, it is difficult to anticipate land use, price, or yield changes from year to year. Similarly lacking are well-trained agricultural economists and statisticians who could provide supporting work and advice to the policy-makers.

When price regulation, minimum wages, credit programs, foreign-trade control, and other policies are extended and agricultural policy is thereby refined, more complete agricultural statistics and economic studies will become indispensable. Resource mapping and evaluation will also become increasingly necessary. Recognition of these needs should encourage immediate strengthening and expansion of teaching and research in these fields.

As a result of the low levels of Mexican agriculture when the process of development began, the persistence of obstacles such as those reviewed above, and the high concentration of government policy in particular areas of agriculture (typically those that at present can be classified as commercial), the agricultural sector presents a particular "dual" characteristic. A fundamental aspect of this, which has persisted probably since the time of the Revolution, is the existence of large portions of the rural population deriving a meager existence from the scant resources at their command. Their incomes are low; their health and nutritional levels poor; their illiteracy rates high--in general, their whole way of life and work is antiquated. At the other extreme, a number of farmers have moved into commercial agriculture, have adopted modern techniques of production, and have obtained sufficient land and capital resources for adequate incomes. The latter probably comprise about 15 per cent of the Mexican farmers and the

former 20-30 per cent. The remaining 55-65 per
cent of the farmers span the whole range between
these extremes but can be considered economically
viable in that, with the proper help, they can
reach the level of commercial agriculture.

This general characterization of Mexican agriculture points to one over-all problem: the still
deficient economic or institutional organization of
the agricultural sector, which operates under heavy
population pressure. Rigidities in the land-tenure
system, inadequate credit policies, deficiencies in
marketing, and so on, along with the very low educational level of the rural population, obstruct
more efficient allocation of resources and rapid
adjustment to changing conditions. These obstacles,
however, the government recognizes and faces when-
ever it is politically feasible to do so.

The fact is that after so many years of revolution and reform, made by and for the peasants
primarily (the revolutionary slogan was "land and
liberty"), and of sustained government action to
promote agriculture, those who have benefited the
least are precisely a majority of the farm population. This is becoming a crucial issue in Mexican
development today. Reportedly, there is discontent
and unrest in many rural areas where living conditions have remained strikingly low, in spite of the
advances achieved on the average.

Fortunately, one of the remarkable features of
the Mexican political system and governing class is
the awareness of and responsiveness to social and
national issues. The problem of rural poverty and
backwardness is recognized and is presently receiving high priority, at least in public statements by
government officials. President Diaz Ordaz, in a
campaign speech in 1963, stated "The problem of the
countryside is the most distressingly grave one in
the political, social and economic horizon of Mexico. . . . The rural sector has supported industrial development and urban growth in Mexico. The
industrial and urban sectors must help in the

improvement of the living conditions of the farming
population. . . ."[4] These statements were repeated
and reinforced in the Presidential Messages in 1965
and 1966; in the last one, it was stated that a top
objective in national development planning is "to
grant priority to the farm and livestock group in
order to accelerate its development and to strength-
en the internal market."[5] During the Thirty-Second
National Convention of Mexican Bankers, in March,
1966, the leaders of the Mexican economy stressed
the relative lag in agricultural financing and
stated the necessity of adopting urgent measures
to channel more resources to agricultural, livestock, and forest activities in order to sustain
the rapid progress of the economy.[6] It is to be
expected, therefore, that these statements will be
translated into public action to promote agricultural development to an even greater extent than
in the past.

POSSIBILITIES FOR GROWTH

The question then arises as to the possibilities and projections for further growth and improvement of Mexican agriculture and as to the needed
programs, investments, and action to realize these
possibilities. The remainder of this chapter is
devoted to a discussion of these issues.

Further growth of agricultural production can
come through either an expansion of the cultivated
land area and pasture lands or increased crop and
livestock productivity.

Some estimates presented in previous chapters
indicate that probably a maximum of 37 million
hectares could be cultivated in Mexico, or about
20 per cent of the total area of the country. This
area would be about two and one half times larger
than the presently cultivated area. If the new
lands, on the average, had yields similar to those
currently obtained, total agricultural production
could be more than doubled simply through addition

of land (and labor) inputs. However, the potentially tillable lands are in areas generally less accessible than has been the case in the past (tropical areas) and/or their incorporation to production requires large capital investments. This is especially true for irrigated lands. It is estimated that approximately 8 million hectares are potentially irrigable in Mexico, or slightly over twice the presently irrigated area, but the additional 4 million hectares represent high-cost, lower-priority projects, because those easier to carry out have been developed in the past twenty years. In fact, despite the large portion of government investments devoted to irrigation, it is estimated that by 1985 only 5.9 million hectares will be under irrigation (see Chapter 7).

Therefore, although there is still considerable potential for increased production through expansion of cultivated land, increasingly greater reliance will have to be put on productivity improvements. Some references have been made earlier in this study to potential yield increases of some crops. Table 44 shows current average yields for the major crops grown in the country and maximum yields obtained by farmers and at experimental stations.

It can be seen that average yields of these crops are about one half the maximum yields obtained by the best farmers and about one third of the maximum experimental yields. These differences tend to be fairly constant in all regions of the country. Therefore, considerable yield increases could be obtained, with presently known technology, simply by stimulating further adoption of improved practices. But, as was argued in Chapter 9, there is no reason to assume that technological development is at a standstill; progress is currently being made in research on the major crops, as well as on crops that are now becoming more important in the Mexican agricultural economy. Thus, considering the still fairly low level of productivity in much of present-day Mexican agriculture, the

available stock of technological knowledge, and the
rapid improvement in average yields of many crops
that has been occurring in the last ten years, op-
timism can be expressed as to the prospects for
substantial increases in agricultural productivity.

Given the lack of reasonably reliable data on
livestock activities, it is not possible to estimate potentials for development, but the widespread
opinion of national experts in this field is that
production could be expanded tremendously through
breeding, pasture improvement, supplementary feeding, adequate disease control, and other better
animal husbandry practices. To the casual observer,
the difference between well-managed ranches and
livestock ejidos, for instance, is so great that
there can be no doubt that great improvements in
livestock production can be achieved through simple
spread of known technology; moreover, livestock research is presently meager, and greater efforts
should easily yield new sources for increased productivity in livestock-raising.

The conclusion, then, with respect to potentials for expanded agricultural and livestock production in Mexico is that these look fairly good
at present, but that the source of increased output
in future years will have to be mainly improved
productivity, in contrast with past years when increases in land, labor, and water were the major
factors accounting for agricultural growth.

Another aspect of future Mexican agricultural
development that must be stressed is the need for
larger farm-family incomes, as distinguished from
larger total output. The importance of this distinction has been discussed earlier; it will become
much more important in the coming years. As the
whole economy continues to develop at a rapid pace,
the agricultural population runs the risk of falling ever further behind in their socio-economic
level, as has been happening in the last decades.
Therefore, investments and programs to promote
agriculture in Mexico will have to lend special

TABLE 44

Average and Maximum Yields of Important Crops, by Regions, 1966

Crops	North Pacific			North			Gulf			Central			Bajio[a]		
	Average	Best Farmers	Experiments Maximum	Average	Best Farmers	Experiments Maximum	Average	Best Farmers	Experiments Maximum	Average	Best Farmers	Experiments Maximum	Average	Best Farmers	Experiments Maximum
Corn															
Irrigated	3.2	6.0	7.5	2.0	5.0	8.0	2.8	5.0	8.0	3.5	8.0	15.0	2.8	6.0	10.0
Nonirrigated	—	—	2.3	0.6	1.0	4.0	1.5	2.5	5.0	1.0	4.0	4.5	1.0	3.0	5.0
Wheat															
Irrigated	3.2	6.0	7.0	2.0	4.5	7.0	—	—	—	2.5	4.5	6.0	2.8	5.0	7.0
Nonirrigated	—	—	—	—	—	—	—	—	—	1.5	2.5	4.5	—	—	—
Rice															
Irrigated	2.3	4.5	6.5	—	—	—	5.0	6.5	7.0	5.5	6.5	7.5	—	—	—
Nonirrigated	—	—	—	—	—	—	2.0	3.5	4.0	—	—	—	—	—	—
Beans															
Irrigated	1.0	2.0	—	0.9	1.2	—	1.2	2.0	3.0	—	—	—	1.8	2.5	3.2
Nonirrigated	—	—	—	0.8	1.2	—	0.8	1.5	2.5	0.4	—	—	0.4	1.2	2.0

[a]This is a subregion within the Central region.

Source: Instituto Nacional de Investigaciones Agrícolas, Department of Extension (direct information).

attention to this issue, and not only to expansion
of total output.

ALTERNATIVE PROGRAMS AND
INVESTMENTS FOR GROWTH

Having reviewed some of the major limiting
factors in Mexican agriculture and the possibilities for continued growth, what policies, programs,
and investments are needed to sustain or speed up
agricultural development? These can be divided
into three major categories: those concerned with
expanding the cultivable land base, those concerned
with raising agricultural productivity, and those
concerned with raising real farm incomes or rural
welfare. Some programs, such as credit or extension services, cut across more than one of these
categories, but they can be conveniently discussed
in terms of their primary objectives.

Land-area expansion is the result of action
by private individuals and public agencies. The
first type occurs mostly in a spontaneous way, in
response to several factors already discussed.
Probably, not much should be done to control this
development, except perhaps to prevent further
incorporation of marginal lands (hillsides, forest
land, etc.) into production, which tends to perpetuate the problems of low productivity and low
income.

Public investment in development of new areas
for cultivation should continue to be an important
activity. Two main spheres of action are open in
this respect: irrigation and development of the
tropical regions.

Irrigation

Considering the existing government plans for
irrigation development, current budget allocations,
and Mexico's long-standing experience, there is no
doubt that irrigation will continue to be a priority

area for public investment. Given the good results
obtained in the past and the predominantly arid nature of the Mexican territory, it seems quite logical to pursue this line of activity with vigor.

Some issues in respect to irrigation development, however, should receive greater attention.
One is the question of whether large-scale projects
or small-scale ones should be emphasized. This entails an economic problem, that is, the cost-benefit
relations for each type of project, as well as a
social one, for typically the small-scale projects
would be located in already-settled areas and would
benefit the lower-income farmers. Another issue
involves the better utilization of water, or allocation at the farm level. Here some questions are
the real cost of water, the price the farmer actually pays, and the development of management practices for optimum water use. Finally, another issue concerns the rehabilitation of irrigation areas
that have deteriorated because of various defects
in the established systems. It is likely that rehabilitation programs may yield large returns with
limited expenditures, and therefore should receive
high priority.

Precise answers for the preceding issues can
only be given after some solid research has been
conducted; hence, at this point, economic research
on irrigation development and water utilization
should be emphasized.

Tropical Areas

As was mentioned earlier in this chapter, the
tropics may hold great promise for agricultural development in Mexico, but little is presently known
about their potential or the best means for utiliz-
ing their resources. Thus, emphasis should be put
on resource mapping and research on the whole range
of biological, technological, economic, and social
aspects of development and settlement of tropical
regions. The greatest need at this stage is to
establish experimental stations in key spots in

these regions and to train technicians who may
later help to conduct the settlement projects. As
noted in Chapter 8, a start is presently being made
in this respect.

The various activities concerned with improving productivity in agriculture can be classified
as technological improvements, improved resource
allocation, and improved product distribution.

Technological Improvements

These refer to the development and adoption by
farmers of new practices and inputs to raise yields
and livestock productivity: crop varieties, artificial pastures, fertilizers, chemicals for disease
and pest control, etc. The three most important
activities that need to be stressed much more than
has been done in the past to raise the technological level of Mexican agriculture are research (crop
and livestock), extension services, and production
credit.

Crop research needs to be strengthened and expanded, for some crops in particular, such as corn,
vegetables, oilseeds, and fruit trees, the last
three categories of crops being those that threaten
shortages in coming years and for which little research has been done. Also, research on some current or potential crops--strawberries, citrus,
tomatoes, avocadoes, etc.--might pay handsomely.
As for livestock research, special emphasis is
needed on improvement through breeding, feeding
alternatives and combinations, disease control, and
animal husbandry generally. The problem of budgets
and salaries for technicians of research institutions is fundamental if research is to be conducted
at the pace and level of quality needed for rapid
improvement.

The existing gap between known technology and
actual practice by farmers is great. Here agricultural extension or technical assistance to farmers
becomes important. It has been shown that these
services in Mexico are quite inadequate at present,

but that they have a crucial role to play, especially among the small and medium-sized farms that
have a reasonable potential to become commercial
units. Improvement of the extension service entails the organization of a system that is more
production-oriented and emphasizes training better
field personnel and production specialists, increased linkage with research, and formulation of
programs geared to the special characteristics of
Mexican agriculture. It is also necessary to provide a budget and salaries that will permit the
service to operate effectively. Since not all this
can be achieved simultaneously, at first, extension
services ought to be concentrated in particular regions, rather than being scattered throughout the
2,000 municipalities of the Republic, as is the
tendency to do at present.

Practically all programs geared to advancing
the level of agricultural technology in Mexico will
be heavily dependent on credit, given the large
number of small farm units and the low income level
of most farmers. Agricultural credit must be expanded to reach substantially more than the present
one quarter of farmers, and it must also be oriented
more to serving as an instrument to bring about improved farm practices and techniques. For this, it
needs to be tied more closely to the extension effort, which would also make the extension service
much more effective.

Better Resource Allocation

There appear to be two important means for increasing productivity through better resource use.
The first is consolidation of small and fragmented
units, including better organization of the ejidos.
This is primarily a land-tenure problem; hence the
needed action at this time would be revision of the
land reform legislation and development of a land
registry, so that the deficiencies obstructing development may be removed.

The second method involves introducing the best
output combination that should be produced. Mexico

may have an advantage in the production of high-
value, labor-intensive crops, such as vegetables,
especially for the export market. Production is
shifting in this direction in the Pacific Northwest,
but many of the irrigated valleys in the Central
region continue to produce mainly corn and beans,
although many better alternatives may exist. Emphasis needs to be put on farm management research
and agricultural planning. These two measures are
also sorely needed to guide the extension and
credit programs.

Improved Product Distribution

Although data on marketing channels, margins,
losses, etc. are very limited in Mexico, existing
partial information indicates that important losses
occur in the passage of many crops from farmer to
consumer, which is reflected in substantial price
differentials at the retail, wholesale, and farm
level. To the extent that these losses can be reduced through improved marketing methods, a larger
volume will be available to the consumer from the
same basic farm resources, resulting in greater
agricultural productivity from a national standpoint. To the extent that some of the gains were
transferred to the farmers through prices, they
would also benefit from improved product marketing.

Turning now to the problem of raising farm incomes, in addition to the preceding measures, which
with an appropriate price policy should result in
larger total revenues for the agricultural sector,
two programs appear to be most important. The
first one concerns the migration of farm people out
of the more marginal areas, either to other agricultural areas (e.g., the new lands to be opened
up) or to urban centers. In this case, the stress
is on speeded-up industrialization, a solution for
the problem of rural poverty that is becoming increasingly evident as the only one that holds real
promise in Mexico.[7] The other program involves the
need to reduce the rate of population growth, not
only in the rural areas, but in the country as a

whole. This again is a problem that more and more
responsible people are facing up to in Mexico, for
they realize the difficulty and the slowness with
which standards of living will be improved at present rates of population expansion.

As a closing note, emphasis should be put
again on education, not only for the technical
elite, but for the farming population in general.
The education needed is not just of the formal
kind, but of a kind that will make the rural people
more aware of their role in the nation's economic
life, that will encourage their group action, political participation, and efforts toward self-
improvement. Unless the agricultural population
offers this kind of active participation, all government programs will have a less than satisfactory
rate of acceptance and progress than is needed to
speed up agricultural development.

CHAPTER **11** SUMMARY
AND
CONCLUSIONS

The total population of Mexico is currently
estimated at 45.7 million people, of which 43 per
cent are rural. The average rate of population
growth over the period since 1950 has been 3.3 per
cent per year, although rural population growth
has been about 1.6 per cent. Gross national product in real terms during the same period grew at
an average rate of 6.2 per cent per year. Thus,
Mexico has experienced a substantial improvement
in real per-capita incomes.

Mexico's agricultural development has been
very good in the period 1950-67, averaging an annual rate of growth of production of 4.0 per cent.
The country has become practically self-sufficient
in all major foodstuffs, while at the same time
more than 50 per cent of her export earnings are
derived from agricultural products, mainly cotton,
livestock, sugar, coffee, henequen, and tomatoes.

Mexico's total cropland area is approximately
24 million hectares, of which 14.5 million are harvested annually. The irrigated area is about 3.5
to 4.0 million hectares. Rangelands cover 80 million hectares. Corn is the main crop, being grown
on half of the total harvested land each year,
followed by beans, cotton, wheat, sugar cane, and
coffee. Cattle are the most important type of
livestock, numbering an estimated 27 million head
in 1964.

203

Characteristic of Mexican agriculture is the small size of most farm units and the dual system of land tenure. About half of the cropland is held in ejidos and the other half in private property.

Agricultural development has not been a homogeneous process in Mexico. Certain regions (notably the Northwest) and the larger farms have made particular progress, whereas the ejidos and very small farms have tended to lag behind. As a result, great differences in productivity exist among farms in the various size and tenure categories, as well as among agricultural regions.

The factors that have determined the remarkable growth in agriculture are principally the expansion of the cultivated land area, which increased by about 75 per cent from 1949-51 to 1964-66, and the increase in yields of practically all crops grown in the country, resulting from several measures. Yields per acre have more than doubled for wheat and cotton, and substantial increments have been obtained for potatoes, beans and corn. Yields of corn and beans, which constitute the basic staple foods of the Mexican people, improved more than 50 per cent during this period.

Probably the most important factor responsible for the increase in both crop area and yields has been irrigation water. Approximately 1.5 million hectares of newly irrigated lands, which is 40 per cent of the total irrigated area of Mexico, were put in production since 1950.

Fertilizer and improved seed varieties are the next most significant inputs accounting for the increase in average yields. Fertilizer use increased almost twenty-fold over the period analyzed. At the present time, practically all wheat and cotton are sown with improved seed; about 10 per cent of the corn crop is planted with improved seed; and many of the small crops show intermediate patterns of adoption. All significant crop-improvement research in Mexico dates from the late 1940's, and commercial-scale production and adoption of improved seeds is a post-1950 development.

On the financial side, agricultural credit expanded about three times in real terms during the period studied, facilitating the means for farmers to adopt the better technology developed by the research institutions. In spite of this expansion in credit, however, less than one quarter of Mexican farmers are served at present by the national and private banks.

Government policy for agriculture has also been highly protective, especially by maintaining firm price supports for the principal food crops, such as corn, wheat, and beans, and discriminatory regulations in agricultural foreign trade. These policies have provided favorable economic conditions and incentives to farmers to increase output.

Other factors that have shown outstanding expansion or improvement, but whose contribution to agricultural development cannot be as easily assessed or quantified, have been agricultural education, extension services, plant and animal protection measures, crop insurance, and limited planning for agriculture.

After this brief outline of the physical features of Mexican agricultural development, which add to an impressive record, attention should be focused on the conditions that helped to make this development possible. Of course, it is to be expected that, in general, output growth will be accompanied by a greater use of inputs, as well as by changes in the production function; but, the fundamental question is how to assure that these changes are put into effect.

In this respect, it is desirable to examine the factors (they could be called nonphysical factors) beyond the quantitative data to see whether some conclusions can be drawn that might also be valid for development in other countries.

Perhaps it would be useful to deal with this aspect by classifying the nonphysical factors as exogenous (which largely escape control by the country itself) and endogenous, further distinguishing between economic and other factors (political, behavioral, institutional, etc.).

The most important exogenous factor in Mexican development is its geographical position, especially its proximity to the United States, which without a doubt is proving to be beneficial for Mexico. The reasons are obvious: The United States provides a large market, and the cost of transportation is lower for Mexico than it is for other countries which are further away (especially for bulky and perishable agricultural products); the proximity allows for easier transference of knowledge, technology, and new or improved inputs; private financial support can be obtained from the United States for the cultivation of certain agricultural products; the employment of braceros has provided opportunities for additional income; there has been a strong direct investment from the United States in agricultural-processing industries; and finally, with regard to the total economy, the tourist trade has turned out to be a very important industry.

Nevertheless, this natural advantage would not be of great significance if it were not for the fact that the internal dynamics of Mexico have provided conditions which have made possible rapid agricultural progress. Several main elements can be identified, among these endogenous factors, as having created favorable conditions for the agricultural development of the country (which are naturally very much interrelated) such as those which follow:

(1) From an economic point of view, the existence of a strong demand for agricultural products, domestic as well as foreign, has been an essential stimulating factor. It is interesting to note that rapid agricultural development began at the same time as industrialization and strong over-all

economic development got under way, in the middle of
the 1940's.   In other words, Mexico presents a good
example of balanced growth, in contrast to the typical situation in other Latin American countries.

Nevertheless, a steadily increasing agricultural demand would not have been sufficient to
stimulate production if relative prices had not
also been favorable to agriculture during the two
decades from 1940 to 1960, according to what can be
deduced from available data on prices.   In other
words, agricultural price inflation provided a
stimulus for Mexican farmers, while the price relation (agricultural prices compared to nonagricul-
tural prices) remained essentially constant, at a
level that allowed reasonable profits for agricultural producers.   This situation permitted at least
the more progressive farmers to introduce technological innovations and, in general, provided an
opportunity for the majority of farmers to increase
the use of all inputs.   The process of technological change in agricultural may have also been more
recently helped by the improvement in price relations for certain inputs, especially fertilizers,
whose real prices have diminished notably.   This
appears to be the explanation for the rapid capitalization of Mexican agriculture (at least for its
private sector), given the relative scarcity of
bank credit and other sources of capital.

(2) Among the other or noneconomic factors,
perhaps the most important one is _time_.   It should
be taken into account that the rapid agricultural
development evident in Mexico since 1950 is the result of a long process of changes (sociological,
economic, institutional, and others) that began in
the 1930's, and possibly even earlier, in the Revolution years.   Development, and particularly that
of agriculture, seems to require a long gestation
period.

(3) The fundamental conditions that should
prevail in the country, during this more or less
long period of _time_ needed for agricultural

development to gain momentum, are <u>political stabil-</u>
<u>ity</u>, <u>social tranquility</u>, and <u>consistency in econom-</u>
<u>ic policy</u>. In general, these conditions have been
adequately met in Mexico, at least from the 1930's,
whereas political and economic instability has been
typical of the majority of the other Latin American
republics during the same period of time.

These general conditions have a great economic
significance, in that they lessen the risk and uncertainty for the producers, as well as for the
government, in such a way that planning and execu-
tion of investment (public and private) becomes
possible, with good probabilities of substantial
returns in the long run.

(4) At this point, another factor should be
introduced, which has been the most publicized aspect of Mexican agricultural progress: the <u>agrar-</u>
<u>ian reform</u>. There is no doubt that the institu-
tional change that took place in Mexico because of
the agrarian reform had an enormous and lasting effect on agriculture, although it is very difficult
to measure this impact and even more to evaluate it.

In the opinion of the authors, the effect of
the agrarian reform on agricultural development was
probably indirect, operating through an increase in
political and social stability in the country (by
changing the status of the landless peasants); providing greater incentives for some farmers and more
security of tenure for others, once the agrarian
policy to be followed was known (which possibly
brought about a greater or better use of land);
forcing the government into continuing support and
protection of the agricultural sector, once the reform and progress of agriculture had become the
cornerstone of the ideology of the Revolution; and,
in time, possibly changing the attitudes and behavior of many of the farmers, making them more re-
ceptive to technological changes.

On the other hand, it is doubtful that the
agrarian reform brought about an immediate or long-
run increase in agricultural production. The data

indicate that productivity is generally lower in
the small farms and _ejidos_ (eminently products of
the agrarian reform) than in the larger units.

(5) Finally, it should be recognized that a
factor of great importance in the agricultural development of Mexico has been the governmental promotion of this sector, that is, the consistency and
continuity of the economic policy regarding agriculture. This is evidenced by the definite position taken by successive governments on the uninterrupted continuation of the agrarian reform, the
investment in irrigation, the policy of bank credit
for the _ejidatarios_ and small farmers, and the
pricing and marketing policies. Although some of
these policies might not be optimum (by whatever
standards one may choose), their consistency and
relative stability has made it possible for producers to face a fairly secure world and to adjust
their decisions in such a way as to try to obtain
maximum economic benefits within the known frame of
reference. In the long run, there is no doubt that
these conditions assist a rapid and sustained agricultural development.

If it is true that in the past these policies
have been developed in a somewhat improvised manner,
without much studying and planning, but by using
good common sense, this procedure has been fairly
effective in Mexico. Nevertheless, as the agricultural sector of the country continues to progress
and reaches levels of greater complexity in its
structure and functioning, it will be necessary to
adopt more sophisticated techniques to guide the
development of agriculture in accordance with the
needs for national economic growth.

In spite of the progress made by Mexico in
developing its agriculture, there are still many
problems left to solve, which limit further growth.
Foremost among these is the persistent poverty of
a large proportion of the rural sector, which results from the agrarian situation: The small size
of most farm units and the organization of _ejidos_

prevent or delay a more effective adoption of the
technology that could increase labor efficiency and
rural incomes. Continuing rural overpopulation
contributes to the difficulty in bringing about the
rapid changes that should be made. All this deter-
mines a persistently low socio-economic level among
a great majority of Mexican farmers, which is a sad
contradiction to the notable increase in total agricultural production experienced during the past
years.

Intimately related to the preceding problem is
the limited use and short supply of capital in agriculture. Agricultural credit reaches only a
small proportion of Mexican farmers, and often it
is the more needy who are unable to obtain financial assistance. Recent large international loans
to the Mexican Government for agricultural credit
are aimed at remedying these deficiencies.

Perhaps the other more serious limiting factor
to a continued rapid growth of agriculture in Mexico is the low level of education in the agricultural sector. About 50 per cent of the rural population is illiterate, and the proportion may be even
larger for the strictly farm population. Higher
technical education is also very limited, and needs
great expansion and improvement to provide technicians to staff governmental programs for the agricultural sector.

Other limiting factors that can be pointed out
in Mexican agricultural development are gaps in research, particularly in the whole range of agricultural economics and in animal husbandry; the inadequate staffing and support for the extension service, which cannot reach most of the farmers in
greatest need of technical assistance and advice;
deficiencies in the marketing of agricultural products and in market information, as well as in the
availability of better inputs in the rural areas;
and limitations in policy formulation and planning
for agriculture. This last factor is largely a
consequence of the lack of more complete and

reliable agricultural statistics, resource inventories and evaluations, economic studies, and of well-trained personnel in the sciences pertaining to these fields.

In conclusion, the factors and conditions that have influenced the rapid growth of Mexican agriculture in the last decades should continue to operate until the whole of the agricultural sector has been raised to the level of commercial agriculture. Naturally, this will require and will cause further changes in the economy; new policies will have to be introduced over a period of time in response to these changing conditions. These should come about in Mexico, given the experience and commitment that the government has in relation to the continued progress of the country's agriculture.

STATISTICAL APPENDIX

APPENDIX TABLE 1

Gross National Product
(millions of pesos)

	1950	1955	1960
Gross national product, 1950 prices	40,577	54,767	73,482
Total population (thousands)	26,433.1	30,849.2	36,003.0
Gross national product per capita, 1950 prices	1,535	1,775	2,041
Gross national product at market prices	40,577	87,349	154,137
Plus: importations of goods and services	6,827	15,101	21,038
Total of goods and services	47,404	102,450	175,175
Less: exports of goods and services	7,234	14,821	17,150
Total internal expenditures	40,170	87,629	158,025

1961	1962	1963	1964	1965
76,038	79,691	84,700	93,200	98,200
37,271.5	38,584.7	39,944.2	40,421	41,755
2,040	2,065	2,120	2,305	2,354
163,757	177,533	192,200	224,600	242,700
21,048	21,791	23,943	28,110	29,318
184,805	199,324	216,143	252,710	272,018
18,291	19,836	21,366	22,957	24,931
166,514	179,488	194,777	229,753	247,087

(Cont'd)

	1950	1955	1960
Distribution of total internal consumption			
Private con- sumption	33,573	71,229	126,806
Public con- sumption	1,769	3,783	7,993
Total con- sumption	35,342	75,012	134,799
Gross private fixed investment	2,185	7,957	14,458
Gross public fixed investment	2,643	4,660	8,768
Total gross fixed investment	4,828	12,617	23,226
Total internal expenditures	40,170	87,629	158,025

Source: Nacional Financiera, S.A.; Banco de México, S.A.

216

1961	1962	1963	1964	1965
133,843	145,129	155,610	180,608	194,571
8,600	9,568	11,157	12,493	13,830
142,443	154,697	166,767	193,101	208,401
13,284	13,452	13,639	19,184	22,601
10,787	11,339	14,371	17,468	16,085
24,071	24,791	28,010	36,652	38,686
166,514	179,488	194,777	229,753	247,087

APPENDIX TABLE 2

Gross National Product by Principal Sectors
(millions of pesos, 1950)

	1950	1955	1960	1964	1965	1966	1967a
Agriculture	5,999	8,417	9,178	10,986	11,579	12,447	12,472
Livestock	2,903	3,460	4,450	5,094	5,267	5,351	5,538
Forestry	263	256	254	277	279	277	298
Fishing	77	86	136	155	147	160	161
Mining	1,243	1,437	1,648	1,670	1,656	1,699	1,728
Petroleum and coal	1,129	1,545	2,346	3,084	3,213	3,316	3,697
Manufacturing	8,437	11,605	17,116	23,522	25,192	25,472	27,508
Construction	1,287	1,757	2,595	3,568	3,507	4,033	4,456
Electricity	370	586	898	1,318	1,443	1,592	1,594
Transportation and communication	1,988	2,851	3,638	4,066	4,265	4,449	4,471
Commerce	10,750	14,233	19,167	24,461	25,806	27,870	29,654
Government	1,294	1,599	1,985	2,620	2,725	2,891	2,905
Other activities	5,320	7,480	10,906	13,794	14,608	15,674	16,750
Total gross internal product	41,060	55,312	74,317	94,615	99,687	105,231	111,232
Less: net interests and dividends paid to foreign countries	483	545	835	1,415	1,487	--	--
Gross national product	40,577	54,767	73,482	93,200	98,200	105,600	112,358

aPreliminary.

Source: Banco de México, S.A.

218

APPENDIX TABLE 5

Exports by Groups and Most Important Products
(millions of dollars)

	1950	1955	1960	1961	1962	1963	1964	1965	1966
Agriculture and livestock	233.9	394.8	352.9	343.6	426.4	380.9	434.3	535.8	548.0
Cotton	87.9	255.7	160.1	162.9	221.2	199.2	173.1	214.7	221.9
Coffee	38.6	104.1	71.7	71.7	70.1	49.1	95.2	78.1	83.5
Tomatoes	2.8	19.0	25.5	14.1	20.2	24.5	34.0	35.1	62.9
Livestock and meat	--	9.2	42.8	57.9	74.4	63.5	41.1	55.3	68.4
Corn	--	3.8	22.0	--	0.1	--	15.9	77.2	46.7
Wheat	--	--	--	--	0.3	5.0	35.8	41.6	3.9
Others	104.6	3.0	30.8	37.0	40.1	39.6	39.2	33.8	60.7
Fishing	19.2	20.3	36.3	46.1	48.2	53.5	55.5	44.6	55.6
Mining	147.2	219.4	157.6	167.3	170.9	174.5	182.4	185.0	185.4
Lead	58.8	53.9	33.6	37.1	26.0	27.4	23.0	27.8	27.6
Sulfur	--	27.8	28.2	29.1	30.3	34.3	37.6	33.6	35.4
Zinc	23.8	28.2	29.5	27.2	28.1	29.8	42.6	42.7	44.9
Copper	23.6	42.0	25.8	19.0	24.4	22.5	14.7	8.1	8.4
Petroleum and natural gas	31.9	51.3	19.9	33.3	38.3	36.9	38.1	39.6	38.6
Others	9.1	16.2	20.6	21.6	23.8	23.6	26.4	33.2	30.5
Manufactured products	33.3	56.7	134.8	168.8	149.1	190.8	201.0	191.0	214.5
Sugar	--	7.2	52.9	68.7	43.4	59.6	76.7	58.9	57.1
Food industry	2.7	8.5	18.3	22.2	22.8	29.4	37.8	37.1	32.6
Henequen fibers	16.2	8.4	17.8	19.7	21.1	25.0	24.0	16.9	10.0
Other textiles	13.6	8.9	15.9	24.3	18.9	15.2	7.8	9.0	29.1
Chemical products	0.2	4.2	16.0	21.6	26.4	30.5	26.4	36.4	40.7
Other manufacturings	0.6	19.5	13.9	12.3	16.5	31.1	28.3	32.7	45.0
Other exports	59.8	118.2	57.0	77.7	104.9	136.2	149.2	157.5	188.9
Total exports[a]	493.4	856.7	738.6	803.5	899.5	935.9	1,022.4	1,113.9	1,192.4

[a]Includes reevaluation estimated by the Bank of Mexico.

Source: Banco de México, S.A.

219

Imports by Groups and Most Important Products
(millions of dollars)

	1950	1955	1960	1961	1962	1963	1964	1965	1966
Consumer goods	115.6	130.4	212.1	222.2	228.9	282.6	300.0	298.5	287.3
Food	43.2	23.8	33.4	27.5	35.9	70.5	4.3	1.9	.7
Automobiles and auto parts	32.9	36.3	87.8	89.4	97.5	113.5	147.4	151.7	137.6
Other consumer goods	39.5	70.3	90.9	105.3	95.5	98.6	148.3	144.9	145.1
Production goods	364.7	1,060.0	974.3	916.4	914.1	957.1	1,192.9	1,261.1	1,317.9
Raw materials and semi-finished products	243.4	296.3	404.0	380.8	378.3	415.8	487.4	550.7	575.6
Textile fibers	9.5	12.2	10.1	10.1	11.5	12.5	20.8	23.0	20.2
Chemical products and fertilizers	10.5	32.7	52.4	53.5	61.2	64.5	57.2	46.8	49.1
Pesticides, insecticides, etc.	4.1	20.8	24.7	22.9	18.0	17.8	14.8	17.8	14.6
Wood pulp and newsprint	10.8	14.4	17.2	16.4	17.6	16.7	21.7	19.1	20.0
Iron and steel products	5.5	19.0	22.2	20.9	16.5	21.9	36.5	41.9	37.1
Petroleum and by-products	12.9	42.0	36.5	27.6	18.6	19.6	26.2	25.5	34.5
Other raw and semi-finished materials	189.1	155.2	240.9	229.4	234.9	262.8	310.2	380.6	400.1
Capital goods	121.3	763.7	570.3	535.6	535.8	541.3	705.5	710.4	742.3
Materials for railroads	7.1	12.2	34.7	23.1	21.0	14.6	25.4	30.1	20.7
Electrical equipment	26.6	9.4	24.3	24.1	31.6	23.7	11.7	14.8	17.3
Tractors, Vehicles and parts	8.4	62.8	92.8	82.0	74.8	97.4	94.1	82.8	71.6
Machinery and parts	21.4	266.6	171.9	165.4	144.2	146.9	247.9	199.8	212.0
Aircrafts and parts	1.3	0.3	28.6	9.7	24.2	12.2	20.9	11.9	17.3
Other capital goods	56.5	412.4	218.0	231.3	240.0	246.5	305.5	378.0	403.4
Total imports	480.3	1,190.4	1,186.4	1,138.6	1,143.0	1,239.7	1,492.9	1,559.6	1,605.2

Source: Banco de México, S.A.

APPENDIX TABLE 5

Geographical Distribution of Commerce
(percentages)

Countries	1950		1960		1964		1965	
	Exports	Imports	Exports	Imports	Exports	Imports	Exports	Imports
United States	86.4	84.4	72.0	72.1	67.3	68.5	62.5	65.8
Canada	0.9	2.3	1.1	2.8	1.0	4.1	0.9	2.4
Other countries of the Western Hemisphere								
LAFTA countries	1.2	0.4	0.9	0.2	3.8	1.1	3.4	1.9
Other Latin American countries	2.4	0.1	2.3	0.8	2.7	0.7	2.2	0.6
European Economic Community	3.3	4.6	9.2	11.7	4.6	13.5	5.8	15.9
European Association of Free Trade	1.3	5.1	3.9	8.1	5.7	6.8	1.4	7.6
Japan	0.0	0.2	7.0	1.4	8.5	1.9	9.4	2.5
Australia	0.7	0.8	0.3	0.8	0.2	1.4	0.3	1.3
Other countries	3.8	2.1	3.3	2.1	6.2	2.0	14.1	2.0
	100.0	100.0	100.0	100.0	100.0	100.0	100.0	100.0

Source: Banco Nacional de Comercio Exterior, S.A.

APPENDIX TABLE 6

Balance of Payments
(millions of dollars)

		1950	1955
I.	**Current Account**		
	a) Exports of goods and services		
	1. Exports of goods (FOB)	493.4	738.6
	2. Gold and silver production[a]	50.5	47.5
	3. Tourism	110.9	118.1
	4. Border transactions	121.9	261.7
	5. Braceros	19.4	24.8
	6. Others	30.5	24.0
	Total exports of goods and services	826.6	1,214.7
	b) Imports of goods and services		
	1. Imports of goods	596.7	883.7
	2. Tourism[b]	6.9	11.9
	3. Border transactions	76.5	151.2
	4. Income on direct foreign investments	66.0	79.6
	5. Interest on official debt	11.2	13.5
	6. Others	22.8	31.3
	Total Imports of goods and services	780.1	1,171.2
	Balance of current account	46.5	43.5

1960	1964	1965	1966[f]	1967[f]
738.7	1,022.4	1,113.9	1,192.4	1,148.0
47.7	46.2	44.3	44.6	--
155.3	240.6	274.8	328.3	364.4
366.0	463.3	499.5	520.9	594.6
36.1	28.9	12.1	11.4	--
28.1	34.8	44.3	55.7	--
1,371.9	1,836.2	1,988.9	2,153.3	2,200.0
1,186.4	1,493.0	1,559.6	1,605.2	1,749.0
40.5	100.2	119.1	136.0	172.0
221.1	276.6	295.1	331.6	363.7
141.6	236.1	236.1	250.0	--
30.4	54.8	62.2	79.9	--
63.0	82.0	94.6	96.5	--
1,683.0	2,242.7	2,366.7	2,499.2	2,663.0
- 311.1	- 406.5	- 377.8	- 345.9	

(Cont'd.)

	1950	1955
II. Capital Account		
a) Long-term capital	66.0	135.8
1. Direct foreign investments	68.6	111.8
Reinvestment	14.6	18.9
New investments	38.0	84.9
Intercompany accounts	16.0	8.0
Dis-investment	--	--
2. Stocks, bonds, notes	- 2.3	- 13.3
3. Credits of Nacional Financiera and other governmental institutions	11.0	57.6
Credits	28.6	101.7
Amortizations[d]	- 17.6	- 44.1
4. Government repayment for debts to foreign countries[e]	- 11.3	- 20.3

1960	1964	1965	1966[f]	1967[f]
120.1	513.8	180.6	286.7	
- 38.0	161.9	213.9	186.1	
10.6	50.2	61.3	69.5	
62.5	95.0	120.1	97.4	
- 5.4	16.7	32.3	19.2	
- 116.5[c]	--	--	--	
- 5.4	- 8.5	11.9	7.5	
188.9	384.4	- 21.5	94.4	
352.1	695.3	344.2	557.4	
- 163.2	- 310.9	- 365.7	- 462.9	
25.4	- 24.0	22.3	11.3	

(Cont'd.)

APPENDIX TABLE 6 (Continued)

	1950	1955
II. Capital Account (cont'd.)		
b) Short-term capital (the reserves of Banco de México are excluded)	43.7	91.2
1. Individuals and enterprises	36.8	61.8
2. Private banks and national institutions of credit	6.9	29.4
Balance of Capital Account	109.7	227.0
III. Errors and Omissions	- 24.7	- 70.4
IV. Banco de México's reserve variation (addition of I, II, and III)	131.5	200.1

aLess the gold and silver used within the country for industrial purposes.

bIncludes expenses of students in foreign countries.

cPreliminary payment for the purchase of foreign electricity companies.

dThe years 1964-65 include credits given to foreign countries for Mexican export promotion.

eThe year 1964 includes an advance payment to the EXIMBANK for a stabilization credit obtained in previous years.

fPreliminary partial data.

Source: Banco de México, S.A.

1960	1964	1965	1966[f]	1967[f]
74.4	62.7			
- 45.9	- 52.8	- 12.5		
120.3	115.5	- 17.3		
194.5	576.5	150.8		290.0
108.0	- 138.5	188.3	65.2	--
- 8.6	31.6	- 21.0	6.0	39.8

Total Financing Provided by Banking System[a]

(millions of pesos)

| Years | Total Financing | To Private Enterprise To Production | | | | | To Federal Government |
		Subtotal	Industry	Agriculture and Livestock	Mining	Commerce	
1950	8,972.7	5'095.3	4,009.6	1,059.9	25.8	1,811.1	2,066.3
1955	17,672.7	11,096.7	8,252.5	2,786.7	57.5	3,390.3	3,185.7
1960	39,780.5	25,673.6	19,798.8	5,811.9	62.9	8,463.6	5,643.3
1961	46,055.9	31,085.4	24,424.1	6,582.8	78.5	9,495.3	5,475.2
1962	53,454.4	38,137.3	30,536.2	7,360.7	240.4	9,704.4	5,612.7
1963	61,251.5	41,250.7	32,800.4	8,237.0	213.3	11,042.8	8,958.0
1964	74,434.9	48,260.6	38,700.0	9,317.9	242.7	13,318.2	12,856.1
1965	87,370.5	53,292.2	42,366.7	10,664.7	260.8	13,608.5	20,469.8
1966	104,629.5	60,120.0	46,945.5	12,547.4	627.1	17,123.2	27,386.3

[a]Excluding operations which did not represent real variations in financing; including credit and bonds of the common fund of certificates of participation of Nacional Financiera, S.A.

Source: Banco de México, S.A.

APPENDIX TABLE 8

Supply of Money and Means of Circulation
(millions of pesos)

December 31	Total Supply of Money	In Circulation			In Checking Accounts
		Bills	Coins	
1950	5,988	2,639	275	3,074
1955	10,517	4,765	319	5,433
1960	16,889	7,312	562	9,015
1961	18,008	7,660	616	9,732
1962	20,274	8,468	676	11,130
1963	23,680	9,555	709	13,416
1964	27,640	11,149	774	15,717
1965	29,519	11,707	800	17,012
1966	32,752	12,778	852	19,122
1967	35,565	10,313	4,425	20,827

Source: Banco de México, S.A.

APPENDIX TABLE 9

Price Index of Wholesale Prices in Mexico City
(210 articles, 1950 = 100)

	1955	1960	1961	1962	1963	1964	1965	1966
General index	156.6	189.4	191.4	194.8	196.0	204.2	208.1	210.8
Consumer goods	155.6	190.4	192.2	199.3	197.8	206.9	211.7	215.8
Food	162.3	203.1	203.1	209.5	208.2	220.6	224.3	228.7
Nonprocessed food	168.0	213.5	212.4	220.6	218.6	234.9	238.5	244.6
Processed food	148.4	178.0	180.4	182.3	183.0	185.7	189.8	190.1
Nonfood	144.4	165.3	170.6	176.4	177.4	180.0	187.0	190.4
Manufactured goods	157.4	188.6	190.4	190.1	193.5	200.8	203.0	203.8
Raw materials	165.5	187.6	188.8	185.2	188.5	197.4	200.8	197.9
Nonprocessed	168.7	169.6	171.7	163.4	166.9	176.7	178.7	172.8
Processed	160.9	213.3	212.8	216.2	219.3	227.0	231.6	233.8
Fuel and power	128.6	179.9	184.9	193.4	198.3	200.9	201.6	206.9
Vehicles and accessories	159.8	208.2	208.8	212.1	213.5	218.9	219.5	232.0

Source: Banco de México, S.A.

230

APPENDIX TABLE 10

Index of the Volume of Industrial Production
(1950 = 100)

Year	All Industry	Manufacturing	Construction	Petroleum and Coke[a]	Mining[b]	Electrical Energy
1955	135.8	137.5	136.5	136.8	115.6	158.3
1960	197.4	202.9	201.6	207.8	132.6	242.6
1961	204.7	210.1	203.6	231.4	127.0	265.6
1962	215.1	223.6	205.8	235.8	128.6	282.8
1963	235.0	244.2	238.1	250.4	133.1	309.9
1964	266.0	278.8	277.2	273.2	134.3	356.0
1965	280.9	298.7	272.5	284.7	133.2	390.0
1966	289.7	301.9	313.4	293.7	136.7	430.2
1967	312.7	326.0	346.2	327.4	139.0	430.8

[a] Includes petroleum and by-products, extraction, refining, and coke.
[b] Includes nonferrous metals, iron, nonmetallic minerals.

Source: Banco de México, S.A.

231

APPENDIX TABLE 11

Total Production of Principal Manufacturing Industries

	Units	1950	1955	1960	1961	1962	1963	1964	1965
Iron ingots	000 tons[a]	227	328	669	758	801	833	926	946
Steel ingots	000 tons	390	713	1,492	1,693	1,711	2,017	2,326	2,455
Cement	000 tons	1,388	2,086	3,086	2,984	3,266	3,680	4,339	4,199
Plate glass	000 sq. yd.	5,055	7,787	7,278	8,502	9,513	8,329	11,462	10,759
Sulphuric acid	000 tons	43	125	249	276	339	387	455	519
Lye	000 tons	8	23	66	71	83	91	95	104
Ammonium sulphate	000 tons	3	70	147	153	157	159	167	200
Ammonia superphosphate	000 tons	15	75	93	104	109	117	123	131
Ammonium nitrate	000 tons	--	--	54	71	124	125	127	94
Synthetic fibers	000 tons	8	17	23	24	25	29	33	35
Cotton material and yarn	000 tons	66	72	102	102	110	115	120	126
Railroad freight cars	units	--	858	1,686	2,274	787	943	1,062	1,206
Trucks and buses	000 units	11	20	22	23	26	26	32	30
Automobiles	000 units	10	12	28	39	41	49	63	67
Radio receivers	000 units	67	190	450	530	555	676	956	1,038
Television sets	000 units	--	--	80	95	90	116	189	211
Refrigerators	000 units	20	36	45	54	55	69	96	114
Gas stoves	000 units	8	105	132	137	157	159	235	286

[a]Metric tons.

Source: Nacional Financiera, S.A., Informe Anual 1966.

APPENDIX TABLE 12

Production of Principal Minerals (metric tons)

	1950	1955	1960	1961	1962	1963	1964	1965	1966
Silver	1,528	1,492	1,385	1,255	1,282	1,330	1,258	1,254	1,306
Gold (kg.)	12,694	11,909	9,339	8,357	7,364	7,401	6,531	6,712	6,641
Sulphur	13,194	518,721	1,328,546	1,244,347	1,447,003	1,554,395	1,725,300	1,585,273	1,701,060
Lead	238,078	210,815	190,670	181,326	193,298	189,987	174,824	170,092	182,071
Zinc	223,520	269,399	262,425	268,973	250,683	239,818	235,603	224,876	219,180
Copper	61,698	54,676	60,330	49,314	47,125	55,861	52,506	55,248	56,429
Manganese	14,460	35,806	71,856	68,704	62,869	54,341	64,089	58,810	31,099
Coal	911,732	1,342,101	1,775,649	1,817,646	1,993,147	2,070,893	2,137,558	2,005,662	2,094,000
Iron ore	297,794	447,353	895,737	1,029,918	1,089,270	1,396,882	1,392,467	1,442,000	1,319,000

Source: Nacional Financiera, S.A., Informe Anual 1967.

APPENDIX TABLE 13

Land Use (millions of hectares)

	1950 Census			1960 Census		
	Total	Private and Federal Property	Ejidos	Total	Private and Federal Property	Ejidos
Tillable land	19.9	11.1	8.8	23.8	13.5	10.3
Irrigated	2.4	1.2	1.2	3.4	2.0	1.4
Irrigated with subterranean water	0.7	0.3	0.4	0.8	0.4	0.4
Temporary crops (unirrigated)	16.0	9.1	6.9	18.3	10.3	8.0
Permanent crops	0.8	0.5	0.3	1.3	0.8	0.5
Pastures	67.4	50.9	16.5	79.1	59.5	19.6
Forests	38.8	30.0	8.8	43.7	35.7	8.0
Productive lands, not under cultivation	7.8	6.1	1.7	11.2	7.3	3.9
Unproductive lands	11.6	8.5	3.1	11.3	8.7	2.6
Total[a]	145.5	106.6	38.9	169.1	124.7	44.5

[a]Area covered by the census.

Source: Agricultural Census, 1950-60.

234

APPENDIX TABLE 14

Land Tenure and Value of Agricultural Production, 1950

Tenure Groups	No. Farm Units (1,000)	Land Area (1,000 ha.)		Avg. Size Holding (ha.)		Value Prod. (mill. pesos)		Avg. Prod. (pesos)	
		Total	Cropland	All Land	Cropland	Total[b]	Crops	Total Farm Unit	Crop Value per ha. Cropland
Ejidos	1,356.2[a]	38,893.9	8,790.9	28.7	6.5	2,581.2	1,913.8	1,903.3	217.7
Private and other property	1,365.6	106,623.0	11,137.4	78.1	8.2	4,051.7	3,226.9	--	--
Less than 5 ha. private	1,004.8	1,362.8	1,279.8	1.4	1.3	587.8	450.5	585.0	352.0
More than 5 ha. private	353.4	85,323.8	9,857.6	214.4					
More than 5 ha. other[c]	7.4	19,936.4		2,694.1	27.3	3,463.9	2,776.4	9,600.6	281.7
Total	2,721.8	145,516.9	19,928.3	534.6	7.3	6,632.9[d]	5,140.7	2,437.0	258.0

[a]Number of land parcels; total number of ejidatarios is 1,328,326 living in 17,579 ejidos.

[b]Includes crops, forestry, and livestock products.

[c]Federal, state, municipal, and other property. These probably include little cropland.

[d]Excludes production in urban areas (poblaciones).

Source: Agricultural Census, 1950.

235

Land Tenure and Value of Agricultural Production, 1960

Tenure Groups	No. Farm Units (1,000)	Land Area (1,000 ha.) Total	Land Area (1,000 ha.) Cropland	Avg. Size Holding (ha.) All Land	Avg. Size Holding (ha.) Cropland	Value Prod. (mill. pesos) Total[b]	Value Prod. (mill. pesos) Crops	Avg. Val. Prod. (pesos) Total Farm Unit	Avg. Val. Prod. (pesos) Crop Value per ha. Cropland
Ejidos	1,523.8[a]	44,497.1	10,329.2	29.2	6.8	7,221.4	5,869.9	4,739.1	568.3
Private and other property	1,345.4	124,587.1	13,477.6	92.5	10.0	13,011.9	8,525.7	--	--
Less than 5 ha. private	899.1	1,328.1	1,259.0	1.5	1.4	1,308.5	823.1	1,455.3	653.8
More than 5 ha. private	438.1	101,503.7	12,218.6	231.7	27.3	11,703.4	7,702.6	26,164.5	630.4
More than 5 ha. other[c]	9.2	21,755.3		2,364.7					
Total	2,870.2	169,084.2	23,816.9	589.1	8.3	20,233.3[d]	14,395.6	7,049.4	604.4

[a] Number of ejidatarios that own land; total number of ejidatarios is 1,597,691 living in 18,699 ejidos.
[b] Includes crops, forestry, and livestock products.
[c] Federal, state, municipal, and other property.
[d] Excludes production in urban areas (poblaciones).

Source: Agricultural Census, 1960.

APPENDIX TABLE 16

Area, Production, and Yield of Principal Crops[a]

Crop	Area Harvested (1,000 ha.)						Production (thousand metric tons)					
	1949-51	1962	1963	1964	1965	1966	1949-51	1962	1963	1964	1965	1966
Corn	4,183	6,372	6,963	7,461	7,718	7,714	3,139	6,337	6,870	8,454	8,678	9,105
Beans	941	1,674	1,711	2,091	2,117	2,240	240	656	677	891	858	1,002
Cotton fiber	731	787	847	809	657	787	252	486	535	565	545	636
Wheat	617	748	819	743	666	683	560	1,455	1,703	1,527	1,599	1,609
Sugar	194	362	378	445	385	390	9,893	21,116	22,327	26,990	23,079	23,400
Coffee	159	314	323	324	285	300	64	140	137	145	159	185
Avocado	8	9	10	10	10	10	61	113	130	132	132	132
Sesame	163	238	251	261	273	281[a]	79	158	169	172	162	176
Green alfalfa	54	101	102	107	106	108	2,331	5,090	5,132	5,532	5,575	5,724
Rice	106	134	135	133	153	155[a]	114	289	296	274	382	390
Peanuts	48	75	75	76	65	67	57	95	93	95	86	95
Cacao	29	68	69	69	70	70	8	29	30	20	21	25
Barley	225	193	232	212	226	233[a]	162	151	186	171	193	228
Oats	80	86	91	91	36	36	56	74	79	80	20	20
Dried chile	19	22	24	25	25	26	15	17	19	21	21	21
Green chile	16	37	40	41	42	43	38	109	123	134	134	137
Chick peas	123	146	105	137	155	145	88	129	97	124	124	146
Henequen	140	177	184	212	185	185	100	156	172	195	175	176
Lemons	10	15	16	19	16	16	69	118	145	166	141	142
Oranges	51	79	78	78	79	80	49	883	855	845	863	880
Potatoes	30	46	50	48	37	38	134	379	414	413	292	319
Bananas, roatan	22	27	30	31	31	31	248	367	413	421	426	435
Bananas, vario	17	31	43	74	44	45	161	344	526	527	534	543
Tobacco	35	52	51	52	52	52	35	67	67	68	69	69
Tomatoes	54	60	61	61	41	42	350	434	443	445	524	529
Total for Mexico	8,328	12,436	13,357	14,234	14,281	14,928						

(Cont'd)

237

APPENDIX TABLE 16 (Continued)

Crop	Yield (kg. per ha.)						Value of Product (million pesos)					
	1949-51	1962	1963	1964	1965	1966	1949-51	1962	1963	1964	1965	1966
Corn	750	995	987	1,133	1,124	1,180	1,235	4,828	6,469	7,990	8,157	8,559
Beans	256	392	396	426	407	447	170	1,080	1,146	1,538	1,459	1,753
Cotton fiber	349	622	632	700	830	809	1,297	3,047	3,378	3,665	3,554	4,170
Wheat	910	1,946	2,079	2,056	2,401	2,400	336	1,300	1,558	1,435	1,487	1,470
Sugar	50,922	58,394	59,074	60,576	59,870	60,000	257	1,194	1,384	1,676	1,477	1,321
Coffee	405	445	425	447	558	616	221	1,069	1,100	1,167	1,193	1,203
Avocado	7,317	12,750	13,050	13,100	13,100	13,000	54	214	217	223	226	229
Sesame	485	662	675	657	593	626	74	313	345	355	338	440
Green alfalfa	43,486	50,352	50,367	51,693	52,500	53,000	105	570	597	685	663	687
Rice	1,732	2,158	2,199	2,070	2,500	2,521	79	291	313	296	417	432
Peanuts	1,166	1,259	1,261	1,261	1,326	1,416	36	115	119	125	114	129
Cacao	274	433	439	293	296	350	34	164	169	113	113	137
Barley	719	784	799	806	852	977	43	101	132	127	145	173
Oats	700	864	868	875	540	592	29	60	68	72	17	18
Dried chile	785	739	771	819	825	830	45	108	125	142	142	147
Green chile	2,379	2,919	3,058	3,218	3,220	3,230	20	114	132	162	150	156
Chick peas	714	884	927	904	802	1,004	45	168	136	174	179	211
Henequen	715	883	934	923	945	950	119	286	324	392	343	352
Lemons	6,602	7,800	8,850	8,850	8,890	8,900	24	120	117	134	119	122
Oranges	9,999	11,100	10,950	10,800	10,960	11,000	121	1,067	705	746	743	774
Potatoes	4,518	8,236	8,276	8,540	7,899	8,308	54	285	344	360	255	288
Bananas, roatan	11,014	13,200	13,660	13,800	13,800	13,800	68	239	276	305	315	330
Bananas, vario	9,280	10,800	12,000	12,000	12,100	12,200	37	229	370	374	390	407
Tobacco	992	1,298	1,310	1,310	1,320	1,325	66	258	271	283	278	282
Tomatoes	6,453	7,188	7,312	7,278	12,609	12,485	177	416	438	469	534	550
Total for Mexico							5,415	20,863	23,741	26,472	27,131	29,521

aData for 1965 and 1966 are preliminary.

Source: Secretaría de Agricultura y Ganadería, Dirección General de Economía Agrícola.

APPENDIX TABLE 17

Livestock Slaughtered, 1956-65 (thousands)

	1956		1957		1958		1959		1960		1961		1962		1963		1964		1965	
	Number	Wt. Tons	Number	Wt. Tons	Number	Wt. Tons	Number	Wt. Tons	Number	Wt. Tons	Number	Wt. Tons	Number	Wt. Tons	Number	Wt. Tons	Number	Wt. Tons	Number	Wt. Tons
Cattle[a]	1,796	274	1,612	245	1,907	291	2,226	343	2,182	336	2,168	322	1,873	298	1,954	314	2,053	332	2,127	343
Exported alive	111	--	350	--	491	--	374	--	396	--	550	--	766	--	554	--	358	--	575	--
Total cattle	1,907		1,962		2,398		2,600		2,578		2,718		2,639		2,508		2,411		2,702	
Sheep	340	5	423	6	584	9	611	9	765	11	1,098	16	895	14	904	15	986	16	976	16
Goats	967	14	622	9	683	10	736	11	893	13	703	10	732	10	749	10	800	11	742	10
Pigs	1,953	114	1,951	114	2,596	152	2,974	174	2,733	160	2,365	139	2,223	140	2,319	146	2,324	147	2,558	163

[a]Includes slaughter in packinghouses for export.

Source: Secretaría de Agricultura y Ganadería, Proyecciones de la Oferta y la Demanda de Productos Agropecuarios en México, a 1970 y a 1975 (Mexico: Banco de Mexico, S.A., 1965); Dirección General de Estadística, Anuarios Estadísticos de los Estados Unidos Mexicanos, 1962, 1965.

239

APPENDIX TABLE 18

Volume and Value of Important Agricultural Exports

	Volume in Tons (thousands)						Value in Millions of Pesos[a]					
	1950	1962	1963	1964	1965	1966	1950	1962	1963	1964	1965	1966
Cotton	163	425	370	347	409	429	761	2,011	2,565	1,547	1,921	2,007
Sugar	21	357	394	525	534	474	20	543	759	959	736	714
Coffee	46	91	67	105	78	92	334	763	620	1,102	791	886
Beef cattle	--	766[b]	554[b]	358[b]	575[b]	589[b]	--	387	540	175	304	262
Fresh meat	11	33	33	27	26	28	17	283	334	245	229	324
Tomatoes	12	136	141	153	161	217	24	67	372	184	195	262
Molasses	118	253	413	512	556	499	5	39	121	161	177	115
Melons	--	50	54	61	71	63	1	103	107	123	152	141
Rosin	--	35	41	32	18	16	6	79	90	71	45	41
Henequen	73	39	110	18	33	31	138	78	413	67	51	42
Cacao	3	12	18	3	9	7	8	55	88	17	42	43
Strawberries	--	19	20	24	39	52	3	65	70	90	120	224
Tobacco leaf	--	4	12	8	5	2	1	31	69	50	45	17
Wheat	--	1	72	575	684	47	--	2	62	447	520	48
Oranges	--	15	47	59	79	26	5	16	55	72	73	22

[a]One peso equals U.S. $0.116 in 1950 and U.S. $0.08 in 1962-66.

[b]Number of head, in thousands.

Source: Dirección General de Economía Agrícola, Resúmen del Boletín Mensual, 1963, and unpublished data.

240

APPENDIX TABLE 19

Mexico: Schools of Veterinary Medicine
and Animal Husbandry

Name of School	Location	Date of Founding
Escuela Nacional de Medicina Veterinaria y Zootecnia, UNAM	Mexico, D.F.	August 17, 1853
Escuela de Medicina Veterinaria y Zootecnia, Universidad de Veracruz	Veracruz, Veracruz	February 1, 1957
Escuela de Medicina Veterinaria y Zootecnia, Universidad de Tamaulipas	Cd. Victoria, Tamps.	September 20, 1957
Escuela de Medicina Veterinaria y Zootecnia, Universidad de Guadalajara	Guadalajara, Jalisco	October 16, 1964
Escuela de Medicina Veterinaria y Zootecnia, Universidad Juárez del Estado de Durango	Durango, Durango	May 3, 1965
Escuela de Medicina Veterinaria y Zootecnia, Universidad de Zacatecas	Zacatecas, Zacatecas	1962
Escuela de Medicina Veterinaria y Zootecnia, Universidad de Tabasco	Villahermosa, Tabasco	1958[a]

[a] Started operations on January 15, 1968.

Source: Personal communication.

NOTES

NOTES TO CHAPTER 1

1. For a more detailed description, see, for example, Nathan Whetten, Rural Mexico (Chicago: University of Chicago Press, 1948), p. 111.

2. See Raúl Benitez Zenteno and Gustavo A. Cabrera, Proyecciones de la Población de México, 1960-1980 (Mexico: Banco de México, S.A., 1966).

NOTES TO CHAPTER 2

1. Enrique Pérez López, "El Producto Nacional" ("National Product"), México, Cincuenta Años de Revolución: La Economía (Mexico, Fifty Years of Revolution: Economy) (Mexico: Fondo de Cultura Económica, 1960), p. 574. Here the gross national product can be found (with 1950 prices) from 1895 to 1950; the following years were modified.

2. It is estimated that foreign investment represented mainly by direct foreign investments amounted to $464 million in 1897, and by 1911 it had quadrupled. See Raymond Vernon, Dilemma of Mexico's Development (Cambridge, Mass.: Harvard University Press, 1963), pp. 42-43. Another estimate tells us that North American investments alone represented more than half of the total national assets; between 1900 and 1911, 66 centavos of each invested peso were invested by foreigners. Alfredo R. Navarrete, "El Financiamiento del Desarrollo Económico," México, Cincuenta Años de Revolución: La Economía, pp. 513-14.

3. Frank Tannenbaum, "La Revolución Agraria en México" ("Mexican Agrarian Revolution"), Problemas Agrícolas e Industriales de México (Agricultural and Industrial Problems in Mexico), Vol. IV, No. 2, April, June, 1952, p. 117. Another estimate is the following: "1 per cent of the country's

population owned 97 per cent of the land; small owners had 2 per cent of rural property, towns and communities owned but 1 per cent of the total land
area; however, small owners, towns and communities
amounted to 95 per cent of the national population
dependent on agriculture and involved in same."
Cited by J. Silva-Herzog, El Agrarismo Mexicano y
la Reforma Agraria (Mexican Agrarianism and the
Agrarian Reform) (Mexico: Fondo de Cultura Económica, 1959), p. 502.

4. See Daniel Cosío Villegas, and other
authors in the series Historia Moderna de México
(Modern History of Mexico), Vol. VII, Book 11, El
Porfiriato, Vida Económica (The Porfirio Diaz Era,
Economic Life) (Mexico: Editorial Hermes, 1965);
also El Colegio de México, Estadísticas Economícas
del Porfiriato (Economic Statistics of the Porfirio
Diaz Regime), 1960.

5. See Raúl Ortiz Mena, "Moneda y Crédito"
("Money and Credit"), in México, Cincuenta Años de
Revolución: La Economía, and Dwight S. Brothers
and Leopoldo M. Solis, Mexican Financial Develop-
ment (Austin: University of Texas Press, 1966),
Chaps I, II.

6. Based on data supplied by Pérez Lopez,
op. cit., pp. 587-88.

7. Navarrete, op. cit., p. 522.

8. Raúl Ortiz Mena, Victor L. Urquidi, Alberto
Waterstone, and Jonas H. Haralz, El Desarrollo Económico de México y su Capacidad para Absorber Capital del Extranjero (The Economic Development of
Mexico and Its Capacity to Absorb Foreign Capital)
(Mexico: Nacional Financiera, 1953), p. 32. However, the figures checked in 1950 (see Figure 1)
indicate that the gross fixed investment represented 11.9 per cent of the GNP.

9. Ortiz Mena, et al., op. cit., p. 391ff.

10. See Brothers and Solis, op. cit., pp.
160-61, 192-93.

11. Roberto E. Anguiano, Las Finanzas del
Sector Público en México (Mexico: Universidad
Nacional Autonoma de México, 1968), p. 150.

12. See the Prospectus of Mexico, External
Sinking Fund Bonds (mimeo.), The First Boston
Corporation and Kuhn, Loeb and Co., July, 1963,
April, 1964, and October, 1965.

13. See the Secretary of the Presidency,
México: Inversion Pública Federal 1925-1963
(Mexico: Direccion de Inversiones Públicas, 1964).

14. See Directorio General (General Directory)
of decentralized organizations, state participation
enterprises, public establishments, commissions,
boards, and institutes depending on the Federal
Government (Mexico: Ministry of National Patrimony,
September, 1964).

15. Horacio Flores de la Peña, "México: Una
Economía en Desarrollo" ("Mexico: A Developing
Economy"), Comercio Exterior, August, 1963, p. 561.

16. The customs tax structure facilitates importation of raw material and especially production
goods. The Law to Promote New and Necessary Industries grants tax exemptions or reductions to industries whose production requires at least 60 per cent
Mexican goods or material. These exemptions are
granted for ten, seven, and five years, depending
on whether the industry is considered basic, semi-
basic, or secondary. See the "Law, Bylaws and In-
structions" of the Diarios Oficiales (Official
Journals) of January and December 2, 1955.

17. See Banco de México, Departamento de
Investigaciones Industriales, Estudios Sobre Susti-
tución de Importaciones (Mexico: Talleres Gráficos
de Impresiones Modernas, 1963).

18.   See P. Lamartine Yates, <u>Regional Develop-ment in Mexico and the Decentralization of Industry</u> (Mexico: Banco de México, 1960).

19.   Flores de la Peña, <u>op. cit</u>., p. 559.

20.   Nacional Financiera, S.A., <u>La Economía Mexicana en Cifras</u> (Mexico: Nacional Financiera, S.A., 1965).

21.   <u>Ibid</u>.

22.   <u>Presidential Message</u>, September, 1966.

23.   See Edmundo Flores, <u>Tratado de Economía Agrícola</u> (Mexico: Fondo de Cultura Económica, 1962), p. 336, and also Moisés T. de la Peña, "El Pueblo y su Tierra," <u>Cuadernos Americanos</u>, 1965.

24.   Leopoldo M. Solís, <u>Apuntes para el Análisis del Desarrollo Económico de México</u> (Mexico: Banco de México, S.A., Oficina de Proyecciones Agrícolas) (mimeo.), p. 72.

25.   See Ana María Flores, <u>La Magnitud del Hambre en México</u> (Mexico: Impresiones Modernas, 1961); Efigenia M. de Navarrete, <u>La Distribución del Ingreso y el Desarrollo Económico de México</u> (Mexico: Instituto de Investigaciones Económicas, Universidad Nacional Autónoma de México, 1960).

26.   Nacional Financiera, S.A., <u>El Mercado de Valores</u>, No. 33, August 15, 1966.

27.   Secretaría de Agricultura y Ganadería, <u>et al</u>., <u>Proyecciones de la Oferta y la Demanda de Productos Agropecuarios en México, a 1970 y a 1975</u> (Mexico: Banco de México, S.A., 1965), p. 4; and United Nations, <u>Boletines Estadísticos de América Latina</u>   (<u>Statistical Bulletins of Latin America</u>), Vol. I. No. I, Vol. III, No. I, 1964 and 1966.

28.   See Commission Economique pour l'Amerique
Latine, <u>El desequilibrio Externo en el Desarrollo
Económico Latinoamericano: el Caso de México, 1957</u>
Vol. II (New York: United Nations).

29.   See Miguel S. Wionczeck, "Incomplete
Formal Planning: Mexico," <u>Planning Economic Devel-
opment</u>, ed. Everett E. Hagen (Homewood, Ill.:
Richard D. Irwin, Inc., 1963); Victor Urquidi, "Development Programming," <u>Statist</u>, London, January 8,
1965, pp. 13-15; and Robert J. Shafer, <u>Mexico:
Mutual Adjustment Planning</u> (Syracuse: Syracuse University Press, 1966).

NOTES TO CHAPTER 3

1.   Secretaria de Agricultura y Fomento,
<u>Regiones Económico Agrícolas de la República Mexi-
cana</u> (Mexico, 1936).

2.   Emilio Alanís Patiño, "Zonas y Regiones
Económicas de México," <u>Problemas Económico-Agrícolas
de México</u>, 1946.

3.   Quintana A. Francisco, <u>Geografía Agrícola
de México</u> (mimeo.), Mexico, 1966.

NOTES TO CHAPTER 4

1.   See Nacional Financiera, S.A., <u>La Economía
Mexicana en Cifras</u> (Mexico: Nacional Financiera,S.A.,
1965), p. 194.

2.   See Clarence Moore, "Agricultural Development in Mexico," <u>Journal of Farm Economics</u>, Vol.
XXXVI, No. 1, February, 1955.

3.   See <u>ibid</u>., and Richard Parks, "The Role
of Agriculture in Mexican Economic Development,"
<u>Inter-American Economic Affairs</u>, Vol. 18, No. 1,
Summer, 1964.

4. Combined Mexican Working Party (Inter-
national Board for Reconstruction and Development),
The Economic Development of Mexico (Baltimore: The
Johns Hopkins Press, 1953), p. 21. Amounts reported
in this study were deflated by an index derived from
GNP figures for the period.

5. See, for instance, U.S. Department of Agriculture, Changes in Agriculture in 26 Developing
Nations, Foreign Agricultural Economic Report No.
27 (Washington: U.S. Government Printing Office,
1965). Among these twenty-six countries studied
by the U.S. Department of Agriculture, only Israel
had an agricultural growth rate superior to Mexico's.

6. Reed Hertford, Some Notes on Mexico's
Agricultural Development, Mexico, November, 1966
(mimeo.). This brief report highlights some of the
findings of a two-year research study, Mexican
Agricultural Development, sponsored by the U.S.
Department of Agriculture and the Agency for International Development still in process.

7. Ibid.

NOTES TO CHAPTER 5

1. The rate of increase in total demand for
agricultural products has been estimated, assuming
an income elasticity for agricultural products of
.56 over the period considered and an annual rate
of increase in per capita real income of 2.9 per
cent, equal to the increase in gross national
product per capita. See Secretaría de Agricultura
y Ganadería, et al., Proyecciones de la Oferta y la
Demanda de Productos Agropecuarios en México, a
1970 y a 1975 (Mexico: Banco de México, S.A.,
1965), p. 42.

2. Ibid., p. 48. See also Chapter 9.

3. Nacional Financiera, S.A., La Economía
Mexicana en Cifras (Mexico: Nacional Financiera,
S.A., 1965), p. 45.

4. Carlos Castillo, "La Productividad de los
Recursos en el Bajío," <u>Problemas Agrícolas e Industriales de México</u>, Vol. VII, 1956, pp. 127-54.

5. Donald Freebairn, "Relative Production
Efficiency Between Tenure Classes in the Yaqui
Valley, Sonera, Mexico," <u>Journal of Farm Economics</u>,
Vol. 45, No. 5, December, 1963.

6. <u>Censo Agrícola Ganadero</u>, 1950.

7. Guillermo M. Medina and Gustavo S. del
Pozo, "Porcicultura Nacional," <u>Panagra</u>, No. 66,
April, 1966.

8. Secretaría de Agricultura y Ganadería,
<u>Informes Anuales</u>, 1963-67. It must be noted, how-
ever, that the agricultural trade data reported by
the Agricultural Secretariat do not agree with the
official trade statistics reported by the Bank of
Mexico. This may be due to the products classified
as agricultural in each case, the prices used, or
the inclusiveness of coverage; at any rate, it is
quite difficult to arrive at a consistent set of
data for agricultural trade.

NOTES TO CHAPTER 6

1. These figures refer to area harvested as
reported by the <u>Dirección de Economía Agrícola</u>,
which is estimated to be about one half of what the
Census reports as "tillable land" (<u>tierras de labor</u>).
Tillable land increased by about 58 per cent between
the 1950 and 1960 censuses.

2. Nacional Financiera, S.A., <u>La Economía
Mexicana</u> (Mexico: Nacional Financiera, S.A.,
1966), p. 45.

3. Secretaría de Agricultura y Ganadería,
<u>et al.</u>, <u>Proyecciones de la Oferta y la Demanda de
Productos Agropecuarios en México, a 1970 y a 1975</u>
(Mexico: Banco de México, S.A., 1965), pp. 1968-69.

4. Ibid., p. 170.

5. William E. Scholes, "The Migrant Worker,"
Julian Samora (ed.), La Raza: Forgotten Americans
(Notre Dame, Ind.: University of Notre Dame Press,
1966), p. 67.

6. Immigration and Naturalization Service,
Annual Report (Washington, D.C.: Government Printing Office, 1965), p. 64.

7. Nacional Financiera, S.A., op. cit., pp.
196-99.

8. Scholes, op. cit.

9. See, for instance, M. A. Durán, "Situación
y Perspectivas del Regadío en México," Crédito
Agrícola (Chapingo, Mexico: Colegio de Postgraduados,
Escuela Nacional de Agricultura, 1966).

10. Ibid., p. 18; and Alanis Patino, "La Irrigación en México," Problemas Agrícolas e Industriales
de México, 1950.

11. Food and Agriculture Organization, Production Yearbook (Rome, 1960).

12. Agricultural Census, 1950, 1960.

13. Secretaría de Agricultura y Ganadería,
et al., op. cit., p. 184.

14. U.S. Embassy, Mexico, Special Report on
Mexico's Fertilizer Industry (mimeo.), April 21,
1966.

15. See, for instance, R. J. Laird and Hector
Lizárraga, "Fertilizantes y Población Optima de
Plantas para Maiz de Temporal en Jalisco," Secretaría de Agricultura y Ganadería, Oficina de Estudios Especiales, Folleto Técnico No. 35, Enero,
1959; R. J. Laird and Horacio Rodríguez, "Fertili-
zación de Maiz de Temporal en Regiones de Guanajuato,
Michoacan y Jalisco," Instituto Nacional de Investigaciones Agricola , Folleto Técnico No. 50, 1965.

16. U.S. Embassy, op. cit., p. 6.

17. R. Ramirez and R. J. Laird, "La Fertili-
zación del Cultivo de la Papa en la Region de Leon,"
Instituto Nacional de Investigaciones Agrícolas,
Folleto Técnico No. 47, August, 1964.

18. Instituto Nacional de Investigaciones
Agrícolas, Guía para la Asistencia Técnica Agrícola
en México (Mexico, 1965).

19. U.S. Embassy, op. cit.

20. Banco Nacional de Crédito Ejidal, Informe
Anual, 1961 (Mexico: Banco Nacional de Crédito
Ejidal, 1964), p. 12.

21. Secretaría de Agricultura y Ganadería,
Informe de Labores 1963-1964 (Mexico, 1964).

22. Secretaría de Agricultura y Ganadería,
et al., Proyecciones, p. 189.

23. Banco Nacional de Crédito Ejidal, op.
cit., p. 11.

24. See Secretaría de Agricultura y Ganadería,
et al., Proyecciones, p. 181.

25. Agricultural and Livestock Censuses,
1950, 1960.

26. Secretaría de Agricultura y Ganadería,
Informe de Labores 1963-1964.

27. Banco Nacional de Crédito Agrícola,
Informe Anual, 1963 (Mexico: Banco Nacional de
Crédito Agrícola, 1964).

28. See Alvaro de Albornoz, Trayectoria y
Ritmo del Crédito Agrícola en México (Mexico:
Instituto Mexicano de Investigaciones Technologicas,
1966).

29. Compañía Nacional de Subsistencias Populares, Informe Anual, 1966 (Mexico: CONASUPO, 1966).

30. Banco Nacional de Crédito Ejidal, op. cit., p. 17.

31. Vicente Cedillo, "Principales Factores del Desarrollo Agrícola en México." (Tésis, Universidad Nacional Aútonoma de México, 1964), pp. 57-61.

32. See Secretaría de Agricultura y Ganadería, et al., Proyecciones, pp. 191-203.

33. Ibid.

NOTES TO CHAPTER 7

1. See Roberto E. Anguiano, Las Finanzas del Sector Publico en México (Mexico: Universidad Nacional Aútonoma de México, 1968), p. 45.

2. For a brief summary and an extended bibliography on this subject, see Robert J. Shafer, Mexico: Mutual Adjustment Planning (Syracuse: Syracuse University Press, 1966), pp. 86-87.

3. Ibid.

4. Ibid.

5. See, for instance, Secretaría de Agricultura y Ganadería, Plan Agrícola Nacional, Etapa 1967-68 (Mexico, September, 1967).

6. See Banco Nacional de Comercio Exterior, Comercio Exterior, May, 1966, pp. 327-28.

7. "Presidential Message," The News, September 2, 1965.

8. Estimates go from 40 to 100 million hectares, but even the highest figure would be

insufficient to satisfy present demands for land.
See Banco Nacional de Comercio Exterior, _Comercio_
Exterior, October, 1965, p. 724.

9.   Norberto Aguirre, "Tierras Disponibles en
México," _Panagra, El Panorama Agrícola Nacional y_
de los Países Latinoamericanos, November, 1965.

10.   _Ibid._, p. 24.

11.   _Ibid_.

12.   Nacional Financiera, S.A., _La Economía_
Mexicana 1966 (Mexico: Nacional Financiera, S.A.,
1966), p. 60.

13.   See Shafer, _op. cit._, p. 90.

14.   _Ibid_.

15.   "Presidential Message," _op. cit_.

16.   Secretaría de Agricultura y Ganadería,
et al., _Proyecciones de la Oferta y la Demanda de_
Productos Agropecuarios en México, a 1970 y a 1975
(Mexico: Banco de México, S.A., 1965), p. 166.

17.   Shafer, _op. cit._, p. 91.

18.   Secretaría de Agricultura y Ganadería,
et al., _Proyecciones_, p. 167.

19.   Banco Nacional de Comercio Exterior,
Comercio Exterior, October, 1965, p. 725.

20.   "Presidential Message," _op. cit_.

21.   Banco Nacional de Comercio Exterior,
op. cit.

22.   U.S. Department of Agriculture, _Agricul-_
tural Policies of Foreign Government, March, 1964;
and U.S. Department of Agriculture, Foreign Agricultural Service, _The Agricultural Policies and_
Programs of Mexico, May, 1964 (mimeo.).

23. See Inter-American Committee for Agricultural Development, Inventory of Information Basic to Planning of Agricultural Development: Mexico (Washington, D.C., 1964).

NOTES TO CHAPTER 8

1. For further description on Plan Chapingo, see Secretaría de Agricultura y Ganadería, Medio Siglo de Progreso Agrícola en México (Mexico, 1967); Secretaría de Agricultura y Ganadería, Plan Chapingo-- Sus Realizaciones y su Proyección (Inaugural booklet) (Mexico, 1967); National Center for Agricultural Education, Research and Extension, Regional Technical Aids Center (Mexico: U.S. Embassy, 1964).

2. Centro de Estudios Educativos, A.C., Boletín Mensual Informativo, Vol. 4, No. 3, 1968.

3. National Association of Directors of Agricultural Schools, Agricultural Education, Investigation and Extension in Mexico: A Preliminary Study (Monterrey, Mexico: Monterrey Institute of Technology and Advanced Studies, 1964), pp. 58-59.

4. Secretaría de Agricultura y Ganadería, Plan Agrícola Nacional, 1965-1970 (Mexico, 1965), pp. 61-62.

5. Centro Internacional de Mejoramiento de Maiz y Trigo, 1966-67 Report, Mexico, pp. 9-10.

6. Secretaría de Agricultura y Ganadería, Plan Agrícola Nacional, 1965-1970, pp. 63-64.

7. Ibid.

NOTES TO CHAPTER 9

1. Secretaría de Agricultura y Ganadería, et al., Proyecciones de la Oferta y la Demanda de Productos Agropecuarios en México, a 1970 y a 1975 (Mexico: Banco de México, S.A., 1965).

2. See "Proyecciones de la Oferta y la Demanda
de Productos Agropecuarios en México a 1970 y 1975,"
Comercio Exterior, March, 1966.

3. Secretaría de Agricultura y Ganadería,
et al., op. cit., p. 30.

4. Comercio Exterior, July, 1966. Statistical
appendix. (Figures are preliminary.)

5. Ibid.

NOTES TO CHAPTER 10

1. See A. T. Mosher, Getting Agriculture
Moving (New York: Agricultural Development Council,
1966).

2. For an excellent review of current land
tenure problems in Mexico, see Fernández y Fernández
Ramón, Notas Sobre la Reforma Agraria Mexicana
(Chapingo, Mexico: Escuela Nacional de Agricultura,
1965).

3. T. W. Schultz, Transforming Traditional
Agriculture (New Haven: Yale University Press,
1964), pp. 175 ff.

4. El Heraldo, Mexico, D.F., August 12, 1966.

5. The News, Mexico, D.F., September 2, 1966.

6. A. Ortiz Mena, "El Desarrollo Agropecuario,
Base del Progreso de México," Panagra, No. 66,
April, 1966.

7. For instance, the well-known Mexican agricultural economist, Edmundo Flores, recently made
the remark: "In the countryside that [the existence
of latifundia] is not the problem. The problem is
rapid industrialization. There are 2 million peasants with rights to receive land, but I think they
must not stay on the land, but we must get them off
the countryside." Quoted in Novedades, Mexico, D.F.,
October 30, 1966.

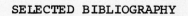
SELECTED BIBLIOGRAPHY

SELECTED BIBLIOGRAPHY

AGRARIAN REFORM AND LAND TENURE

Alamis Patiño, Emilio; López Bermudez, José; and
    Mesa Andraca, Manuel. "Problemas de la
    tenencia y aprovechamiento de la tierra en
    México," Problemas Agrícolas e Industriales
    de México, Vol. V, No. 4. Mexico, 1953.

Alcérreca, G. Luis. Apuntes para una reforma al
    Código Agrario de 1942. Mexico, 1961.

Andrade, M. Carlos. "La tenencia de la tierra y
    la evolución política de México," Revista de
    Economía, Vol. XXIV, No. 10. Mexico, 1961.

Arriaga Ponciano, Molina Enriquez, Andrés; Cabrera,
    Luis y Bassala, Narciso. "El pensamiento
    agrario en México," Problemas Agrícolas e
    Industriales de México, Vol. IV, No. 2.
    Mexico, 1952.

Centro de Investigaciones Agrarias. Modificaciones
    necesarias a la legislación agraria y formas
    de organización campesinas. Ponencia presen-
    tada al Congreso Nacional Agrario. Mexico:
    Talleres Gráficos de la Editorial Comaval,
    S.A., 1959.

Chavez P. de Velázquez, Martha. El derecho agrario
    en México. Mexico: Editorial Porroa, S.A.,
    1964.

Covarrubias, José. "La trascendencia política de
    la reforma agraria," Problemas Agrícolas e
    Industriales de México, Vol. V, No. 3.
    Mexico, 1953.

261

De la Peña, Moisés T. "Problemas demográficos y agrarios," Problemas Agrícolas e Industriales de México, Vol. II, No. 2. Mexico, 1950.

_____. "El pueblo y su tierra," Mito y realidad de la reforma agraria en México--Cuadernos Americanos. Mexico, 1964.

Departamento de Asuntos Agrarios y Colonización. Seis años de política agraria del Presidente Adolfo López Mateos, 1958-1964. Mexico, 1964.

_____. Manual de tramitación agraria. Mexico, 1964.

Deutsch, Herman. El ejido y la integración de México. Mexico, 1960.

Diaz Soto y Gama, Antonio. La cuestión agraria en México. Mexico: Universidad Nacional Autónoma de México, 1959.

Durán, Marco Antonio. Del agrarismo a la revolución agrícola. Mexico, 1947.

_____. "Las funciones de la propiedad de la tierra en la reforma agraria mexicana," El Trimestre Económico, Vol. 31, No. 122. Mexico, 1964.

Eckstein, Salomón. El ejido colectivo en México. Mexico: Fondo de Cultura Económica, 1966.

Fernández y Fernández, Ramón. Economía agrícola y reforma agraria. Mexico: Centro de Estudios Monetarios Latinoamericanos, 1962.

_____. "Una doctrina sobre reforma agraria," El Trimestre Económico, Vol. XXIX, No. 1. Mexico, 1962.

Garcia Treviño, Rodrigo. "Agrarismo revolucionario y ejidalismo burocrático," Problemas Agrícolas e Industriales de México, Vol. V, No. 4. Mexico, 1953.

Gill, Tom. "La crisis de la tierra en México,"
    Problemas Agrícolas e Industriales de México,
    Vol. IV, No. 1. Mexico, 1952.

Girault, Manuel. "El ejido; callejón sin salida,"
    Problemas Agrícolas e Industriales de México,
    Vol. V, No. 4. Mexico, 1953.

González Roa, Fernando. "El aspecto agrario de la
    revolución mexicana," Problemas Agrícolas e
    Industriales de México, Vol. V, No. 3.
    Mexico, 1953.

Hornedo, Eduardo. "El latifundio en México,"
    Investigación Económica, Vol. XIX, No. 76.
    Mexico, 1959.

Instituto Mexicano de Investigaciones Económicas.
    La cuestion de la tierra. Mexico, 1962.
    4 Vols.

McCutchen McBride, George. "Los sistemas de
    propiedad rural en México," Problemas Agrícolas
    e Industriales de México, Vol. III, No. 3.
    Mexico, 1951.

Manzanilla Schaffer, Victor. "La reforma agraria
    mexicana," Revista de Economia, Vol. XXIX,
    No. 5. Mexico, 1961.

Melendez, Hugo Tulio. Estudio comparativo de la
    reforma agraria de México y Yugoeslavia.
    Mexico, 1965.

Mendieta y Nuñez, Lucio. El problema agrario de
    México, 5a. ed. Mexico, 1946.

Muñoz, Carlos. "La tenencia de la tierra y la
    evolución política de la tierra," Revista de
    Economía, Vol. XXIV, No. 11. Mexico, 1961.

Rea Moguel, Alejandro. México y su reforma agraria
    integral. Antigua Librería Robredo. Mexico,
    1962.

Rodríguez Adame, Julián. "Antecedentes y realiza-
    ciones de la reforma agraria mexicana," Prob-
    lemas Agrícolas e Industriales de México, Vol.
    V, No. 4. México, 1953.

Rojo Gómez, Javier. "Los problemas del campo,"
    Comercio Exterior, Vol. XII, No. 9. Mexico,
    1962.

Romero Espinosa, Emilio. "La reforma agraria en
    México a medio siglo de iniciada," Cuadernos
    Americanos. Mexico, 1963.

Rosa Pérez, Manuel de la. "La reforma agraria
    en México y su impacto en la mano de obra del
    campo." Tésis. Escuela Nacional de Economía.
    Universidad Nacional Aútonoma de México.
    Mexico, 1964.

Silva Herzog, Jesús. El agrarismo mexicano y la
    reforma agraria; Exposición y crítica. Mexico:
    Fondo de Cultura Económica, 1959.

Simpson, Eyler N. "El ejido: única salida para
    México," Problemas Agrícolas e Industriales
    de México, Vol. IV, No. 4. Mexico, 1952.

Soberón Martínez, Oscar. "La reforma agraria y el
    desarrollo económico de México," Problemas
    Agrícolas e Industriales de México, Vol. V,
    No. 4. Mexico, 1953.

Tannenbaum, Frank. "La revolución agraria en
    México," Problemas Agrícolas e Industriales
    de México, Vol. IV, No. 2. Mexico, 1952.

Whetten, Nathan L. Rural Mexico. Chicago: Uni-
    versity of Chicago Press, 1948.

Wylie, Kathryn H. "Mexico's Agrarian Reform,"
    Foreign Agriculture. Washington, D.C., Feb-
    ruary 18, 1961.

U.S. Foreign Agricultural Service. Land Redistri-
    bution in Mexico. Washington, D.C., 1961.

AGRICULTURAL CREDIT

Bodegas de Depósito, S.A. Instrumentos que unen el
    crédito, a la producción y al comercio; los
    certificados de depósito y los bonos de prenda.
    Mexico, 1966.

Compañía Nacional de Subsistencia Populares, S.A.
    Sistema de compra, almacenamiento y venta de
    cosechas que fué antecedente para la creación
    de CONASUPO. Mexico, 1962.

Dávila, José Ma. El crédito agrícola y la banca
    privada. Mexico, 1950.

Durán, Marco Antonio. "Crédito agrícola y tenencia
    de la tierra," Problemas Agrícolas e Industri-
    ales de México, Vol. IV, No. 3. Mexico, 1952.

Fernandez y Fernandez, Ramón. "Anotaciones sobre
    procedimientos en el crédito agrícola mexicano,"
    Revista el Trimestre Económico, Vol. 31, No.
    121. Mexico, 1964.

Garcia Garcia, Manuel. "El crédito agrícola en
    México." Tésis. Escuela Nacional de Economía.
    Universidad Nacional Aútonoma de México.
    Mexico, 1965.

Gómez Gronillo, Moisés. "La agricultura nacional y
    el crédito ejidal." Tésis. Escuela Nacional
    de Economía. Universidad Nacional Aútonoma de
    México. Mexico, 1952.

Gónzalez Santos, Armando. "El crédito en el
    noroeste," Problemas Agrícolas e Industriales
    de México, Vol. II, No. 1. Mexico, 1950.

Hernández Arredondo, Eulogio. "Funsión económica
    del almacenamiento de granos en México. Tésis.
    Escuela Nacional de Economía. Universidad
    Nacional Aútonoma de México. Mexico, 1965.

Kuri Breña, Daniel. "Bases para un sistema de crédito agrícola," Problemas Agrícolas e Industriales de México, Vol. VI, No. 2. Mexico, 1954.

López Barragán, Francisco. "La UNPASA, sus funciones y el desarrollo de la industria azucarera," Revista de Economía, Vol. XXI, No. 5. Mexico, 1958.

Montes Ledesma, José. "El crédito agrícola supervisado en México." Tésis. Escuela Nacional de Economía. Universidad Nacional Aútonoma de México. Mexico, 1964

Serna Maciel, Eligio. "El seguro agrícola y sus repercuciones en la economía; el caso de Veracruz." Tésis. Escuela Nacional de Economía. Universidad Nacional Aútonoma de México. Mexico, 1963.

Silva Herzog Flores, Caludio. "Algunos aspectos del crédito ejidal." Tésis. Escuela Nacional de Economía. Universidad Nacional Aútonoma de México. Mexico, 1965.

AGRICULTURAL EDUCATION, RESEARCH,
AND EXTENSION

Aragón Omar. "Evaluación de la demostración agrícola a partir de la adopción de cinco técnicas en la población rural del area de influencia del C.I.A.B." Tésis. Ingeniero Agrónomo, Escuela Nacional de Agricultura. Chapingo, Mexico, 1966.

Canizales D., Juan Antonio. "Medios de información existentes en el noroeste de México y su aprovechamiento por propietarios, colonos y ejidatorios del valle del Yaqui." Tésis. Escuela Superior de Agricultura "Antonio Narro." Universidad de Coahuila. Mexico, 1966.

Chena G., Rodolfo. "Perceptions of Extension Work
    in Mexico." Ph.D. Dissertation. Cornell Uni-
    versity. 1963.

Lara, Victor. "La parcela escolar como un medio
    para la enseñanza y adiestramiento sobre
    nuestras técnicas agrícolas." Tésis. In-
    geniero Agrónomo, Escuela Superior de Agricul-
    tura "Antonio Narro." Universidad de Coahuila.
    Mexico, 1966.

Magdub, Abdo. "La difusión y adopción del cultivo
    de la soya en el valle del Yaqui." Tésis.
    Escuela Nacional de Agricultura. Chapingo,
    Mexico, 1964, and "Cloze Procedure in Spanish."
    M.S. Thesis. University of Wisconsin .1966.

Martínez V., Gregorio. "Completion of Pictorial
    Messages by Illiterate, Semi-Literate and Lit-
    erate Farmers in Central Veracruz, Mexico."
    Ph.D. Dissertation. University of Wisconsin.
    1967.

Martínez V., Gregorio, and Myren, Delbert T.
    "Alcance e impacto de la página agrícola de
    'El Dictámen' de Veracruz," Folleto Técnico
    47. Instituto Nacional de Investigaciones
    Agrícolas. September, 1964.

Myren, Delbert T. "Integración del mercado rural
    en la economía nacional en México," Comercio
    Exterior, Vol. 17, No. 9. September, 1967.

National Association of Directors of Agricultural
    Schools. Agricultural Education, Investiga-
    tion and Extension in Mexico: A Preliminary
    Study. Monterrey Institute of Technology and
    Advanced Studies. Monterrey, Mexico, 1964
    (English and Spanish editions).

Ortega Andapia, Alfonso. "La revista Agricultura
    Técnica en México como medio de información
    científico-técnico: una encuesta realizada
    entre su lectoría nacional." Tésis. Escuela
    Nacional de Agricultura. Chapingo, Mexico, 1962.

Reding J., Jesús Martínez. "La difusión y adopción del maíz híbrido en cuatro municipios del estado de Guanajuato." Tésis. Escuela Nacional de Agricultura. Chapingo, Mexico; and "A New Readibility Formula for Spanish Language." M.S. Thesis. University of Wisconsin. 1965.

Ruanova Hernández, Alfonso. "Readibility and Content Analysis of Selected Mexican Farm Magazines." M.S. Thesis. University of Wisconsin. 1959.

Secretaría de Agricultura y Ganadería. Memoria de Labores. Mexico: Talleres Gráficos de la Nación. (Published each year to report on education, research, and extension activities of the various dependencies of the Secretariat.)

AGRICULTURAL POLITICS

Albores Rovelo, Rafael. "Lineamientos de una política pesquera en México. Tésis. Escuela Nacional de Economía. Universidad Nacional Aútonoma de México. Mexico, 1965.

Betancourt Moguel, Ruby. "La industrialización del ejido." Tésis. Escuela Nacional de Economía. Universidad Nacional Aútonoma de México. Mexico, 1965.

Chirino Martínez, Jaime. "Imposición a los ejidos en el estado de Sonora." Tésis. Escuela Nacional de Economía. Universidad Nacional Aútonoma de México. Mexico, 1965.

Fernández y Fernández, Ramón y Acosta, Ricardo. Política Agrícola. Mexico: Fondo de Cultura Economica, 1961.

Hinojosa Ortiz, Manuel. "Reflexiones sobre una politica agraria," Investigación Económica, Vol. XXI, No. 82. Mexico, 1961.

Larios Tolentino, Juan.   "La organización de la
    economía agrícola, factor de la reforma
    agraria mexicana." Tésis. Escuela Nacional
    de Economía. Universidad Nacional Aútonoma
    de México. Mexico, 1965.

Miramontes Estrada, Hilario.   "Estudio para la im-
    plantación del Seguro Social para trabajadores
    del campo en la cuenca del Tepalcatepec."
    Tésis. Escuela Nacional de Economía. Universi-
    dad Nacional Aútonoma de México. Mexico, 1964.

Moreno Sánchez, Manuel y otros.   "Política ejidal."
    Escuela Nacional de Ciencias Políticas y
    Sociales. Universidad Nacional Aútonoma de
    México. Mexico, 1960.

Ramirez, José Ch. Defensa Azucarera. Mexico, 1954.

Secretaría de Agricultura y Ganadería. Dirección
    General de la Pequeña Propiedad Agrícola.
    "Tésis nacionales en materia agrícola ganadera
    y forestal." Mexico.

Taboada, Edmundo. "Los problemas agrícolas en la
    planificación," Revista de Economía, Vol. XXIV,
    No. 10. Mexico, 1961.

Tamayo, Jorge L. El problema fundamental de la
    agricultura mexicana. Mexico: Instituto
    Mexicano de Investigaciones Economicas, 1964.

IRRIGATION

Alanis Patiño, Emilio. "Las tierras de riego,"
    Problemas Agrícolas e Industriales de México,
    Vol. II, No. 2. Mexico, 1950.

Chávez Orozco, Luis. "La irrigación en México,"
    Problemas Agrícolas e Industriales de México,
    Vol. II, No. 2. Mexico, 1950.

Gómez, Marte R. "Los riegos en México," Problemas
Agrícolas e Industriales de México, Vol. II,
No. 2. Mexico, 1950.

Herrera Gómez, Hugo. Redituabilidad de las obras
de riego por bombeo en la región central del
bajío. Mexico: Banco Nacional de Crédito
Ejidal, S.A., 1954.

Núñez Estrada, Carlos. "El aprovechamiento de los
recursos hidráulicos y sus repercuciones en el
desarrollo económico de México." Tésis.
Escuela Nacional de Economía. Universidad
Nacional Aútonoma de México. Mexico, 1964.

Orive Alba, Adolfo. "Las obras de irrigación,"
México, Cincuenta Años de Revolución: La
Economía. Mexico: Fondo de Cultura Económica,
1960.

_____. La política de irrigación en México.
Mexico: Fondo de Cultura Económica, 1960.

Secretaría de Recursos Hidráulicos. Los recursos
hidráulicos de México; su relación con los
problemas agrícolas y económicos del país.
Mexico, 1961.

_____. Dirección General de Distritos de Riego.
Departamento de Planeación, Investigación y
Estadística. "La distribución de la propiedad
y la forma de asociación de los usuarios en los
distritos de riego," Informe Estadístico, No. 9.
Mexico, 1955.

_____. Dirección General de Distritos de Riego.
Departamento de Planeación, Investigación y
Estadística. "Función económica y social de
los distritos de riego," Memorandum Técnico
No. 89. Mexico, 1954.

_____. Dirección General de Distritos de Riego.
Departamento de Estadística y Estudios
Económicos. "Los recursos hidráulicos de

México y su relación con los problemas
agrícolas y económicos del país. Proposiciones
para establecer las bases de su desarrollo y
planeación futuro," Memorandum Técnico Nos.
181 y 193. Mexico, 1962.

MISCELLANEOUS

Banco Industrial de Jalisco, S.A. Estudios económicos referentes al estado de Jalisco.
Mexico, 1964.

Beteta, Ramón. Tierra de chicle. Mexico: Editora
México Nuevo, 1951.

Flores, Edmundo. Tratado de economía agrícola.
Mexico: Fondo de Cultura Económica, 1962.

Guerra, Edmundo. Historia de la Laguna. Mexico:
Editora Torreón Coah, 1957.

Martín Echevarría, Leonardo. La ganadería mexicana.
Mexico: Banco de México, S.A., Departamento
de Investigaciones Industriales, 1960.

Morán Walch, Olga Elena. "Educación y desarrollo
económico." Tésis. Escuela Nacional de
Economía. Universidad Nacional Autónoma de
México. Mexico, 1965.

Quesada, Alejandro. La pesca. Mexico: Fondo de
Cultura Económica, 1952.

Reina Celaya, Alfonso. "Nuevo plan para la producción y exportación de ganado," Comercio
Exterior, Vol. X, No. 11. Mexico, 1960.

Reyna González Roberto. "El problema agrícola de
la Comarca Lagunera." Tésis. Escuela
Nacional de Economía. Universidad Nacional
Autónoma de México. Mexico, 1965.

Rojas Coría, Rosendo. Tratado de cooperativismo
mexicano. Mexico: Fondo de Cultura Económica, 1952.

_____. "Introducción al estudio del cooperativismo, ensayo metodologico." Mexico: Talleres Gráficos de la Nación, 1963.

Vogt, William. "Los recursos naturales de México (continentales renovables) su pasado, presente y futuro." Mexico: Sociedad Méxicana de Geografía y Estadística, 1965.

Yañez Pérez, Luis. Mecanización de la agricultura mexicana. Mexico: Instituto Mexicano de Investigaciones Económicas, 1957.

Zamora Millán, Fernando (ed.). Diagnóstico económico regional. Mexico: Secretaría de Economía e Instituto Mexicano de Investigaciones Económicas, 1959.

PRICES, MARKETS, AND FOREIGN TRADE

Amaya Díaz de León, Ma. del Refugio. "La agricultura y el mercado interno en México." Tésis. Escuela Nacional de Economía. Universidad Nacional Aútonoma de México. Mexico, 1956.

Banco Nacional de Comercio Exterior, S.A. Hechos, cifras, tendencias. Mexico, 1960.

_____. Comercio de México con Centroamérica. Mexico, 1964.

Castellanos, Francisco X. "Notas sobre el mercado del algodón," Comercio Exterior, Vol, IX, No. 4. Mexico, 1959.

Escalante Cortina, Daniel. Mercado del camarón mexicano en Estados Unidos de América. Mexico, 1962.

Flores de la Peña, Horacio. "Agricultura mexicana," Comercio Exterior, Vol. VIII, No. 7. Mexico, 1958.

Guillón Díaz, Pedro. Regulación de los precios, del ingreso agrícola. Mexico: Banco Nacional de Crédito Ejidal, 1955.

Ortega Cruz, Leopoldo. "El control de precios y su importancia en la economía del país." Tésis. Escuela Nacional de Economía. Universidad Nacional Aútonoma de México. Mexico, 1965.

Padilla, Pablo. "Elasticidad en la oferta de la producción agrícola total en la República Mexicana," Boletín de Estudios Especiales, Vol. XI, No. 132. Mexico, 1958.

Soto Angli, José M. "El mercado regional de Tehuacán." Tésis. Escuela Nacional de Agricultura. Chapingo, Mexico, 1961.

Vázquez Morales, Mateo. "Análisis estadístico de la demanda de trigo en México." Tésis. Escuela Nacional de Agricultura. Chapingo, Mexico, 1963.

PRODUCTION AND AGRICULTURAL DEVELOPMENT

Amorós G., Roberto. El Presidente Alemán y la industria del café en México. Mexico: Comisión Nacional del Café, 1949.

Amorós G., Roberto, and Pablo Duque, Juan. La Comisión Nacional del Café. Mexico: Comisión Nacional del Café, 1950.

Attolini, José. Economía de la cuenca del Papaloapan. Mexico: Instituto de Investigaciones Económicas, 1951.

Cano Luebert, Sergio Luis. "La productividad de la República Mexicana." Tésis. Escuela Nacional de Economía. Universidad Nacional Aútonoma de México. Mexico, 1958.

Cedillo Vázquez, Vicente. "Principales factores del desarrollo agrícola en México (1925-1960)." Tésis. Escuela Nacional de Economía. Universidad Nacional Aútonoma de México. Mexico, 1964.

Círculo de Estudios Mexicanos, A.C. La situación agrícola nacional. Mexico: Editoro Círculo de Estudios Mexicanos, 1957.

Delgado Navarro, Juan. "Desarrollo económico y justicia social; equilibrio entre la industria y la agricultura," Revista de Economía, Vol. XXV, No. 1, Enero. Mexico, 1962.

Durán, Marco Antonio. "Condiciones y perspectivas de la agricultura mexicana," Trimestre Económico, Vol. XXVIII, No. 1. Mexico, 1961.

_____. "La revolución agrícola en las tierras de temporal," Problemas Agrícolas e Industriales de México, Vol. VIII, No. 3-4. Mexico, 1956.

_____. "Agrarismo y desarrollo agrícola," Revista Investigación Económica, Vol. 23, No. 92. Mexico, 1964.

Echevarría, Leonardo M. "Progresos recientes de la agricultura mexicana," Revista de Problemas Agrícolas e Industriales de México, Vol. VI, No. 4. Mexico, 1954.

Eckstein Raber, Salomón. "Planeación económica y agricultura; investigación de campo realizada en Ixtapalapa, D.F." Tésis. Escuela Nacional de Economía. Universidad Nacional Aútonoma de México. Mexico, 1957.

Fernández, Antonio. "El algodón, algunas consideraciones sobre su cultivo, industrialización y comercio en la República Mexicana," Boletín de Estudios Especiales, Vol. XI, No. 131. Mexico, 1958.

Fernández Flores, Humberto. "El sector agrícola,
    la inversión y la demanda externa como factores
    dinámicos que influyen en el nivel de la activi-
    dad económica de México." Tésis. Escuela
    Nacional de Economía. Universidad Nacional
    Aútonoma de México. Mexico, 1960.

Fernández y Fernández, Ramón. "El ciclo general de
    la agricultura," Boletín de Estudios Especiales,
    Vol. VI, No. 12. Mexico, November, 1956.

Flores, Edmundo. "Reforma agraria y desarrollo
    económico," Revista de Investigación Económica,
    Vol. XII, No. 2. Mexico, 1952.

Fondo de Garantía y Fomento para la Agricultura,
    Ganadería y Avicultura. Criterios básicos del
    programa de rehabilitación y mejoramiento
    rural encomendado al Fondo de Garantía y
    Fomento para la Agricultura, para pequeños
    productores agrícolas y ganaderos y vinculados
    con la "Alianza para el Progreso." Mexico,
    1963.

Gallart Valencia, Antonio. "El papel del sector
    agropecuario en el desarrollo económico de
    México." Tésis. Escuela Nacional de Economia.
    Universidad Nacional Aútonoma de México.
    Mexico, 1963.

Garcia Ruiz, Federico, and Ignacio González, Monreal.
    La industria de la piña. Hawaii, Filipinas
    México. Mexico: Banco de México, S.A., 1957.

González, Arturo. "Las posibilidades de desarrollo
    de la actividad pesquera," Comercio Exterior,
    Vol. XII, No. 8. Mexico, 1962.

Hopkins, John A. "Los salarios y la productividad
    del trabajo agrícola en México," Problemas
    Agrícolas e Industriales de México, Vol. II,
    No. 2. Mexico, 1960.

276   THE AGRICULTURAL DEVELOPMENT OF MEXICO

Loredo G., Joaquín. "Producción y productividad
     agrícola en México," México, Cincuenta Anos de
     Revolución: La Economía. Mexico: Fondo de
     Cultura Económica, 1960.

Martín Echevarria, Leonardo. "Progresos recientes
     de la agricultura mexicana," Problemas Agrí-
     colas e Industriales de México, Vol. VI, No. 4.
     Mexico, 1954.

Mercado Díaz Carlo, Florentino. "Productividad
     agrícola y desarrollo economico de México."
     Tesis. Escuela Nacional de Economia. Univer-
     sidad Nacional Aútonoma de México. Mexico,
     1964.

Mesa Andraea, Manuel, and Alanis Patino, Emilio.
     "La agricultura en México," Problemas Agrí-
     colas e Industriales de México, Vol. III,
     No. 1. Mexico, 1951.

Monroy Sevilla, Horacio. "La apicultura como
     fuente económica en México." Tésis. Escuela
     Nacional de Economía. Universidad Nacional
     Aútonoma de México. Mexico, 1964.

Nacional Financiera, S.A. La Nacional Financiera
     en el desarrollo económico de México, 1934-1964.
     Mexico: Nacional Financiera, S.A., 1964.

Nolasco Armas, Margarita. "Agricultura y desarrollo
     económico," Revista de Economía, Vol. XXV, No.
     12. Mexico, 1962.

Ortega Ortega, Juán. "La mecanización de la agricul-
     tura en el desarrollo económico." Tésis.
     Escuela Nacional de Economía. Universidad
     Nacional Aútonoma de México. Mexico, 1964.

Ortíz Mena, Raúl, Urquidi, Victor L., Waterstone,
     Alberto, and Haralz, Jonas H. En desarrollo
     económico de México y su capacidad para
     absorber capital del extranjero. Mexico:
     Nacional Financiera, S.A., 1953.

Paz Sánchez, Fernando. "Estructura y desarrollo
    de la agricultura en México." Tésis. Escuela
    Nacional de Economía. Universidad Nacional
    Aútonoma de México. Mexico, 1964.

Pérez Ruiz, Antonio. La Agricultura en México.
    Madrid: Editora Cultura Hispánica, 1953.

Sánchez Córdoba, Carmen. "La agricultura y el
    desarrollo económico en México." Tésis.
    Escuela Nacional de Economía. Universidad
    Nacional Aútonoma de México. Mexico, 1957.

Secretaría de Agricultura y Ganadería, et al.
    Proyecciones de la Oferta y la Demanda de
    Productos Agropecuarios en México, a 1970 y
    a 1975. Mexico: Banco de México, S.A., 1965.

Secretaría de Economía. La economía mexicana en
    1954 y 1955. Mexico: Talleres Gráficos de
    la Nación, 1956.

Secretaría de Recursos Hidraúlicos. Dirección
    General de Distritos de Riego. Departamento
    de Estadística y Estudios Económicos.
    "Análisis económico de dieciocho productos
    agrícolas importantes del país." Memorandum
    Técnico No. 198. Mexico, 1963.

_____. Dirección General de Distritos de Riego.
    Departamento de Planeación, Investigación y
    Estadística. "Planeación agrícola, su aspecto
    económico y social." Memorandum Técnico No.
    89. Mexico, 1956.

Silva Alvarado, Martín. "Productividad en la in-
    dustria azucarera." Tésis. Escuela Nacional
    de Economía. Universidad Nacional Aútonoma
    de México. Mexico, 1965.

Uribe Ruíz, Jesús. Problemas y soluciones en el
    desarrollo agrícola de México. Mexico:
    Academia Mexicana de Ciencias Agrícolas, 1964.

278   THE AGRICULTURAL DEVELOPMENT OF MEXICO

Valle Prieto, F. Hector del. "Plan piloto de
    desarrollo en el distrito de Jojutla, del
    Estado de Morelos." Tésis. Escuela Nacional
    de Economía. Universidad Nacional Aútonoma
    de México. Mexico, 1964.

Vellalon Rodríguez, Pedro. "Desarrollo regional y
    desarrollo pesquero (El caso de la region
    noroeste)." Tésis. Escuela Nacional de
    Economía. Universidad Nacional Aútonoma de
    México. Mexico, 1965.

PRODUCTION ECONOMICS

Andrade, Francisco J. "Resultados financieros,
    recursos y técnica del sector ejidal con
    operación individual del Valle del Yaqui, Son."
    Tésis. Escuela Nacional de Agricultura.
    Chapingo, Mexico, 1960.

Andrade, Francisco J., and Freebairn, Donald K.
    "Economía agrícola en el Valle del Yaqui,
    Los ejidatarios individuales." Folleto
    Técnico No. 49. Instituto Nacional de In-
    vestigaciones Agrícolas. Mexico, 1965.

Castillo, Carlos Manuel. "La economía agrícola én
    la región del Bajío," Problemas Agrícolas e
    Industriales de México, Vol. VIII, No. 3-4.
    Mexico, 1956.

Elías Barragán, Efrén. "Análisis económico de las
    explotaciones agrícolas en el Bajo Papaloapan."
    Tésis. Escuela Nacional de Economía. Uni-
    versidad Nacional Aútonoma de México. Mexico,
    1966.

González Romero, Vicente. "La pequeña propiedad
    en la zona de Celaya." Tésis. Escuela
    Nacional de Agricultura. Chapingo, Mexico,
    1963.

González Santos, Armando. La Agricultura.
    Estructura y utilización de los recursos.
    Mexico: Fondo de Cultura Económica, 1957.

Herrera Gómez, Hugo. "Análisis económico de la
    unidad agropecuaria de Cananea," Boletín de
    Estudios Especiales, Vol. XIII, No. 147.
    Mexico, 1958.

Silos Alvarado, José S. "Evalue la administración
    de su rancho," Circular CIANO, No. 20. Insti-
    tuto Nacional de Investigaciones Agrícolas.
    Mexico, 1964.

_____. "Estudio económico de fincas agrícolas en
    el Distrito de Riego del Alto Río Lerma."
    Tésis. Escuela Superior de Agricultura
    "Antonio Narro." Torreón Coah., Mexico, 1958.

Silos Alvarado, José S., and Freebairn, Donald K.
    "Economía agrícola del noroeste. La agricul-
    tura en el sistema de pequena propiedad,"
    Folleto Técnico No. 48. Instituto Nacional
    de Investigaciones Agrícolas. Mexico, 1964.

Silva Rodríguez, Hector J. "Las colectivas en el
    Valle del Yaqui, Son. (Organización, estruc-
    tura y resultados económicos en tres años
    agrícolas)." Tésis. Escuela Nacional de
    Agricultura. Chapingo, Mexico, 1964.

Torres Téllez, Wenceslao. "La productividad de los
    recursos en la zona agrícola de Celaya, Gto."
    Tésis. Escuela Nacional de Agricultura.
    Chapingo, Mexico, 1964.

STATISTICS

Anaya Cárdenas, Raúl Enrique. Las estadísticas
    nacionales del Comercio Exterior. Mexico:
    Editora Grabados e Impresores, 1963.

Comisión Nacional del Café. Estadística del café.
    Mexico: Talleres Gráficos de la Nación, 1957.

Chihuahua, Departamento de Economía. Compendio
    estadístico del Estado de Chihuahua 1957-1958.
    Chihuahua, 1959.

Comisión del Papaloapan. <u>Compendio estadístico de
la Cuenca del Papaloapan</u>. Mexico, 1960.

Dirección General de Estadística. <u>Anuario estadístico de los Estados Unidos Mexicanos</u> (Series
anuales). Mexico, 1958.

_____. <u>Censos Agropecuarios</u> (varios). Mexico.

_____. <u>Compendios estadísticos</u> (Series anuales).
México.

_____. <u>Cuarto censo de transportes 1955</u>. Resumen
general. Mexico, 1959.

_____. <u>Mexico en cifras 1959</u>. Mexico, 1959.

_____. <u>Primer censo ejidal, 1935</u>. Resumen general.
Mexico, 1937.

_____. <u>Tercer censo agrícola ganadero y ejidal 1950</u>
Resumen general. Mexico, 1956.

Dirección General de Pesca. <u>Resumen de actividades
pesqueras, 1952-1957</u>. Mexico, 1958.

Gleason, Ruben. "Principales estadísticas en los
aspectos económico y social," <u>Sociedad Mexicana
de Geografía y Estadística Boletín</u>, Vol. LXXXI,
Nos. 1-3. Mexico, 1958.

Gómez Guerrero, Isaias. "Estadísticas agrícolas."
Tésis. Escuela Nacional de Economía. Universidad Nacional Aútonoma de México. Mexico,
1951.

Instituto Mexicano del café. <u>Estadísticas del
café, 1958</u>. Mexico, 1958.

Nacional Financiera, S.A. <u>La economía mexicana en
cifras</u>. Mexico, 1965.

Padilla, Pablo. "Censo de sociedades locales de
crédito ejidal," <u>Boletín de Estudios Es-
peciales</u>, Vol. XIII, No. 154. Mexico, 1959.

_____. "Censo de sociedades locales de crédito
   ejidal," Boletín de Estudios Especiales, Vol.
   XII, No. 133. Mexico, 1958.

Secretaría de Recursos Hidraúlicos. Dirección
   General de Distritos de Riego. Departamento
   de Estadística y Estudios Económicos. Informes Estadísticas (Series anuales). Mexico.

Secretaría de Industria y Comercio. Dirección
   General de Pesca e Industrias Conexas.
   Estadísticas pesqueras concentradas, 1956-1961.
   Mexico, 1964.

Unión Nacional de Productores de Azúcar, S.A.
   Estadística azucarera. Mexico, 1961.

ABOUT THE AUTHORS

Eduardo L. Venezian is Program Advisor on Agricultural Economics for The Ford Foundation in Mexico and Central America, headquartered in the Foundation's Mexico City office. Before joining the Foundation in 1965, Mr. Venezian was an economist with the Department of Economic Affairs of the Organization of American States. He has participated in country evaluation missions and reports for the Committee of Nine of the Alliance for Progress and for the Inter-American Committee for Agricultural Development. He has traveled extensively throughout Latin America.

Dr. Venezian is also a Visiting Professor at the Agricultural Economics Center of the Post-Graduate College of the National School of Agriculture, Chapingo, Mexico. He formerly was with the Department of Economics and Sociology at Iowa State University. Dr. Venezian studied at the Catholic University of Chile and received his Ph.D. degree in agricultural economics from Iowa State University.

William K. Gamble is also with The Ford Foundation in Mexico City as a Representative and Program Advisor on Agriculture for Mexico and Central America. He previously served as an agricultural advisor to the Government of Burma for eight years and has been a consultant on agriculture for programs in several countries in the Orient and in Latin America. Mr. Gamble taught at North Dakota State University and at Iowa State University.

After studying agricultural education and agronomy at Iowa State University, Mr. Gamble received his Ph.D. degree from Cornell University.